MOCTU

and the

Mammoth People

Neil Bockoven

Published by Waldorf Publishing

2140 Hall Johnson Road

#102-345

Grapevine, Texas 76051

www.WaldorfPublishing.com

MOCTU and the Mammoth People:

An Ice Age Story of Love, Life and Survival

ISBN: 978-1-64255-077-1

Library of Congress Control Number: 2018943869

To my father, who instilled in me a love of learning

Acknowledgments

I didn't plan to write this book. The inspiration for it came as I was doing research into why Neanderthals died off so quickly after we, Early Modern Humans, arrived in Europe about 45,000 years ago (we are also a prime suspect in the demise of three other human species: Homo erectus, Denisovans, and the Hobbit people of Flores). A small portion of the research I did is represented in the annotated references at the back of the book. To all those authors and websites, I thank you for your fascinating research and insights. A few of the "rock stars" of this group are worthy of special mention: Chris Stringer, Erik Trinkaus, Thomas Higham, and David Reich.

After realizing that there was a great story to be told, I gained early and valuable encouragement from Kimberly Shelton and Ryan Bockoven, both of whom also offered helpful edits. Other early readers or book promoters were Fred and Erma Bockoven, Eric Bockoven, Marti Sturm, Larry Morrison, Jeff Eckert, Steve Vealey, Stella Maria Saldarriaga, Amy Martin, Steve Schaps, Al Haertlein, Doug Beveridge, Karen Weidenaar, and Scott and Susy Gorham. I thank them all for their support.

I have been lucky my whole life, and my luck held as I chose a very fine editor, Marlene Adelstein, who made the manuscript markedly better. Perhaps my most fortunate choice was that of Waldorf Publishing. CEO Barbara Terry is dynamic, entrepreneurial, and a joy to work with.

Above all, my thanks and love go to my wife, Denise, who was not only my greatest critic, but my most ardent supporter. Without her forbearance and help, this book wouldn't have been written.

And finally, special thanks to those first, intrepid Early Modern Humans that entered Europe and began our adventure with the Neanderthals so long ago.

"And it came to pass, when they were in the field, that Cain rose up against Abel his brother, and slew him."

Genesis 4:8

Author's Note

Our forefathers, Early Modern Humans (EMHs), probably reached southeastern Europe no earlier than 45,000 years ago and perhaps 4,000 years later still.[1,2, 128] It's likely that EMHs and Neanderthals in Europe overlapped in time by less than 5,000 years (roughly 45,000 to 40,000 years ago) before Neanderthals became extinct.[115]

The rapid demise of the Neanderthals has been attributed to many possible factors, including genocide by EMHs, infection from EMH-carried disease, competition for food and resources, and climate change (although the Neanderthals made it through numerous periods of substantial climate change over the previous 250,000 years). The fossil record indicates that Neanderthals disappeared only after EMHs moved into their territory.[24] Analysis of a deep, sharp scratch on a rib of Shanidar 3, an adult male Neanderthal who lived in present day Iraq more than 50,000 years ago, suggests he was hit by a spear thrown by an EMH, according to Duke investigators.[3] Based on the brief overlap in time of EMHs and Neanderthals in Europe, the fossil evidence, the rapid and truly massive extinction of large animal species following EMH entry to the Americas and Australia, and the xenophobic nature of early (and many would say current) man, I'd bet that genocide played a key role.

However, EMH-carried disease is also a likely cause and

is consistent with the data. In the early 1500's, Cortés unintentionally brought smallpox to the Aztecs and saw a die-off of between 60-90%.[86] The Aztec empire went from 30 million people to 3 million in just a few years, by some accounts. During the early 1600's, European settlers in New England saw a near eradication of the surrounding Native Americans as epidemics swept through the Massachusetts and Algonquin tribes, killing 90% or more of them.[82, 84]

A great deal of research has substantiated that EMHs and Neanderthals inter-bred, and the average non-African person of today owes between 1-5% (generally 2-3% for Europeans, and higher for East Asians) of their genetics to Neanderthals.[5, 6, 69] Neanderthal genetics have given us some good things like an increased ability to fight viruses, and perhaps red hair[116] (my first girlfriend, Heather, had red hair). But the Neanderthal genes also brought along some real negatives, including predispositions for type 2 diabetes, lupus, biliary cirrhosis, depression, nicotine addiction, actinic keratosis, and Crohn's disease.[11, 12, 13, 15, 16, 30, 31] So, for my Crohn's disease I can "thank" my distant great-great-great-etc. grandfather Og.[117]

The story of Moctu takes place 45,000 years ago. Although some disagree, a host of researchers has concluded that something happened around that time that dramatically and beneficially impacted EMH development and their resultant diaspora out of Africa.[118, 127] Humans successfully made it north into Europe[119] and they were off to the races, overwhelming the Neanderthals and other hominids and spreading to all parts of the globe. Certainly population blossomed, and in what Jared Diamond has popularized as the Great Leap Forward, technology, culture, art, and music expanded more in the short period thereafter than it had in the past million years. Even if some of these technological and cultural breakthroughs had happened earlier, the intensification of them is undeniable.[127]

What caused this explosion of creativity and success?

Various researchers have proposed a genetic change (or changes), for example to the FOXP2 gene, which allowed for better language skills.[13, 25, 29, 130] Others have called on our interactions with the Neanderthals for better (e.g. technology transfer and modest beneficial gene flow),[2, 11, 12, 16, 31] or for worse (Neanderthal predation that forced us to become the shrewd, and at times, bloodthirsty race we are).[24]

We'll probably never know for certain the cause, or causes, of the transformation, but that hasn't stopped us from speculating. A single breakthrough, such as mastery of fire starting, or the atlatl (spear thrower, which allowed for greater range and safety during hunting) could have played a major role. A small but consistent advantage can make all the difference—just a one percent difference in mortality could have led to the extinction of Neanderthals and the supremacy of EMHs in as little as 30 generations or about 1,000 years.[23]

As I grew up, typical depictions of Cro-Magnon/EMHs featured fair-skinned, fair-haired, blue-eyed people that looked like current-day northern Europeans. Neanderthals, on the other hand, were stooped, darker skinned, darker haired, more ape-like and, let's face it, uglier.[27, 28] It's only been within the last decade that our perceptions of Neanderthals have begun to change based largely on genomic research, which indicates that European Neanderthals probably had some blue-eyed, strawberry blondes, that in the right garb could easily pass by unnoticed on the streets of New York or Berlin.[22, 30] Okay, they didn't have the art, culture, tool making, and probably language skills to the extent that EMHs did. But recent genetic findings, as well as archaeological discoveries have had an enormous impact on our image of these people and reversed some long-held misconceptions. In this book, I've tried to strike a balance that shows EMHs as more advanced in many things but suggests that Neanderthals had a lot to offer too.

Did EMHs have more advanced language skills than Neanderthals? We can't be sure, but the answer is—probably.[37, 38] Basque is the oldest European language (the only Pre-Indo-European language of Western Europe), and there is a reasonable chance that it has the greatest similarity to the EMH language of 45,000 years ago.[39, 41] Genetic evidence exists for this as well; the R1b haplogroup, which originated in Paleolithic times, is more pronounced in the Basque population.[10, 39, 41, 43, 44] I've therefore used more than a dozen Basque words, or derivations, for the EMH Nerean people's (there's one—a derivation of Nerea means *mine* or *my people* in Basque) words and names. Another is etxe (pronounced *etseh*, meaning '*home*' in Basque), which is the name of their shelter.

In 1980, I was enthralled by Jean Auel's *Clan of the Cave Bear*, as were millions of other readers. The story takes place about 30,000 years ago, largely in present-day Ukraine where EMH and Neanderthal cultures encountered one another. At the time, Auel was praised for maintaining a high level of authenticity in her characters' lifestyles, cultures, and technologies. Recent discoveries and genetic breakthroughs, however, have changed our image of her characters' appearances, and have pushed back the age of Neanderthal extinction (from ~28,000 to ~40,000 years ago). So, we've learned that many of Ayla's accomplishments and discoveries happened long after Neanderthals were gone.

In this book, all accounts and descriptions of animals (rhinos, aurochs, caribou, wolves, mammoths, saber-tooth cats, etc.) have been extensively researched and are realistic. Pictures of many of these beasts may be found in the center of the book. All were present in Italy 45,000 years ago.[71, 72, 73, 95] In fact, even more recent images (from 17,000-36,000 years ago) of these animals can be found in the caves of Lascaux and Chauvet in France, as well as elsewhere in Europe.

Based on the most recent archaeologic research, I've endeavored to make this novel as (pre-) historically accurate as possible regarding the tools and technology in use around

45,000 years ago. For instance, domestication of the horse had not yet happened, and dogs were either not widespread or non-existent.[45, 101] The bow and arrow were yet to be invented[48] while atlatls, or spear-throwers, were more likely in use.[50, 51, 52]

Archaeological evidence for when humans learned the ability to create fire is more problematic. Clear use of fire by humans dates back at least 400,000 years, and perhaps as far back as 1.8 million years.[67] Fire probably played an important role in evolution, allowing humans to extract more caloric value from food, thereby fostering the development of larger brains.[68] But early fire use was undoubtedly opportunistic, that is, taken from a natural fire, transported to a hearth, and kept alive. I've taken the finding of transported embers found on the 'Otzi' Iceman as evidence that fire starting was difficult and perhaps impossible even as recently as 5,300 years ago.[62,108] That said, it's hard to imagine Neanderthals surviving in places like ice age Germany for at least 250,000 years, relying solely on opportunistic fires.

I strongly encourage you to look over the annotated references at the end of the book and the amazing pictures in the middle before reading the story. Key portions of the references have been bolded, so it just takes a few minutes. It'll reinforce that essentially everything in this book is based on factual evidence. Besides documenting the topics mentioned above, the references discuss many other subjects such as Neanderthal spear thrusting versus throwing, cannibalism, Neanderthals having better eyesight, a prehistoric flint mining site near Verona, Italy, and the earliest musical instruments yet discovered.

I hope you enjoy this story.

PART ONE

MOCTU OF THE NEREA

Main Characters and Places

- Moctu – Young man of the Nerea people

- Nerea – Name of Moctu's tribe (means *mine* or *my people* in Basque)

- Etseh – Large rock overhang that the Nerea used for shelter (means *home* if spelled etxea)

- Jabil – Good young hunter; adversary to Moctu; wants leadership position in Nerea

- Jondu – Young hunter who is Jabil's ally

- Ordu – Leader of the tribe

- Alta – Moctu's mother

- Nuri – Young dark-haired woman of the Nerea

- Avi – Young fair-haired woman of the Nerea

- Nindai – Lame young man training as a healer

Map of Nerea Activities

(Map modified from "More Images of Northern Italy" website)

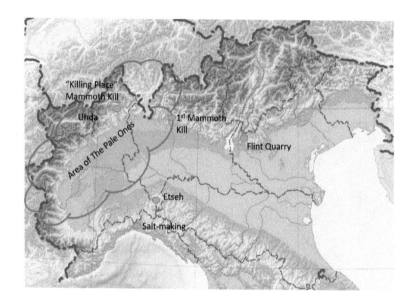

Northern Italy, about 45,000 years ago…

Chapter One

As the burly men charged into the herd of caribou, Moctu could see that they were different, very different, and a chill rippled down his spine. These must be the Pale Ones—the "People Eaters" that Jona and the older hunters warned him about when he was younger.

Now a tall, well-muscled youth of 14 summers, Moctu remembered his father's description of the abandoned dwellings of the beasts which had contained piles of charred human bones that had been split for their marrow. They had eaten people—lots of them. He shuddered recalling the nightmares that followed, where he and two friends were captured and eaten by the creatures. His mind flashed on the dead raven he'd seen this morning—certainly a bad omen, now proving true.

Moctu could tell the men were huge. Not tall, just… thick… and Spirits—they charged right into the herd where even the cows could kill with their antlers. They were fearless! Things were happening so fast. He could see three of the men stabbing and slashing. The caribou were confused, but some began to break to the south toward him, retracing steps they'd taken this morning.

He needed to get to the valley narrows fast. He had to

make a kill—his people needed it—and if he could set up there, he thought he'd get a shot. Having spent most of the day tracking and running after the herd as it moved northward, Moctu felt the muscles of his legs groan in complaint as he sprinted toward the nearby spot where the stream and meadows funneled between low hills. But as he got there, the panicked beasts rounded a hill and arrived at almost the same time. They'd picked up unbelievable speed and thundered toward him in full stampede now just half a stone's throw away!

"Ooooh shit!" he hissed through clenched teeth.

A turbulent sea of antlers was headed straight at him. Coming here had been a bad idea—he wasn't going to make it! It momentarily occurred to him that even if he did survive and was only injured, the Pale Ones would probably get him—and they would *eat* him.

Chapter Two

The day had started out well. The morning air had been crisp and the ground cool as Moctu flattened himself against the scattered rubble and short grass and peered over the crest of a low hill. He had used this hill before to scout caribou and other prey as they grazed on the grass, moss and low shrubs near the stream toward the middle of the valley. The winter had been harsh, however, and this spring season hadn't brought the numbers of game as in the past. Moctu grinned with satisfaction as he counted at least seven hands of caribou, including four small calves. He touched the wolf-tooth talisman hanging from his neck and whispered, "Thank you, Spirits, for bringing game, and so many—our hunting group will be pleased." His smile broadened as he imagined how excited the hunters would be.

It had been nearly half a moon since his people, the Nerea, had fresh meat, and everyone was tired of chewing on stringy dried remnants of past hunts. Watching the animals, Moctu began to evaluate options on the best way to attack the herd. It would be good to have a plan to recommend to Ordu and the rest of the hunting party when he got back to alert them. He felt honored that Ordu had given him this role—to scout the west valley for game. He was one of the youngest allowed to participate in the hunt having not yet reached his 15th summer. Although thin, he was tall and strong for his age, and Ordu said he was becoming a great hunter.

Moctu couldn't spend much time planning because he needed to get back so that the bigger hunt effort could be implemented. All the men would be pleased, especially Ordu, a huge man and gifted hunter but partially hobbled by a glancing blow from a wounded auroch two summers ago. He walked with a limp but still covered distance quickly and was nearly as good as before. Recently, Ordu had carried a worried countenance as game sightings had been sparse, and the tribe, already thin from the winter, was getting hungrier. This was supposed to be the fat season when his people built up their strength and weight to survive the next winter.

As Moctu turned to leave, he stopped, motionless. Something was wrong. The herd was suddenly alert and nervous, staring toward the south. Although that direction was downwind, perhaps wolves or cave lions were approaching and had been seen or heard by the caribou.

What the…? He studied an odd, wounded, or sick caribou slowly and clumsily limping through the grass toward the main herd. It was only moments before Moctu recognized that the creature was a man wearing a caribou skin, and he knew immediately who it was. Jabil, only two years older than Moctu, was moving in for an attempt at a kill.

You hyena dung, Moctu thought. You're going to ruin the hunt. We're supposed to get the larger group involved when we see this many animals—and you know it.

Jabil had been told to scout the valley to the south, but he was here instead, jeopardizing the chance to kill multiple caribou. Moctu was torn between his responsibility to get back to the others and his disbelief as he watched Jabil ruin the hunt.

Jabil edged closer to the herd and was now within range of the southernmost caribou, a mid-sized female with a calf nearby. The cow was just nosing her calf into moving when he rose up gracefully and flung a spear at her with his atlatl. The herd immediately surged away northward, but the spear took the cow between the shoulder and belly. It grunted loudly in pain and turned away but couldn't keep up with the rest of the herd. Jabil shed his caribou cloak and pursued the stricken cow. The calf which had remained close to its mother finally turned and ran after the herd now barely discernable through a dust cloud in the distance. Jabil, however, was keeping pace with the wounded cow.

Moctu had seen enough and turned back to inform the hunting party. "Jabil, you slime scum," he muttered as he began running. He wondered what he should say to Ordu and the men. If he didn't handle it right, they'd just think he was being jealous. That was when he saw it—a dead raven on the trail, a bad omen. This was a definite sign, and he was going to have to be very careful about what he said.

Jabil was Ordu's nephew, and it was well known that he and Moctu had quarreled several times in the past. Jabil was tall with high cheekbones and chiseled good looks. He moved with the self-assured poise of a leader. But he considered Moctu a rival for both the best mates and a future leadership position in the tribe, and he took every opportunity to belittle and sabotage him. The older boy had once wrestled him to the ground and pounded his head savagely against a rock while taunting him. Two older men had to pull Jabil off him. That was after Moctu and Nuri, a cute thirteen-year-old girl, had been talking and laughing with each other.

Jabil had won acclaim with the tribe a year ago when he was key in locating a cave bear den, smoking it out and, with some help, killing it. The cave bear was enormous, weighing the equivalent of nearly two hands-worth of hunters, and it had been loaded with prized fat and rich meat. Jabil had been awarded the skull and fur to keep at his hearth to remind everyone of his accomplishment, made all the more remarkable by his relative youth. Even Jabil's fox totem had been changed to the bear totem.

But today it was just a selfish attempt for glory. Sure,

he'd get a kill, but he probably ruined their chance to bring down lots of caribou—something that could have really helped the tribe.

Cool wind blew Moctu's long, wavy brown hair back as he picked up speed on a downhill stretch. The men were going to be pretty upset about losing such an opportunity. It was *his* valley to scout so they might even blame Moctu. If he wasn't careful, however, criticizing Jabil would only seem petty. Moctu slowed, thinking through alternatives. He'd just say what he saw with no comment. He decided that was best.

When he found the hunting party, they were seated on some boulders around a small fire but were in a state of readiness. Samar, a dark-bearded bull of a man, bellowed a friendly jab in his deep voice.

"So one of our sorry scouts is finally back—what do you have for us?"

Moctu noticed that Tabar, his stepfather, was also there, and he nodded to him.

"I've seen seven hands of caribou in the middle of the west valley. Jabil has wounded or killed one," Moctu said, trying not to show any of the outrage that he felt. He was gratified when Ordu and some of the other men snorted in surprise and disappointment upon hearing of Jabil's action.

"Seven hands?" Ordu asked. "And the herd—what of it?"

"It's moved north... out of sight," Moctu replied, which prompted more grumbling among the men.

As the group moved out, Ordu asked again, "Seven hands of caribou?"

The men were soon running easily toward the west valley along a narrow trail through a low sedge of scrub oaks, beech, and small conifers. When they crested the hill, they could see in the distance the tiny shape of Jabil working on gutting and cleaning the caribou. As Moctu had mentioned, the rest of the herd was no longer visible.

As they pulled up closer to Jabil, he called out, "I've made a good kill—the tribe will finally have some fresh meat to eat."

"How many were in the herd?" Ordu pointedly asked.

"There may have been as many as two hands."

Moctu remained quiet knowing that the expert trackers in the group could tell that there had been many more which was soon pointed out by Samar.

"There are tracks for at least five, maybe seven hands of caribou here," he said. "Why did you make a lone attack when we could have made kills that would feed the tribe for a moon?"

Jabil seemed ready for the question. "I've made a good kill here which should make everyone happy. I had to act quickly because wolves were threatening to scare the herd."

Ordu shot a glance at Moctu, and he shook his head imperceptibly rejecting the comment. Ordu instructed several of the men to help with the cleaning and butchering. In a low voice, he asked Samar to scout the area for wolf sign. He told Moctu and Nabu, a tall, skinny, quiet young man known as the fastest runner in the tribe, to track the caribou to the north to see if they could be found within a suitable hunting distance.

Chapter Three

Moctu had a hard time keeping up with the lithe and laconic Nabu who ran almost effortlessly. He ran up the hills as easily as Moctu ran down them. They spoke little, focused on their running and on the ground to avoid the occasional cobbles that could easily turn an ankle. After running for half the morning, they stopped for water at the stream. Their bronze bodies dripped with sweat, and their hair was wet even before they began scooping large handfuls of cold water over themselves. They still hadn't located the herd, but the tracks and dung were extremely fresh now and indicated they were close. Continuing on, the two traversed along the side of a low hill then crested a higher one before finally sighting the herd in the medium distance.

The caribou had found a small portion of the valley where the dry, cobble-strewn ground had given way to darker, richer earth where thick knee-high grass and clover grew. It appeared the herd was settled in and wouldn't be moving for a while. They carefully counted about eight hands of caribou, and there was also a smaller group of red deer not far from the main herd. The young men were elated. This was wonderful, perhaps life-saving news for the tribe. Although not the huge herds of hundreds or sometimes thousands of caribou from years ago that they'd been told of by the older hunters, this was the most game anyone had seen for many moons.

"It took us so long to get here, and only one of us needs to go back," said Moctu. "Want to pitch pebbles to see who has to do it?"

Both young men knew that whoever had to go back was likely to be too exhausted to join the hunt after running here, there, and back. So, they pitched pebbles to see who would stay—which of them could land their pebble closest to the gray sandstone boulder about 20 feet away.

"Thank you, Spirits!" Moctu whispered to himself, briefly closing his eyes in relief as Nabu's pebble hit the rock and bounced beyond his. "Sorry, Nabu—sorry that either of us has to go back."

"Ah, don't worry friend, I enjoy running," Nabu said with a smile. With that, the lanky, soft-spoken, young man picked up his spear and started back to alert the hunting party. After he'd gone, Moctu drank deeply at the stream and chewed more of the stringy jerky. The sun was fully up, and he found it hard to keep his eyes open. Despite the excitement at the prospect of the coming hunt, Moctu was really tired. Including his early morning scouting, he'd covered a lot of ground today. He began to plan the coming hunt in his mind.

It would be late afternoon at the earliest before the other hunters got there. If it was evening, they'd wait until daybreak—it would be too dangerous in the dark. At dusk, the herd was even more unpredictable, and it was easy to lose footing on the uneven ground.

The wind was still from the north, and there was good cover from the boulders and the tall grass down there. As long as enough men came with Nabu, they could break into three separate groups—one each to the south, east, and west. Each group would creep close to the herd, and they'd attack it from several sides. The herd would be confused, and the men could keep throwing shafts while it milled around trying to figure which direction was safe. It would probably break toward the north again, but not before they killed or wounded a bunch of them.

His plan in place, Moctu continued to watch the herd. They seemed stable and unlikely to move soon. He began to daydream in the warm sun. His thoughts turned to Nuri.

She was pretty... really pretty with that long, lustrous, dark hair and her big, brown, doe-like eyes. He paused imagining her face. She had all her teeth... and a nice smile. She was a hard worker, and she was friendly, well-liked by everyone. She would make a good mate.

Then there was Avi. He refocused on the other girl he often thought about. With her light brown hair and those beautiful, intriguing eyes. They were like green fire—a vision of her dazzling eyes came to him, and he smiled. She was really pretty, a good worker and well-liked too. He remembered once, when helping Avi carry firewood, she smiled at him and said that he was very strong. He'd been at a loss for words and hadn't responded. Both girls seemed to like him, and both were nearing their first menses and would be placed with mates soon.

His thoughts were interrupted by a change in the herd. They'd stopped grazing and were looking to the northwest. He strained his eyes in that direction to see what had made the herd suddenly nervous. Was it cave lions? He used his hands to block the sun from his eyes as he looked, but he could see nothing of concern. Some of the central animals gradually went back to grazing while the peripheral, mostly male caribou, remained alert continuing their watch.

Moments later he saw movement in the tall grasses. Actually movement in two separate areas to the northwest. As he continued to watch, he saw for the second time today a man in a caribou skin moving toward the herd.

Spirits—not again, he thought. It couldn't be Jabil, but who...?

Then another man in a skin appeared a stone's throw to the south of the first. This couldn't be his tribe's hunting party.

There was another group, a different tribe involved. He was fascinated because he was rarely exposed to other peoples except at the flint quarry where several tribes would assemble each time one hand of years had passed.

Could be our sister tribe, he conjectured. Twelve members of Ordu's tribe had moved out two years before. The group included both Ordu's oldest son, as leader, and Moctu's uncle. Ordu's tribe had grown to number more than eighty members making it difficult to find enough game and roots, nuts and berries to feed them all. The tribe's women were forced to range ever farther to gather enough wood for the hearth fires. So, with the consent of Ordu and the elders, the party of twelve had moved to the south for potentially better chances.

But these hunters had come from the north or northwest. So who were they? Maybe the Lion People? They were a large clan that lived to the east, whose shaman wore a cave lion skull and whose men each wore a lion claw around their neck.

He now noticed movement to the northeast of the herd. So perhaps it was the Lion People. The wind would carry the scent of at least some of these hunters toward the herd, and they'd react when they felt threatened. Our hunt will be ruined again, Moctu worried. He began to creep closer to the herd himself. If they spooked, they'd likely move south toward him. Maybe he could bring one down.

The herd was now focused on the threat from the northeast. All the caribou had stopped eating and were watching the man in the caribou skin gradually move closer. Less noticed, the men to the northwest were also moving closer. Even covered by their skins, Moctu could tell that these were big men, perhaps even larger than Ordu. The herd began to amble slowly away from the threat to the northeast. Suddenly not just one man but two rose up from the northeast and charged the herd yelling and barking, making sounds that Moctu had never heard before. The herd broke to the south and west whereupon the hunters to the west rose up and charged into the herd, stabbing with long, thick spears.

Spirits—those aren't men, they're... the Pale Ones, Moctu thought. The People Eaters. His mind flashed on the dead raven he'd seen earlier that morning—it had certainly been a bad omen.

Chapter Four

He sprinted to get nearer to the herd where the valley narrowed. He had to get a shot. But the panicked, confused beasts had coalesced and now moved south with desperation in full stampede. They'd picked up incredible speed and rounding a low hill, thundered toward him.

Focusing his attention on the animal approaching a nearby boulder, he hurriedly set the back of his heavy spear in the rocky ground at his feet. The charging bull was immediately upon him, and he felt the thick shaft bend as it impaled the beast in the chest. The animal continued forward careening over and to the right side of Moctu falling awkwardly before being run over by another caribou. There were more behind, and on they came.

Moctu leapt for the closest cover—a waist-high boulder, and he barely made it just as another beast rushed by, so close that it kicked gravel on him. The air was filled with dust and the smell of animal musk and fear. The wounded animal was up and struggled onward but slowed the remaining herd. That probably saved Moctu's life. Pressed hard against the boulder, Moctu felt more than heard the rumbling move past him. He unclenched his eyes and teeth to find he was surprisingly unharmed. As he watched the receding herd, he realized that he had a shot if he hurried. Moctu's hands were shaking as he fitted a shaft onto his atlatl and flung it at the trailing animal. He was gratified to hit it but couldn't tell if it would kill or even slow the beast. Looking to the north, he saw the Pale Ones just one hillock away. He could see that they'd made some kills, and he could see that they were watching him. An involuntary shudder went through him, and he gripped his atlatl tighter.

They had killed their nearby wounded animals, and two of them were celebrating, waving their thick, bloody spears in the air. There were at least five of them, Moctu counted, and he could see they were stocky and powerful. The smallest of them, he decided, studying the one who had knelt and was already gutting one of the caribou, might even be a female.

Two of them were staring at him, the largest of them pointing his way. Waves of alarm swept over Moctu as the creature seemed to be pointing to either side of him. Were they going to try to flank him? He nervously scanned his immediate area to make sure there weren't more of them attempting to circle around him. He could outrun them—he was sure of that, but he wanted his caribou. He'd gotten at least one. Moctu knew the one he speared was dying. "He's mine," he whispered fiercely. At the thought that these odd beasts might try to take his kill, his near-panic was largely replaced by an indignant sense of resentment. They're *not* getting *my* kill, he thought as he placed a shaft in his atlatl.

He turned his back to them and moved away following the herd and the wounded animals. He'd keep an eye on the People Eaters, but now it was time to finish his kills. Moctu was glad that the animals had moved south again, taking them away from the group of Pale Ones and closer to his tribe's hunting party. He broke into an easy run following the trail of the herd and gained quickly on three straggling animals.

The first caribou he came to was a large bull with a deep gash in his chest, and he was foaming blood from his nose and mouth. This was a wound inflicted by the Pale Ones, so by rights, it was their kill. The beast had now stopped, and he decided to leave it alone and follow the other two wounded animals. They stopped together, both exhausted, about the distance of three atlatl throws farther on. They were far from the main herd that had now moved westward out of a break in the valley toward the lowlands. He could see his heavy spear protruding from the chest of the bull. He'd missed the heart, but it would be a fatal strike nonetheless. The other animal, a female, had his lighter shaft buried deeply at an angle between her stomach and haunch. The bull was listing, about to collapse, but the female still had some fight left. He got within range and threw the shaft in his atlatl with all his strength. It buried itself deep in her chest, and with a grunt, she went down to her knees.

Wounded animals were unpredictable and extremely dangerous. His father, Jona, had been mortally wounded from having his leg broken by a downed and motionless auroch that he moved in to dispatch. It had seemed dead, but suddenly whipped its head around breaking his father's leg completely with two bones protruding sickeningly through the skin. Jona had died in great pain, with a high fever a quarter moon later despite the best efforts of Jelli, the medicine woman. Moctu was a young boy at the time, but he still remembered his father moaning in delirium and his mother Alta's consuming grief. He tried not to think too much about his father because it still saddened him.

The bull died first, but Moctu threw another atlatl shaft into it to be sure. His heavy spear was so deeply buried in the bull's chest, he was only able to extract it after sitting, placing both feet on the bull, and pulling with all his strength. Examining the point, Moctu was pleased to see that it was still secure and undamaged. Elation swelled within him as he regarded the two motionless caribou. This was the most meat he had ever managed to bring down.

Using the spear to prod the female, he ensured that she too was dead. His animals dispatched, he looked back toward the big bull wounded by the Pale Ones. It was now down, and he was dismayed to see that two of their hunters, their long spears in hand, were moving cautiously toward it—and him. They were still a good distance away, but Moctu worked frantically to retrieve his shafts from the animals, and he positioned his spear prominently at the ready.

His heart was beating fast, and he was trembling, but he scowled in their direction with his jaw set and his teeth clenched. The People Eaters were not going to take his body back with the rest of their kills today—and they weren't getting either of his caribou. He touched his wolf tooth amulet as the two Pale Ones moved ever closer, baring their teeth, and holding their spears threateningly.

Moctu put a shaft in his atlatl and readied another one. If they rushed him, he'd hit the closest one with a shaft and then use his big spear against the other. As the two neared their animal, they stopped and stared at him. From this distance, Moctu could see where the creatures got their name—their skin, though hairy, was eerily white. Even their hair was light colored. It looked as though they'd been left in the sun too long and bleached like an old caribou skull. He could tell their legs were slightly bowed, but they walked easily enough. Less than two atlatl throws separated them, and he could make out more details he hadn't seen before.

They looked so powerful—bigger than Nerean men, but maybe not as tall. Their shoulders and forearms were massive. They were so hairy… and… Spirits! That one had red hair. Was that real? Did he put red ocher in his hair to make it that color? That would be difficult, because it pretty much covered his whole body.

They wore crude, ill-fitting animal skins, not the woven nettle and hemp fiber cloth that his tribe favored in the spring and summer seasons. They seemed as intrigued with his appearance as he was with theirs, and they continued to stare.

He hoped his trembling wasn't noticeable as he gestured to their animal and then to them. He then pointed down at his two animals and touched his chest. They seemed to understand and nodded. One of them uttered an unintelligible grunt and moved his hand strangely. That one quickly speared their downed bull again with a strong thrust, then knelt and began to gut and clean it. The other Pale One just stood and glared at Moctu.

Moctu was stunned at the power of the spear thrust he'd just witnessed, and he immediately altered his earlier plan. He didn't stand a chance fighting close-up with either of those... He couldn't bring himself to call them men. If they rushed him, he'd hit the first one with an atlatl shaft, then run and hit the other one from a distance. But they were not getting his caribou, he thought emphatically.

He positioned himself where he could watch them while beginning to gut and clean his animals. The work was even more tedious than usual because of the need to keep careful watch on the Pale Ones and his surroundings. His bull weighed as much as two big men, and the female was almost as big, so this would dramatically help his tribe even if no further kills were made. He watched the sun sink lower on the horizon and was heartened by the prospect of his hunting party getting ever nearer.

The Pale Ones finished cleaning their animal much faster than he could have, and Moctu was relieved when they began to drag the carcass away back toward their group to the north. Theirs was a bigger bull than his—it must have weighed more than three men before the cleaning. The two Pale Ones handled it easily, however, and moved away at a quick pace. Moctu finished cleaning his bull, and as he continued working on the female, his thoughts focused on the Pale Ones and all he'd seen today. Including the bull that the two had dragged away, their hunters had killed at least three animals.

What kind of camp did they have? How far away was it, and how many of the creatures were there? How much of a threat were they? Ordu and the others of his hunting party would be enthralled to hear about his interaction with the creatures, and he was anxious to tell them what he'd seen.

He looked to the north and could still see the two Pale Ones pulling the carcass. They were far away now, and no more of their party could be seen. He wondered where his hunting party was. Moctu hoped they were close and had brought along some of the tribe's boys and women to help cut and carry the meat back. They'd be especially helpful if the hunters managed to make more kills. He'd gotten his start like that—as a pack boy traveling with the hunters.

Chapter Five

Moctu finished gutting the female and ate a hunk of warm, raw liver after first raising it toward the sun and thanking the Spirits. He began the laborious task of removing the hide and collecting the valuable rope tendons and sinews used for sewing. Women would later beat the sinews into fibrous masses from which strands could be removed for thread and string.

His mind wandered back to the hunt two years ago during which he'd won the respect of the older hunters. Game had been scarce near Etseh, so Ordu organized a long-range hunt with eight men and four boys. The group became dispirited as they traveled far northward for nearly half a moon, but saw little in the way of large game. They managed to feed themselves by killing smaller game such as ducks, turtles, fish, and beaver.

They circled to the east toward the Dorne River when they spotted a herd of about three hands of aurochs. The hunters killed four of the cattle—a black "mossy horn" bull and three reddish-brown cows, but Ordu was wounded while helping bring down the bull. It was a large one weighing more than ten hunters, whereas the cows were about half that size. The kills would provide a huge amount of meat, and there was a great deal of work to be done. While some of the men cared for Ordu, the rest began to clean and butcher the animals as well as build several travois to help carry the meat back to their people.

The hunters decided to send some of the meat back with the boys who would then bring others in the tribe back to help. The extra rest would be good for Ordu. It was a simple trek to the south—it would take three, maybe four days, for the boys to get back to Etseh with a travois of meat. With Moctu in charge, the four boys set off at daybreak the next day dragging meat weighing more than two large men on the travois. Moctu was glad that one of the other boys was Palo, his best friend who was a tall, strong, hard worker. The other two, Seetu and Sokum, were a summer younger, and while both were extremely skinny, they were affable and good workers.

The boys had made good progress through the lowlands the first day, and Moctu was hopeful that they could reach home in two more days. Moctu chose the highest ground he could find, a low hill on which to make camp. It was fireless because Samar, the fire-master, had unfortunately allowed the skull ember to go out a few days earlier. The skull ember was a mixture of charcoal and animal fat that slow-burned inside the wolf skull protected from the wind and weather. It was used each evening to start the campfire, so since it went out, the hunters and boys had suffered with only cold camps. Fire was precious to Nereans because it couldn't be created. Fire came from the Spirits. It had to be harvested from fires started by their lightning strikes. The main fire at Etseh was kept burning continually. Moctu had never seen it extinguished in his whole life.

It was the evening of the second day out when the boys were chilled by the nearby howl of a wolf, which was soon joined by many others. Moctu anxiously clutched his talisman, a wolf totem, because a lone wolf had been killed by his father, Jona, on the day he was born. Moctu knew that wolves most often stayed away from humans, but if there was freshly slaughtered meat around, they could become very aggressive.

The two younger boys were close to panic since there

wasn't a fire to keep the wolves away. Moctu calmed them by stopping early at a bald hilltop and setting the boys to work gathering large piles of cobbles. Since there were no trees or brush nearby, the hilltop would be more easily defended than any place they'd come across that afternoon. Moctu strained to remember everything his father Jona, the tribe's best wolf hunter, had told him about wolves.

"Let's see, they're agile, crafty, and hunt cooperatively, and like most animals, they're best shot at from the side," he remembered.

"Trust the Wolf Spirits. They are your totem—they are on your side and will guide you through trying times," Jona had told Moctu.

Well, now is one of those times, Moctu thought, but will the Wolf Spirits side with me over their own kind? The boys took stock of their weapons—four heavy spears, two atlatls, and twelve throwing shafts. The boys agreed that Moctu and Palo were the best at using atlatls, so they split the shafts between the two of them.

"Don't throw your heavy spears. Keep them with you for close thrusting work, if it comes to that," Moctu instructed the boys. The wolf howls were closer now, and there seemed to be dozens of them. Palo was trying to show bravery, but Seetu and Sokum were becoming unnerved. Moctu had them practice throwing the rocks which seemed to give them a little added confidence.

It was dusk when the first wolf was spotted, and several others soon joined it. The ones they saw were huge, nearly the weight of a grown man and thickly furred. Night fell, and the stars and half-moon shone brightly allowing the boys to see the shadowy, fast-moving shapes of the wolves as they circled them slightly more than an atlatl throw away. The smell of fresh auroch meat was driving the beasts into a frenzy, and they gradually moved closer.

The boys seemed buoyed and chuckled nervously when

Moctu yelled at the wolves, "Come try and take our meat, and we'll make worm's-meat of you."

The wolves edged ever closer and began to make darting runs toward the boys' circle. Spirits! There were so many!

"Some of them are coming within throwing range now, so throw a rock if you have a good target," Moctu told the younger boys. Both Seetu and Sokum threw almost immediately but hit nothing. Moctu saw a big wolf begin a move toward them and drew back his arm to throw but hesitated thinking how few shafts they had. So many wolves! I should wait for a better opportunity, he thought. He saw Palo draw his throwing arm back, but he too hesitated. Seetu and Sokum were throwing rocks but rarely hitting wolves. The wolves were quick and skittered away from the bouncing rocks, but they'd be back almost immediately. The young boys were losing hope and beginning to panic. Twice more Moctu raised his atlatl, but the agile beasts seemed to sense his intention and dart away just before he threw.

He wondered if they were reading his mind. How can they know when I plan to throw? Are the Wolf Spirits helping them and working against me, against us?

Palo had missed with two shafts. The wolves were fast and nimble, and the darkness made it harder to track their movements. Moctu reverently touched the wolf paw print charm carved on his caribou antler atlatl and prayed desperately for the great Wolf Spirits to help him against these marauders. I'll throw at the next beast that darts close to us that gives me any kind of side angle shot, he decided. The younger boys were terrified, and even Palo was losing his nerve with his lack of success.

Moctu saw a large gray beast begin a charge, and he let fly with a shaft that struck it, penetrating the fur and burying itself deep in the creature's left haunch. It wasn't a kill, but the boys cheered nonetheless. The stricken wolf yelped loudly and turned, disappearing into the dark where there was fierce growling and snarling.

"Sometimes wolves will turn on their own wounded comrades, especially if they're very hungry," Moctu remembered Jona saying. From what Moctu could hear, that was happening in the darkness lower down the hill.

Although the night was cool, Moctu was sweating profusely. They'd been defending against the wolves for a long time, and their pile of stones was much smaller. Moctu and Palo had both thrown two more shafts but missed. Occasionally one of the boys would hit a wolf with a rock causing the animal to yelp and retreat briefly, but there was no overall change in the attitude of the pack. They wanted the meat. Moctu realized they had only five more shafts and a small pile of rocks. "All right Palo. Wait until they get close... really close before using these last shafts. We have to make them count."

Moctu decided he would hold off on throwing his last three shafts until the rocks were gone. It didn't take long for that time to come.

"That was the last of the rocks," Seetu yelled, his voice a higher pitch than usual.

"So now take up your spears, but don't throw them," Moctu stressed.

With no more rocks coming their way, the wolves seemed to get more aggressive, and several would charge at one time. "That's some of the cooperative hunting you told me about," Moctu murmured to his father's spirit. "But please... help us find a way to beat these beasts."

Palo threw again, just missing, a finger's width below the throat of a huge, light-gray wolf. He was down to just one shaft. The boys were demoralized from the seemingly endless attacks. All their rocks and most of their shafts were gone and only one wolf had been wounded. Moctu threw another of his shafts, but it glanced harmlessly off the heavily furred back of a wolf. One of the wolves charged in close, and the younger boys thrust their spears at it. It grabbed Sokum's spear in its jaws and ripped it from the boy's hand, dragging it out of sight.

"We can't let that happen again," Moctu warned the boys. "Have to keep a firm grip on our spears and not let them be pulled away by the wolves."

Jona, we're down to three shafts and three spears, he thought, with at least a dozen of these ravenous wolves almost on us. They're relentless. We're doing our best, but I don't think we can beat them.

Moctu took a deep breath and fitted one of his two remaining shafts on his atlatl. He again waited for one of the beasts to start a charge, and he threw it hard. He knew as it left that it would hit. The atlatl magnified the throwing power, and the shaft buried in the chest of the wolf. Its paws went under and, carried by its momentum, it rolled to within a few feet of the boys' line of defense and lay motionless. The boys cheered once again, and the wolves seemed to back away. Moctu fitted his last shaft onto the atlatl and said to the younger two boys, "One of you… Seetu, you're closest. See if you can spear that wolf and drag it back to our line." But the wolves were snarling, and neither Seetu nor Sokum, who had Moctu's spear, seemed inclined to act on his request. Palo stepped in, quickly putting down his atlatl and with his heavy spear, thrust it into the belly of the wolf ensuring it was dead. Palo dragged the hundred-pound beast the short distance back to their defensive line and again took up his spear thrower."

Good job, Palo," Moctu said. "Sokum, pull the shaft out so we can use it again, but be careful not to break it."

The wolves were back again, and Seetu thrust his spear to parry a charging wolf only to again have it bite the spear. It growled savagely trying to pull it away. As Seetu hung on grimly to the spear, the wolf who weighed about as much as the boy pulled him off his feet and began to back up. It snarled loudly as it dragged both the spear and boy slowly away.

Seetu made a wailing cry and Moctu, who had only a frontal shot, threw his last shaft hard at the animal and was gratified to see it bury in the left eye socket of the wolf. It released the spear and went down motionless. Seetu scrambled back still holding his spear which made Moctu smile with pride for the boy. The two other boys had happily cheered Moctu's shot and seemed to regain their failing morale. The shaft had been extracted from the dead wolf they'd pulled within their lines, and it was given to Moctu who could make out in the dark that the flint head was loose but still attached. He fitted this shaft in the atlatl and waited for the next charge.

It never came. The pragmatic wolf pack decided this target wasn't worth the trouble and dissolved into the night. The boys were exhausted but thrilled that the wolves were gone and they were still alive and well. They were charged with adrenalin and loudly gushed with praise for Moctu.

"We'd be dead if not for you," Seetu said, pointing both forefingers at him. "You killed two wolves and wounded a third."

"You were great, and the people will be proud of you. They'll hear of this, I promise," Palo said.

Moctu was embarrassed but pleased and deflected the praise by saying, "You all impressed me with your courage, but I'll tell you, when Seetu didn't let go of that spear as that giant beast was pulling him down—that took some real courage." The boys laughed at the memory, and Seetu glowed with pride.

There was lots of talk and laughter, but the nervous energy rapidly drained from them all, and Moctu found himself dead-tired. He forced himself and the boys to gather in the other dead wolf and extract the shaft and collect the few stones that were not too far out.

Morning came and after breakfasting on chunks of raw auroch liver and heart, the boys scouted for the missing spear and shafts. They found most of them, including the shaft in the partially eaten corpse of the third wolf. The other wolves had indeed finished off one of their own. That carcass was useless, but Moctu gutted the two other dead wolves and put them on the travois near the auroch meat but separate. The furs were good, and the wolf meat would likely be eaten, but it was gamey and probably best made into jerky for eating during the lean times.

It was a long day's trek, especially after the previous night's battle and not much sleep. In the evening, however, they began to recognize the very familiar geography closer to Etseh, and they buoyantly pressed on. It was dark when a lookout heard them and called out, and soon many of the clan were coming to meet them. There was rejoicing when the auroch meat was uncovered, and the three other boys began telling what had happened.

Sokum summed things up saying, "Moctu saved us and the meat. We'd be dead if not for him!" Moctu's mother, Alta, was there and beamed with pride. The tribe feasted that night, and speeches were made around the main fire about the bravery of the boys—especially Moctu. Nuri smiled at him every time their eyes met, each time looking down shyly afterward. Everyone enjoyed the fresh roasted meat, and the whole tribe seemed happy—except Jabil.

Chapter Six

Moctu's thoughts were broken by a shout from Nabu and the hunters. They were soon upon him and he said, "The main herd has headed westward through that break in the valley and toward the lowlands."

Ordu immediately sent Nabu, who'd already had a full day of running, and another scout in that direction to see about remaining hunting possibilities.

"What is it with you young hunters?" Samar complained. "Why did you attack the herd before we got here? Spirits! We've been running all day long."

As Moctu told them in detail what had happened, he saw Ordu's eyes narrow. The men's disappointment quickly turned to amazement tinged with a bit of skepticism. Ordu sent Tabar and another man north to scout for evidence of the Pale Ones and information on their strength and whereabouts. The rest of the men finished cleaning and prepping the meat for transport back to Etseh.

It was late evening by the time the hunters got back to Etseh. Even from a distance, the men could see the small hearth fires that lit up the length of the deep, gently sloping overhang that sheltered the Nerea. Anxious to get back, the hunters picked up their pace, and they were soon gathered around the central fire while the women prepared their food and drink. The simmering stew of fresh meat, pinon nuts, onions, wild grain, and herbs gave off a wonderful smell. Most of the hunters, however, were grumpy. Besides being tired and hungry, they were disappointed that most of them hadn't been involved in the kills—they'd been unsuccessful locating the remainder of the herd that had moved through a pass in the valley, continuing far westward toward the lowlands.

Each night the men listened respectfully to the "Song of the Tribe" chanted by Nindai, a young man who'd been lamed by a fall from a tree at an early age. Since then, he'd been trained as a medicine man by Jelli and her predecessor, Mago. Nindai's chanting was interspersed with his adept playing of an eagle-bone flute. In the background, outside the circle, Jelli beat a rhythm with a thick stick on a section of hollow log. Before Mago died two winters ago, the nearly blind, white-bearded healer had taught Nindai to play the flute expertly. Tonight, the pounding rhythm and the rich, wafting notes seemed to penetrate deep within the men. All seemed moved by the haunting tones and melodies, the flickering fire, and swirling smoke which set an ethereal mood.

> First was the Earth with her beautiful mountains, streams and sky
> We are the Earth Mother's People
> Then was born the sun which comes every morning where the mountain and sky meet
> We are the Earth Mother's People
> Then was born the moon to teach woman, yet to come
> We are the Earth Mother's People
> Then came the stars in beautiful design
> We are the Earth Mother's People
> We were birthed by Earth Mother, discharged from the deepest cave
> We are the Earth Mother's People
> First came man, then woman. From them, all others
> We are The Earth Mother's People

We stand on the Earth's fullness, we enjoy all that is good
We are the Earth Mother's People
She has placed the trees, animals, fire, and sparkling
stones here for our use and pleasure
We are the Earth Mother's People
From Mother Earth we came to wander this beautiful
land
We are the Earth Mother's People
To Earth we return where Mother Earth cares for us
We are the Earth Mother's People.

After Nindai had finished there was quiet while the men once again processed the words and dealt with their innermost thoughts.

Finally, at a sign from Ordu, Samar rose and broke the silence.

"Seven hands of caribou," he said scowling. "Not far from Etseh. And we got... one. Why? Because there were wolves? No. We scouted for wolf sign and found none." He looked scornfully at Jabil who was toying nervously with a long, thin braid that extended from his right temple.

Many of the other hunters were equally infuriated that Jabil had ruined their chances for a larger kill, and Ordu rebuked him sternly. Jabil seethed with barely contained rage, staring in turn at Samar and Ordu. Two older men stood to remind the hunters that Jabil had located and killed the cave bear just one year before and today had indeed killed a good-sized caribou. That seemed to soften the mood of the men. It was clear, however, from what Ordu said, that there would be some punishment for Jabil, at a minimum excluding him from scouting and hunting for at least a half moon. He'd have to do women's work—which any man loathed—including gathering firewood, cleaning, skinning, drying meat, and foraging for nuts and edible plants. Not what a cave bear killer expected to be doing.

Ordu nodded at Tabar, who had scouted the area north of where Moctu had made his kills, and he stood.

"At the northern kill site, we found evidence of the Pale Ones," he started.

This was what the tribe really wanted to hear about. The men quieted and were riveted to Tabar's words. Women on the outskirts of the fire circle edged closer to listen in.

"It's clear that they made three kills there and that the animals were gutted, cleaned, and dragged away to the north. At least five individuals—five Pale Ones were involved, and one left this." He held up a crudely made, broken sandal, and the curious men around the fire leaned in and strained to get a better look.

Ordu then nodded at Moctu, indicating he should speak about all that he had seen of the Pale Ones. Moctu was honored to be asked by Ordu to speak to the gathered men. Interest was even higher in his comments because he'd seen the creatures. Women defied convention and crowded near the fire to hear what he had to say.

"They're big," Moctu began. "Bigger than Ordu or Samar, at least in the shoulders and arms. Not as tall, though. They're hairier than we are, but it's light-colored—and they are too—their skin looks bleached—and I saw one that has red hair." This caused some consternation, as no one there had seen a person with red hair before.

"They used caribou skins to cover themselves to get close to the herd and came at the herd from several directions. They didn't use atlatls, or throw their spears, but charged into the caribou herd slashing and thrusting. Afterward, they came close enough to me that I could see their clothes—just pelts that were crudely strapped together. They never really threatened me, but they retrieved one of their kills not far from mine. The Pale Ones spoke only in grunts and sign language—nothing I could understand. They gutted their large bull quickly, and two of them pulled it away to the north with ease."

Ordu praised Moctu for his two kills, and he could see Jabil again fuming with jealousy and anger. Jondu, a young, black-haired hunter who spent much of his time with Jabil, arose unbidden and loudly, and stormily asked what was to be done about the Pale Ones.

"These are the People Eaters! They take our scarce game. They're not like us, and we can't trust them. They could attack us. We have to destroy them first."

As strident as this speech was, there did seem to be a high level of unease and concern among the men around the fire and the eavesdropping women on the periphery. Everyone seemed a bit unnerved by the Pale Ones. Most of the older men spoke in turn, and there was a consensus for action of some type. Suggestions ranged from an attack by all the men of Nerea to a scouting party that would identify how many of the Pale Ones there were and where and how they lived. Most men favored the latter strategy, and Ordu seemed to lean toward it, but he wanted more time to think on the subject.

Two days later, Ordu sent four men, including Nabu, to the north to try to determine the Pale Ones' location and numbers. The men scouted for more than half a moon without seeing any of the Pale Ones, or their fires. They found two old sites the creatures had occupied. One was a shallow cave and overhang shelter much smaller than Etseh, and the other a remarkable structure of mammoth skulls, tusks, and bones over which, presumably, they'd stretched animal skins. In both, the men found evidence of only five or six hearths, indicating these encampments had far fewer inhabitants than Etseh which had at least fifteen hearths. This news seemed to largely relieve the apprehensions of the Nerea. Visions of being overrun by hordes of Pale Ones now seemed highly improbable, and most largely dismissed the matter. Jabil, Jondu and a few others, however, continued to lobby for action against the Pale Ones citing the threat they posed to the tribe. After the third time that Jabil or Jondu had spoken of the need for war against the Pale Ones, Ordu formally dismissed the issue.

"Keeping our people fed is a much more pressing need," he said. "There are those among us who have never experienced a starving time, a winter of death. It changes you. We cannot spare the men needed for a successful war effort."

On their trip north, the scouts had seen a distant herd of two hands of horses, as well as several rhinoceroses. Game was still scarce near Etseh, so based on the scouting information, Ordu determined that another long-range hunting trip should be made. He chose eight hunters, including Moctu. Jabil was excluded as part of his punishment. While the hunters were away, another group, mostly women, would be sent to the sea for the annual Gatza, or salt-making effort. Salt was important to the tribe for preserving meat, but making it was a slow, tedious effort. It entailed gathering an enormous amount of firewood to burn while gradually evaporating large quantities of seawater to make the crystalline salt. Women did almost all the work while a couple of men guarded them and hunted or fished for food.

"Since both the Gatza and our hunting trip will each take a half a moon or more, they'll be done at the same time to limit the time couples and families are apart," Ordu said. This would help preserve harmony within the tribe, something that Ordu's father, a former leader, had instructed him was almost as important as the feeding and safety of the tribe.

Chapter Seven

Tomorrow's the day, Moctu thought smiling, his heart beating faster as he planned what to take on the hunt. The sun had just crested the eastern mountains, dappling the trees and nearby hills with soft amber light but leaving most of the world still shadowed. Returning from his morning ablutions, Moctu slowed as he found his way blocked by Jabil and Jondu. To him they looked like twins, each wearing the same harsh expression—a cross between a sneer and a scowl. Like Moctu, both were broad-shouldered and well-muscled. But they were each heavier than he was and about a thumb taller. Moctu knew this was trouble, but he found that he was more annoyed than worried.

"Why should a boy who hasn't even undergone his manhood rites go on a hunting trip?" Jabil snarled. He was referring to the fact that Ordu and the elders had rewarded Moctu's bravery and leadership in fighting off the wolves two years before by giving him manhood status without the arduous rites that boys normally had to endure.

"Isn't my handprint on the Wall of Warriors?" Moctu asked. This question seemed to irritate Jabil even more. Most of the tribe had cheered when Jelli blew red pigment mixed with charcoal on Moctu's outstretched hand after he'd placed it on the sacred wall. About 40 handprints of Nerean warrior-hunters past and present were preserved under a small overhang near Etseh. Moctu had placed his hand just below the print of his deceased father, Jona. But Jabil and Jondu, whose handprints were also there, had been rankled then and were more so now, especially after being excluded from the upcoming hunt. Jabil spit at Moctu's feet.

"You're no warrior, you're a little boy."

Irritation and frustration overwhelmed Moctu, and he replied in kind, spitting at Jabil's feet. The action inflamed both the bigger young men, and bellowing with indignation and rage, they attacked Moctu. He ducked Jabil's charge and brought his head up into Jondu's chin as he absorbed a wicked punch to his ribs at the same time. Jondu fell backward and sat in the dust, stunned and bleeding, having badly bitten his tongue. By then Jabil was back at Moctu pummeling him in the face and neck. The boys fell to the ground, and Jabil was on top still battering Moctu's face with vicious punches. Moctu fended some of the punches with his left hand and with his right delivered a powerful blow to Jabil's left eye. But the older boy soon gained control and was then rejoined by Jondu who held Moctu's right arm down while Jabil continued hammering Moctu's head.

Jabil was there above him beating him savagely, and then he wasn't, as a man flew into him from the side ripping him off Moctu and careening off to the left. Moctu suddenly found his left arm free and delivered a stinging punch to Jondu's nose which dislodged him from Moctu's pinned arm. Another man was there now separating the young men. There was a lot of yelling, and Moctu saw that Samar had been the one that had wrenched Jabil off of him and Tabar was the man separating him from Jondu. Moctu's nose was bleeding, one eye was partially swelled closed, and one of his front teeth was loose—the thing that worried him the most. He knew that losing teeth was a grave misfortune as they were critical for chewing, tool-making and general appearance. Moctu was pleased to see that Jondu's nose was also bleeding, and some blood had seeped from his mouth, and Jabil's eye was red and puffy. The men, joined by others, angrily and roughly marched the young men back toward camp. The three were brought in front of Ordu who sat near the fire.

"What started this fight?" Ordu asked, his calm voice masking an irritation and displeasure that his clenched teeth betrayed. He focused his gaze on Jabil.

"He spit at us!" Jabil blurted.

"He hit us first!" Jondu quickly followed.

Moctu, his face a wreck and his nose still bleeding, remained quiet as his tongue investigated his loose tooth.

Ordu watched him for a moment then said, "Interesting—I've rarely seen where one boy attacked two older, larger boys at once." He paused, thinking, then said, "But we will not fight among ourselves, and you will all be punished. Moctu, you won't be going on the hunt tomorrow." Moctu looked down, and Jabil flashed a grin. "And you two," Ordu continued to the others, "will accompany the women on the salt expedition where you'll do nothing but carry water and firewood." The grin left Jabil's face, and Jondu let out an audible sigh.

After Ordu's decree, all retired to their family hearths. As Moctu's mother cared for his facial wounds, he was overcome by a powerful headache and an overwhelming weariness. He was soon asleep on his furs. Alta, heavy with Tabar's child, mixed poultices and applied them to Moctu's wounds while he slept. He slumbered all that day and through the night, and when he awoke his headache was gone, and he was ravenous. He hungrily ate some caribou stew, wincing occasionally when his loose tooth hit a tough piece of meat, and he drank some bitter-tasting tea that Alta had prepared that morning from willow bark and yarrow.

Alta gently dabbed more poultice on his facial wounds, worriedly noting his bruised, swollen cheeks and blackened eyes. But Moctu could still see well, and even though his face, shoulders, and arms ached, he went out to stretch his legs and get away from the smoky air of the hearth. The hunting party had left at first light, and although Moctu was deeply disappointed not to be with them, he realized it was probably for the best. His wounds would heal faster with rest and Alta's poultices, and he might not have been much help the way he felt. Shortly after leaving his family's hearth, Palo joined him.

"I've been watching for you since yesterday—I heard what happened. I can only imagine how bad Jabil's fists hurt today," Palo said grinning, trying to lighten the mood. Moctu found that it hurt to smile, but he appreciated Palo's companionship. Almost every person they passed stared at Moctu's bruises and black eyes.

"When you're healed up we'll get them back," Palo said, his jaw set. "We can take them separately, two on one like they did to you, or two on two. I don't care."

"Thanks, Palo, let me think about that for a while. Jabil's the one I'd like to get. The dung-face won't leave me alone. But I'm already in a lot of trouble."

They passed a woman scraping a hide who twisted to get a better look at Moctu's battered face. "I'm sick of this," he said. "Let's get our atlatls and get out of here and go practice."

Palo smiled and nodded. "Meet you at the practice meadow."

Chapter Eight

They were soon flinging their practice shafts at a stump about three or four fallen-tree lengths away. The practice shafts had crude stone points that gave them the appropriate weight and aerodynamics but didn't risk any of the finely worked points that took longer to make. Moctu could make about two hands of good stone points in one afternoon's effort (Samar could do almost twice as many in that time), but it was laborious, and the flint supply wasn't nearby. In fact, it was a good four- or five-day trek to the northeast crossing three rivers to get high-quality flint. Breaking a point, or worse yet, losing a shaft in the tall grass was distressing.

Moctu and Palo competed on who could throw the far-thest, who could throw closest to the stump, and who could throw one hand of shafts separately, past the stump the fastest. The sun was bright in the blue sky, the air was crisp and clear, and the practice with Palo was stimulating and fun. Moctu found that his shoulders quit aching and his stress melted away.

After Moctu hit the stump with a throw, Palo whistled softly and said, "You're really good, and you're getting better every time we practice. You could win the atlatl competition when the tribes meet again at the flint quarry. Even if Lehoy of the Lion People is there."

"You too," said Moctu. "I think you'll be tough to beat."

He remembered that every five years at least three tribes would meet for a reunion, to mine flint, and to trade goods and often young women or girls. Counting back, he realized that the next meeting was less than two years away. That meeting would likely be four tribes including the new one led by Ordu's son.

"But Lehoy won it easily last time," Moctu reminded Palo. "And I bet he's gotten even better. We should keep practicing."

The boys were trying to find an errant shaft when Palo discovered something wondrous. He'd moved toward a small grove of trees when he saw a large group of bees angrily circling a portion of a dead tree that had fallen. About two-thirds of the tree was still standing, and bees swirled around the top of it as well.

"Moctu! Hey Moctu, quick—come take a look at this!" On closer inspection, they discovered that the tree had broken off at the entrance of a beehive and the downed portion had honeycomb within it! The boys had only rarely had the opportunity to taste honey and only in very small portions. Here were several fist-sized slabs, and after dragging the downed section of tree farther away, they feasted on the honeycomb, savoring the exquisite, super-sweet taste.

"We need to save some of this for others in the tribe," Moctu said in-between licks when they'd eaten about half of it.

"Right," Palo responded.

But shortly thereafter, the honeycomb was gone, and they found themselves licking chunks of the wood broken away from the hollow trunk.

"There's probably a lot more honey up there," said Palo pointing to the broken top of the tree where numerous bees still buzzed furiously about twenty feet up. The boys gathered their atlatls and shafts and ran back to Etseh with the news of the beehive. They first went to Nindai who, even though lame, could still climb trees. He was skilled with using smoke to make bees less aggressive while taking their honey. Although his right leg was more than a finger's length shorter than his left, he still had strength in it. He was pleased to hear of the bees and excitedly began his preparations for extracting the honey. He set aside his cane, the bottom of which was covered with a thick hide wrap which Moctu assumed was there to help cushion the shocks from Nindai's uneven gait.

"I'll wrap myself in thin furs and woven cloth and stand before a fire until the clothes are saturated with smoke," Nindai said. "Then we'll gauge the wind direction and in a good place near the honey tree, we'll pile a fire with wet wood. We'll get the smoke billowing up to the hive, and finally, I'll strap on these gourds and climb the tree." It sounded simple and safe, but in fact, he'd gotten stung so many times in past honey extractions that he was nearly immune to the stings. The stings still hurt, but they wouldn't be life-threatening, even though he'd likely be stung many times. He was extremely cheerful, and Moctu realized this was as close to dangerous hunting or fighting as Nindai ever got. From what Moctu had seen, Nindai had the heart of a warrior, just not the body. This was one of the few times Nindai could be a hero to the tribe.

Word had gotten out, and soon there was an audience watching Nindai's preparations, everyone hoping to get a taste of the precious honey that might be recovered shortly. With many of the tribe gathered around the honey tree to watch, the event went pretty much as Nindai predicted, although at one point his face seemed to be engulfed in bees. With the help of an auroch skin belt, he climbed the tree, the bees remaining rather docile to that point. When he started scooping honey out of the hive, they swarmed, and there seemed to be a black cloud around him. His exposed skin around his face and hands looked black and furry with bees. Moctu shivered with the thought of all that stinging, but Nindai had soon scrambled back down the tree with four large gourds full of the treasured nectar hanging from his neck by cords of sinew. Some of the bees still followed him, and his face and hands were red with welts, but his smile showed success.

With the crowd noisily following, Nindai used his cane to help himself limp back to Etseh and to the hearth of Ono, Jondu's father, who'd been left in charge while Ordu was on the hunting trip to the north.

Ono called to him as he came up. "Nindai, I honor your brave effort. Were you successful?" Nindai held up the four gourds, and the group behind him cheered with expectant enthusiasm. His hands had been stung so many times, they appeared to be one continuous welt, and despite his relative immunity, they'd swelled to nearly twice their normal size. He was experiencing extreme pain, and his hands trembled slightly as he set the gourds carefully near Ono's feet. Even with the intense pain, Nindai maintained his composure and seemed to be enjoying the attention and acclaim.

"Ono, I present this honey to you and ask your aid in distributing it fairly to the tribe."

"I've already given this thought," Ono replied, "and the division will be by hearths. Each hearth will get an equal share, except that the hearth of Nindai will get a double portion." Although there was a little grumbling from those from large hearths, most thought this split was equitable, and the division was completed.

Chapter Nine

That same morning, Jondu lingered by the large rocks at the base of Etseh's overhang casually inspecting his atlatl shafts and the leather holder which contained them. A deerskin headband kept the young man's long, wavy black hair from covering his deep-set dark eyes. The hunters had left at first light, and it was now after breakfast. The women were beginning their daily tasks and chores. For a while, he idly watched two women preparing caribou hides, glad that he didn't have to do the dirty, tedious work himself. The hides had been scraped of all flesh and gore then buried for nearly half a moon to help loosen the hair. Now, the women were taking the stiff, soiled skins and scraping them again. The next step would be to soak them in stale urine for half a moon to help remove the rest of the hair. To his left, he noticed a third woman working to increase the suppleness of a smaller strip of nearly finished hide by pulling it back and forth around an upright pole.

Switching his focus back to his shafts, he checked each one to see that the point was secure, the shaft wasn't warped, and the fletching was well attached. Although he continued to appear occupied, it would be clear to anyone who saw his occasional furtive glances that he had other purposes. As he waited for something or someone, he gingerly tested his tongue which he'd deeply bitten during his fight with Moctu. It seemed to be healing, but it still affected his swallowing and speaking. Even though he and Jabil had given Moctu a good beating yesterday, he promised himself that he'd repay Moctu for this injury.

It wasn't long before the girl for whom he'd been waiting passed by unaware of his attention. It was Avi, and she was on her way to the west woods, carrying some skins to help her gather a large load of firewood. Jondu waited for her to get some distance ahead, and then stealthily followed her. It was a bright, pleasant morning and she was wearing a light, woven grass wrap. She had a leather strap tying her long, light brown hair behind her. Jondu's excitement grew as he followed her. This was better than hunting.

The forest had been stripped of dry wood and branches close to Etseh, so Avi moved farther into the interior, gathering some wood into piles as she went. She'd pick up these piles on her way back. She jumped and let out a small cry as Jondu called out to her.

"Avi, I've come to help you."

"Oh, Jondu, you startled me! I didn't know you were there."

"I'd like to… to help you," he said coming up to her.

She noticed he had an odd smile on his face. "I'd be glad for your help," she said a little nervously. "You're very strong, and together we can carry a lot of wood."

"We can carry a lot of wood later," he said pressing his body against hers. "Right now, I want you."

"But Jondu, I've yet to reach womanhood."

"That'll come soon enough. You're a woman to me," he said, grinding his hardness against her.

"No Jondu, please. It's wrong. Please."

But he was already stripping her wrap from her and forcing her to a leafy patch on the ground. She pushed at him and raised her voice.

"No Jondu, don't—this is wrong."

She was scared, he could see it. She was fighting him

but perhaps not as much as he'd anticipated. Maybe that was because he was so much stronger than she was, and she knew it was pointless. He stripped off his clothes while holding her down with his right arm. She was still pushing at him, and he was hugely excited. He had never been this hard.

She was whimpering a little now, saying, "Please Jondu, please don't do this. You'll hurt me."

He positioned himself between her legs and thrust inside her, gasping with the pleasure of it. She was sobbing quietly but no longer fought him. Grasping her buttocks, he pushed her against himself, ramming into her again and again. It didn't take long before he felt an overwhelming force welling up within him, and he exploded inside her, letting out a moan of staggering satisfaction.

Jondu rolled off Avi, staring up at the forest canopy, breathing heavily. "That wasn't so bad now, was it?"

Avi said nothing and remained motionless as she also stared up at the trees towering over them.

"That was *good*," he continued. "You're really pretty, and I want to do this again soon."

Avi was awash with confusing, conflicting emotions and thoughts. A strong feeling of violation and betrayal was moderated only slightly by a degree of... what? Was it gratification at being desired and complimented or happy consternation that the act hadn't hurt as much as she'd expected or something else?

Chapter Ten

Avi reached Nuri's hearth and breathlessly called out to her. Nuri came out from behind a group of skins hung on a horizontal pole where she'd been weaving reeds into baskets. Avi came up close to her and whispered, "I really need to talk with you alone—can you come now?" Soon they were away from the group of hearths, and Avi, still out of breath said, "Jondu just took me!" Nuri was surprised because taking a girl before her menses, although not forbidden, was strongly discouraged.

"How did it happen?"

"When I went to gather firewood—he surprised me in a secluded spot. He's very strong. It wasn't bad—as bad as before anyway."

"What?" Nuri exclaimed, swatting Avi's arm. "You never told me that. What happened before?"

"Well, it happened once before, last summer, when Ono found me gathering wood. That time was awful. It was painful—I bled—a lot," Avi reflected quietly.

"Jondu's father took you last summer?" Nuri said shocked, trying to keep her voice calm.

"Yes, but Father went to him that evening and told him it was unseemly—to take a girl before her menses—and to stay away from me. Father was very angry."

"And did Ono stay away?"

Avi nodded.

"Will you ask your father to force Jondu to stay away?"

"Yes—I'm sure Father will be even angrier because Jondu's of the same family as Ono. But I'm not sure Jondu will listen to him. He said he'd see me often in the future. But the Spirits favor me. Jondu leaves on the Gatza expedition tomorrow and will be gone for at least half a moon, and my menses will come soon, and Ordu will place me with a mate. It may even be Jondu. If it's not him, my new mate will keep him away. I just hope it won't be Ono. I really hate him, and he already has two mates anyway. I don't want an old man, even if he is an elder or a great hunter. I want a younger man like Jabil or Moctu. They're both strong and good hunters. Even Jondu would be all right, I guess. He's strong too, and I don't want to be a second or third mate at Ordu's or especially Ono's hearth."

"I've heard that a second mate gets a lot more *attention,*" Nuri teased.

"I don't want more *attention,*" Avi said in a near whimper.

Nuri was immediately sorry she'd teased her. "I too will soon get my menses and be placed with a mate. I've been worried about the exact same things." She touched her talisman, a red hawk feather she wore at her neck between two carved ivory rings, and said, "I've prayed to the Spirits that I don't get placed with an older man." Nuri's thoughts wandered to Moctu, with whom she felt a connection. But Jabil and Jondu were better than most of the other alternatives, and girls didn't get to pick mates, so she and Avi would have to hope for the best and be resilient no matter to whom they were assigned.

"I guess we should be grateful that we're not coming of age near the time when the tribes meet at the flint quarry. Then we'd be traded to a different tribe, and we'd be leaving our families and friends," Nuri said. "I would dread that—going to a strange, new tribe."

"Yes, there is that," Avi admitted. "I'd hate it too."

The girls were quiet for some time lost in thought. "Well, I need to get going. I have to help my mother process hides."

Nuri scrunched up her face at the thought of working the hides in stale urine. "Are you going to tell her about Jondu?"

Avi paused at the hearth entrance. "Yes, I guess I should tell her before Father, so she can help keep him from getting too angry."

Nuri spent the rest of the day thinking about Avi's misfortune and their collective predicament. She'd been lucky—in part due to her protective father and mother—and had never yet been taken by one of the men. She knew what to expect from hearing and, at times, seeing her mother and father, and other mates in the tribe coupling. Also, her mother had instructed her on what would happen and what to do. Her thoughts kept coming back to Moctu—she wondered how he was doing after the fight. She'd seen his bruised face and blackened eyes, and now would be a good time to visit him. She'd take him some special stew to help him recover. It was a good opportunity to talk with him and get to know him better. If word got out that she was fond of Moctu, maybe Ordu would consider that when placing her with a mate. It couldn't hurt.

Chapter Eleven

"Hello, Nuri—welcome," Alta called out as Nuri neared the hearth.

"Hello, Mother Alta. You look happy and strong. When is the baby due?" Nuri asked using the tribe's respectful "Mother" designation for women who'd given birth.

"Should be any day now. And it can't come soon enough for me." Alta's broad smile and cheerfulness belied her stated impatience. She had gone a long time without having a baby and was clearly enjoying the experience and the anticipation of having a newborn again.

"Is Moctu here? I've brought him fresh stew which I hope will help his healing," Nuri said a little shyly as she came closer. She offered the generous portion of hot, savory, meaty stew in a thick leather vessel to Alta.

"This smells wonderful. I'm sure he'll love it," Alta said. "Especially coming from you," she added after a moment. "He ought to be back soon—he's with your uncle, Samar, making spear points this afternoon."

"Is he feeling better? His bruises looked so painful. It was awful—two against one like that."

"Yes, that was unfair," Alta said matter-of-factly, but still wishing she could have been at the fight wielding her grinding stone. "But Moctu's recovering rapidly."

"That's good," Nuri said. The women were each seated

on one of the thick logs that, along with stacked stones, divided the hearth from the neighboring ones and made up the lower third of the room's walls. Skins draped over horizontal wooden poles completed the partition. After a pause in the conversation, Nuri said, "Mother Alta, may I ask you about the time when you were first given a mate?"

"Certainly, what would you like to know?"

"Well… it's… it's just…" Nuri stammered, trying to formulate the question. "Was Jona the one you wanted? Or was there someone else you would have preferred?" There was a long silence while Alta reflected, and Nuri felt like she'd overstepped her bounds.

Finally, Alta said, "Well, as you know, I came from the Gurek tribe when I was about your age. I was so young and scared. I wanted to stay with my own tribe, near my own family. Yes, there were some younger Gurek men that I would have preferred at the time, but I… I was naïve and young and not aware of some of the traits that are more important in a man. Jona was older, yes, and perhaps not as attractive as some of the younger men, but he was kind, and he had honesty, bravery, and loyalty. Each time the tribes would meet I would see the Gurek men and I was glad I had Jona. And he was a very good hunter and provider. All these things become ever-so-much more important to a woman when she has a baby to care for. Having said all that, there are some younger men in this tribe that would make excellent mates."

Nuri thought she saw Alta wink at her.

While she was thinking on Alta's comments, she heard Moctu approach and call out, "The stew smells good. I'm very hungry." He came into the hearth area. "Oh… hello, Nuri."

"Hello, Moctu, I hope you're feeling better," Nuri said, and she was mad at herself as she felt a blush come over her.

"Nuri's made you some delicious smelling stew to help your bruises heal," Alta said with a smile. She enjoyed watching the interaction between the two young ones.

"Oh, um… that's really nice of you—it does smell wonderful," Moctu said. "I'll eat some of it right away. I was hungry before, but smelling it makes me even hungrier."

Nuri smiled broadly at the compliment. "Your bruises look much better. I hope they don't hurt anymore."

"No, nothing hurts anymore," Moctu said, although his tooth still hurt. But he was pretty sure it would be all right. "This is great stew," he said after several large mouthfuls. "You're a very good cook."

Nuri blushed again and looked down with a smile. The conversation slowed as Moctu ate the stew appreciatively. Although it had been entertaining, Alta decided to leave them alone so they could talk without her around. She excused herself, saying she was going to get some reed materials from a woman a few hearths away.

After she'd gone, and as Moctu finished the stew, Nuri said, "It was wrong for them to both fight you at once." Moctu nodded but said nothing. He appreciated the comment and realized that he didn't feel nervous talking with her. "It seems so unfair," she continued. "But you made them pay a price—you hurt them badly."

"Uh huh," Moctu said smiling, "I'm sure I must have. I hit Jabil's fists brutally with my nose several times."

Nuri laughed despite the horrible image that came to mind. Moctu was having a good time, and he enjoyed making her smile. She was so pretty—especially when she smiled.

"Do you remember when we were young, and we'd go on lizard hunts around the ledges and rocks to the south?" she asked.

"We caught so many that some days they'd make up most of the meat in our evening stews," Moctu recalled. "Plus a few vipers here and there."

"I never liked the snakes," Nuri shuddered.

"You just have to watch out for the sharp end. Catch them by the tail, and whip the heads on the ground. The meat was good."

"Those were such good days," Nuri said.

"There'll be lots of good days to come," Moctu replied. "With a few cuts and bruises along the way."

"You've gone from being a good snake hunter to bringing down two caribou and scaring off the People Eaters."

Moctu shrugged. "I didn't scare them off—they just went about their business and left me alone. But they seemed as interested in me, or us, as we are with them."

"Do you think they're a threat like Jondu and some of the other hunters do?" Nuri asked.

"I don't know. I don't think so. They left so quickly—it seemed like they just wanted to be left alone. But we need to be cautious and stay guarded."

They both were quiet for a little while contemplating the Pale Ones. "Anyway, you've gone from being an excellent lizard hunter to providing caribou for the whole tribe," Nuri said smiling.

"And you've turned into a beautiful woman." Moctu couldn't believe he'd just vocalized that thought and was immediately embarrassed. Nuri, too, was embarrassed but very pleased at the comment. There was an uncomfortable silence, and both seemed grateful to hear Alta returning.

As Alta came into the hearth area, Nuri said, "Well, I need to be getting to my work. Goodbye Mother Alta, Moctu—it was good to see you both."

"You're welcome anytime Nuri, and thank you for the stew," Alta said.

"Yes… thanks, it was delicious," Moctu said, still a little embarrassed by his earlier comment. Alta picked up on the slight falter in his voice and eyed him curiously. She felt like she knew the gist of what had transpired and couldn't restrain a smile.

Chapter Twelve

"I make this promise to the Spirits," Jabil said to Jondu as they pulled a travois of food and supplies and trudged behind the five women. "One day I'll make Ordu pay for this humiliation."

"It could be worse," Jondu said, pointing at the two men who were there as guards for the women. Both were older men who provided little oversight for the two younger ones, which would probably give them opportunities to explore and hunt instead of just gathering firewood and water as directed by Ordu. Jabil grinned and nodded.

"I like the way you think, Jondu. By the time we make it to the sea, those two will be exhausted, and they'll give us no trouble."

"Now if we just had some girls or unmated women, we'd have all we need," Jondu said. "I took Avi in the west woods a day ago. It was great—she fought a little but didn't seem to mind it much. I told her I'd be 'helping her gather firewood' more often in the future."

"You took her before her menses?" said Jabil, surprised. "Ah… you waited until her father was on the hunting trip with Ordu. You're a cunning one Jondu. But stay away from Nuri. I have plans for her. I may help her with some 'firewood gathering' myself sometime soon."

The comment sidetracked Jabil's thoughts for a moment. It would serve two purposes—he could take Nuri in the woods and anger Moctu all at the same time. It was perfect. He recalled the way Nuri had looked at Moctu two summers before at the evening fire after he'd fought the wolves. The image of it still bothered him. She'd seemed infatuated with Moctu, and that had probably made Jabil hate him even more than Moctu getting special treatment and being excused from his manhood rites.

When the little dung pile was laughing with her a few moons after that, I taught him a lesson—beat him senseless before I got pulled away, Jabil thought with satisfaction. And here again a few days ago. I could have killed him. Probably would have if I hadn't been stopped. Several times now Nuri's seen how much stronger I am. Jabil was sure Moctu wanted Nuri. But that wasn't going to happen.

"Nuri and Avi will both get their menses soon and be placed with mates by Ordu," Jondu said.

"Ordu's a disgrace." Even the mention of his uncle made Jabil angry. "He's taken half the tribe's warriors on a hunting trip north and sent half of the remaining warriors to the western sea for salt. Now, Etseh or either of the smaller groups could be overrun and slaughtered by the People Eaters. He's just foolish. He worries about feeding the tribe but there won't be a tribe to feed if the Pale Ones come."

"Yes," Jondu agreed. "We need to find the Pale Ones and exterminate them before they catch us off guard and kill us or take our women. When we last saw them, they were hunting just one day away from Etseh. That's too close. They killed game that should have been ours. And they spooked the rest of the herd." Jondu realized that comment might offend Jabil for his earlier transgression of the same nature, and he continued quickly, "They've got to be eliminated. We have to find them and kill 'em."

Their thoughts and conversation were interrupted as the group came to a broad, fast-moving stream that they needed to ford. Getting the supplies and women across these streams was always the hardest and most dangerous part of the trip. The two young men were strong, competent workers, however, and the effort was accomplished with no losses or injuries.

Chapter Thirteen

It was late afternoon when Alta finished her basket weaving and irritably eyed the vole that scurried along the rocks near the front of her hearth. Etseh was overrun by rodents lately. The little creature disappeared into a hole at the base of a rock that was now fronted by a small delta of recently dug, reddish brown earth. It had come from the direction of a basket along the wall in which she kept chestnuts and acorns.

She would get the children to flush him out. She recalled the roving band of gourd-carrying kids that canvassed Etseh several days before looking for fresh vole holes. They poured small amounts of water into the holes to see where the water came out, usually several feet away and downhill. Once the escape hole was found, the children dowsed the top hole with large volumes of water until the rodent emerged from either the front or back hole. Then they stomped or clubbed the mouse and added him to their pile for use in the evening stew.

Smiling at the thought, Alta stood to start preparations for the evening meal. She missed Tabar who was away with Ordu on the hunting trip to the north. She worried much more now about the safety of the hunters on these trips, especially when Tabar and Moctu were involved. Her first husband, Jona, had been mortally wounded on such a trip. Even now, remembering that time was almost unbearable. However, after the appropriate mourning time had passed, Tabar wanted her for a mate, and Ordu and the other elders agreed. Tabar had been good to her and Moctu. Alta gradually found that her feelings for Tabar, while different, were every bit as strong as the ones she'd held for Jona. Moctu seemed to like and respect him too.

Moctu would be back soon from hunting with Palo, and he'd be hungry. She hoped he'd been able to kill something this time. Even a rabbit or a marmot would help. None of the hunters had found any large game near Etseh since the caribou had come and gone. There was talk that one or more of the Spirits had been angered and were no longer sending game. But which Spirits? There were Spirits in everything—not just the grasses and trees, or the birds and land beasts, but also in the flowing streams and clouds that moved overhead and made living shapes. Even rocks had Spirits and could form into sacred shapes on the mountains that sometimes helped with fertility or hunting. Jelli and Nindai had recently painted themselves and performed elaborate rituals, ones that placated the Spirits in the past. Maybe they'd work again.

As Alta retrieved some onions from a basket in the corner of the hearth area, she felt a gush of fluid between her legs. "Have I lost control of my…? Spirits! No—it's my baby coming. My water broke!"

She needed to alert Jelli and then go to the Red Hearth where women stayed when they had their menses and where births were undertaken. She wasn't overly worried since she had wide hips, good for child-bearing, and since Moctu's birth hadn't been a difficult one. She asked those in the nearby hearths to tell Moctu what had happened. After grabbing some woven cloth and other birthing materials, she said a prayer to her owl totem and the Earth Mother for protection and headed for Jelli's hearth.

"I've been expecting you, Mother Alta," Jelli said as Alta approached her hearth. "I saw in a vision that you'd have your baby before the moon became full. I've been busy making all the potions and giving the preliminary prayers. Nindai," she motioned at the young man grinding herbs in the corner, "will handle everything in my absence. Let's go." She grabbed a basket of food, potions, and woven materials and headed for the Red Hearth, not bothering to look if Alta was following her. Alta was having contractions now and watched Jelli walk away as she waited for one to pass. Jelli was one of the oldest women in the tribe and very slight of frame, but still sprite-ly, with a confident, commanding presence. Alta followed her to the Red Hearth where Jelli began arranging furs around a shallow birthing hole over which Alta would ultimately squat while delivering her baby.

Jelli was already chanting in soft tones, imploring Ama, the Earth Mother Spirit, to be with them and make the de-livery easy. Alta went through another contraction, and Jelli came over to check her and massage her abdomen.

"This one's different from Moctu," Jelli said thinking out loud as she rubbed the swollen belly. "I feel a foot down low—that's not helpful."

They both heard Moctu's call from beyond the hearth, "Mother, are you all right?" Men weren't allowed in the Red Hearth but could follow the birthing progress from outside.

"Yes, I'm fine, and Jelli is with…" Alta's voice cut off abruptly as a powerful contraction swept over her. She let out a soft moan and caught the eye of Jelli. Birthing women were discouraged from any loud screams or moaning because it would make the child weak-natured and could attract evil spirits.

The afternoon progressed but Alta did not. Jelli checked her again and pronounced that the birth opening was still too small. She'd been almost constantly massaging Alta's abdo-men while softly singing and chanting. Darkness had fallen, and Jelli stood back.

"The baby is positioned wrong. I'll give my most pow-erful prayer and then try to move it from both the outside and the inside." After a long, partially chanted, partially sung prayer, Jelli again felt the abdomen. "I'll be pushing from the inside. I need you to push down here." She positioned Alta's hands to the left side of the abdomen. She inserted the fingers of both her small, but powerful hands into Alta's vagina and said, "Push hard now."

Alta again let out a soft moan as both women pushed at the baby. The baby didn't move.

"I can feel the baby's bottom, but you don't have enough fluid inside for it to move around," Jelli said. "The baby's locked in this position. We'll wait until your opening is as large as possible and the baby will be born the way it is."

Fear shot through Alta. "Will my baby live? Will it be all right?"

"Only the Spirits know that. And I feel Jona's spirit intervening. It may help if you assure his spirit that your first-born, Moctu, will continue to have your favor no matter if this child is a boy or a girl." Alta nodded, but Jelli continued, "You must say it out loud, and give your best prayer. I'll be back soon," and she left the Red Hearth.

Outside she found Moctu, who'd been occasionally calling out encouragement to his mother.

"How is Mother Alta?" Moctu asked anxiously.

"The situation is serious. The Spirits are not allowing the baby to position correctly. It's unfortunate that Tabar is not here."

"What can I do to help?"

"I think your father, Jona's spirit is intervening. Your mother is right now beseeching his spirit to allow the birth, but you can help too," Jelli replied.

"I'll do anything."

"Good," Jelli said with an almost imperceptible smile, and she led him to an empty hearth nearby. She pulled out three bone needles and said, "We will show Jona's spirit with an Odel-emit, a sympathetic blood-letting, that you wish for and support the birth of this baby. Now strip off your bottom clothes and kneel down." At the sight of the bone needles, and the mention of stripping off his "bottom clothes," Moctu's breath caught, but he did as he was told.

He'd heard about Odel-emits, but they were rare. It was something that the men sometimes joked about—that something was "worse than an Odel-emit." Jelli pulled a large piece of bark from a woven bag and put the smooth side up, resting on his upper thigh. "Now place your penis on the bark," she directed. Moctu had a moment of hesitation but complied. She deftly pinned the skin of his member to the bark with one of the needles. The pain coursed through him, but he fought the urge to give voice to it. Blood dripped from the wound, as she took another needle, and chanting loudly, pinned the other side of his penis. Moctu watched in fascinated horror and riveting pain as she lifted the skin on the upper side of his member and ran the final needle through it. "There," she said. "Now you hold the bark and tell your thoughts to Jona's spirit. Let him know you support the birth of this baby and have now shown it with the Odel-emit. After you're done, when you want, you can leave the bark here, but keep the needles in until the birth is complete. I'll return to Alta." With that, she left him staring disbelieving at his injured penis.

Alta labored through the night and into the early morning when Jelli instructed her to squat low over the shallow pit and bear down while rolling her abdomen muscles. Jelli, lying facing upward, slipped her fingers inside Alta and pulled downward on the baby.

The pain for Alta was unbearable, but she kept herself from screaming, letting out small whimpers and moans. After a long time in this position, exhausted and drenched in sweat, she said, "I'm so tired. I must sit. I *have* to rest."

But Jelli said, "The baby's buttocks has come through. Keep pushing!" Soon the legs were through and unfolded, and only the head remained. "You must push hard—it will be over soon," Jelli encouraged as she carefully held the body of the baby to protect the neck.

Alta ground her teeth together and softly moaned, "Aaaaaaaggg," giving a last great push. The baby's head came out and it was over.

As Alta rested with her healthy baby, Jelli left the Red Hearth to find Moctu. He was sitting in the hearth where she'd left him with a partly congealed puddle of blood beneath him. The bark lay separated to one side of him, but the needles were still in, and he was still oozing blood.

"Your blood sacrifice has been successful," Jelli told him with a weary smile. "You may remove the needles after thanking Jona for your new sister, Zaila."

Chapter Fourteen

They'd fully stocked the women with sea water and firewood, and now Jabil and Jondu saw their opportunity. One guard was staring toward the south only half-awake, and the other guard was standing in the surf trying to spear small fish. They quickly broke for the rugged hills along the coastline to the north. A good hike later and they were perched atop one of the hills enjoying the wide view. The sea was beautiful—seemingly endless, a deep azure blue that got ever greener toward the shore where white frothy waves ran periodically along it.

The boys stared entranced for some time before Jabil said, "Maybe we can see some game from here." He stood and scanned the landscape, using his hands to block the sun from his eyes. Jondu did likewise, and they both saw it at the same time.

"There's a large overhang with a cave there," said Jondu pointing.

"I see it. Let's go scout it."

After clambering down a rock scree, they came to a small trail through the scrub oaks and hornbeam that seemed to lead toward the site. The trail made them more alert. They checked carefully for tracks but found none. Nonetheless, both young men were measurably more cautious and aware of their surroundings, and proceeded slowly. They came around a rocky bend in the trail and could see the approach to the cave area.

Stopping to watch for a long moment, the two strained their ears for any sound that would indicate activity at the site.

They gradually became convinced that no one was there, and that it was safe to investigate the cave and overhang. With a short climb, they were up the slope and inspecting what had clearly been an inhabitance with multiple hearths. There were at least five hearths, but these were smaller, shallower and simpler than Nerean hearths and would have cooled more quickly as the embers subsided overnight. The place appeared to be long-abandoned. For several moments, neither Jabil nor Jondu spoke as they became absorbed in kicking through the refuse which was unlike any they'd seen before—a burned leather pot, remnants of oddly woven reed baskets, and a few strangely chipped broken points.

"These are not of the Nerea or any of our sister peoples. These are of the Pale Ones. They've been here, maybe less than one summer ago," Jabil said.

"They're getting too close, constantly encroaching farther onto our land. They're becoming more of a threat every day," Jondu said with conviction. "We can't just watch irresponsibly as more and more of them get closer and closer. These are the People Eaters. They'll either overrun us or completely wipe out our game. And Ordu does nothing about it. He's a fool."

"Yes, this is really troubling," Jabil said. "I was thinking that as Ordu's tribe got larger, and another division took place, that you and I could lead the new group here as its leaders. Now I'm not sure that we'd be safe in this place." They got to the cave opening on the northern side of the overhang. What started out as a large, vertical fracture in the rock got wider farther in. There were numerous spider webs at the entrance which suggested a relative lack of recent use, but they waited to let their eyes get used to the dark before they went inside with their heavy spears at the ready. In addition to their worries about the Pale Ones, they also had concerns about cave bears or lions.

A few steps inside, they found a narrow ledge on which a small pile of rocks had clearly been arranged. Their eyes gradually grew more accustomed to the dim light from the entrance, and they could make out more features of the interior. They saw a mound of earth and rocks about halfway in, on which lay a rod-shaped object about the size and shape of a man's forearm. Moving to it, Jabil picked up the item which turned out to be the broken, top portion of a heavy spear, the shaft much thicker than spears of the Nerea. Besides several more, small piles of rocks, there was nothing else of much interest in the shallow cave. Outside, they studied the spear. It had clearly been used. It was blood-stained, but the flint point, more triangular, much different from theirs, was undamaged. Only the thick staff had been broken, a hand's breadth above the point.

"It's so massive!" Jondu remarked with a mixture of alarm and amazement. "The Pale Ones must have huge hands and arms to wield such a weapon."

"Yes, that matches what we've heard from those who have seen them recently," Jabil said, avoiding the mention of Moctu's name.

"Was that a burial mound?"

"Probably, and it could contain items of interest, but the Spirits might get angry if we disturb it," Jabil replied.

"Do they even have Spirits? Do the Spirits even concern themselves with the Pale Ones?"

Jabil ignored the questions and wondered aloud, "Maybe this spear was broken during a hunting incident in which the Pale One was killed. Maybe that's why it was placed on his burial site." He put the spearhead and a discarded, broken sandal, like the one Tabar had found after the caribou hunt, into his leather pack.

"What do you plan to do with those?"

"I'm not sure yet, but they could prove useful in the future," Jabil said. "We must tell no one of this place or what we've seen. Ordu has heeded none of our warnings. This new evidence—this place—and how the Pale Ones intrude ever closer won't move him to action. It's pointless. We need to find another way. And I have the beginnings of a plan which could work."

"What is it?"

"I'll tell you when I've figured out a few more things," Jabil replied.

Chapter Fifteen

It had been more than a day since Samar had spotted the small group of mammoths far in the distance moving north toward the east-west, snow-capped mountain range that the Nerea called the Alpeetans. The hunters had excitedly moved out toward them but were slowed by having to cross a wide, cold, fast-flowing stream. Several of the men had been washed a short way down the stream as they tried to cross. All the hunters were chilled, wet and tired when they got to the other side, so they stopped briefly to warm up and dry out by a fire. Even though the mammoths had been moving at a good pace north toward the foothills and its maze of valleys, woods, and scattered ice sheets, Ordu was confident that the animals' tracks could be easily followed and the hunters would be able to overtake them. They had started after the mammoths again and, sure enough, Tabar and Nabu had come upon the tracks and alerted the others, and the group's pace had quickened in pursuit.

"We're making good progress," Samar said as he felt a small bit of one of the immense piles of dung that one of the beasts had left. He squeezed the material between his fingers, checking the moisture content. "I think they're a little more than a half day ahead of us. We've gained on them but it's almost dusk, so we'll not catch up to them today." The men were tired and made camp but remained excited by the prospect of the upcoming mammoth encounter. Mammoths were huge—a full-grown one was twice as tall as a man at the shoulder, and its meat could feed the Nerea for an entire summer. The men checked and rechecked their spears, atlatls, and shafts that evening as they envisioned tomorrow's hunt.

At first daylight, the hunters had eagerly resumed trailing the mammoths, and about midday they reached the foothills. The beasts had moved into a valley and east of a lake fed by an alpine glacier to the north. Ordu was troubled to see that several brown vultures circled high in the sky far ahead around a bend in the hills. Nabu, who could easily outpace the other men, was sent ahead to scout and determine what was attracting the vultures.

It was late afternoon when he returned saying, "We're not alone. One of the mammoths has been killed and partially butchered. A large bull. It's not far ahead. The hunters who killed it are no longer there. There are blood trails leading away to the northwest."

A buzz went up among the hunters, and they anxiously scanned the surrounding hills.

"It's the Pale Ones," said two of the men at the same time, but with no evidence.

"They haven't had long to kill and butcher the beast," Ordu stated. "They're still near and are likely watching us."

"They may be returning to their home to bring back more warriors to meet us," said Samar uneasily.

"I don't think so," said Nabu. "If it is the Pale Ones, our earlier scouting indicated there weren't that many of them."

"All right," said Ordu, waving a hand at the group. "We'll proceed carefully to the kill site but not before Tabar scouts these hills to the east. They represent the greatest threat of ambush."

Tabar left immediately, and the men continued nervously talking amongst themselves. They watched Tabar's progress intently as he easily climbed the hills, stopping occasionally to scan the surrounding area. It wasn't long before he was at the top of the easternmost hill, and waved the all-clear sign. Nabu led the men forward, and they were soon at the kill site throwing rocks to scare off the vultures. No hyenas or wolves had arrived yet. It was indeed a large bull, large enough to feed the Nerea for several moons if the meat, fat, and organs could be harvested. The animal had already been partially cut up and disemboweled. The trunk, tongue and two front legs were gone, the shoulder hide had been ripped back, and parts of the rich shoulder meat and fat layers had been removed.

Samar showed Ordu a blood-stained, crude stone hand axe that had been found and they both agreed that this was the work of the Pale Ones. The remains of a large fire still smoldered not far from the open belly of the animal.

"They probably killed the beast yesterday afternoon and worked all through the night by the light of the fire," Samar said. "They knew we were coming so they left shortly before Nabu got here."

"How many of them were there?" Ordu asked.

"Tabar says from the tracks it looks like there were at least six, and maybe as many as eight," Samar replied.

"So their hunting party may be as large as ours, and they may have other warriors nearby," Ordu said. "We have to work fast. We'll butcher enough meat—well, all that we can carry on several travois, but stay no longer than that. And we'll post scouts to avoid a surprise attack. Keep your weapons at the ready. Samar will stoke their fire, and we'll work through the night as they did," he continued. "But there'll be no looking into the fire. We need to stay alert for attack, and eyes that have viewed a fire can't see as well in the dark."

The men labored all through the afternoon and night, largely ignoring the howls of nearby wolves except for building the fire larger. They continued working through the morning with two of the men entering the immense cavity of the mammoth and carving slabs of meat and fat which they passed to a man outside. The men were tired and slippery with gore but pushed on enthusiastically. Tabar, while washing offal from his hands and arms, made a happy discovery when he found several huge hunks of meat, including one of the front legs, several feet deep in the ice-cold lake, weighted down with large rocks. Ordu checked with the scouts repeatedly throughout the day, but none had seen any sign of the Pale Ones.

The men stopped working only long enough to gorge themselves on slightly cooked heart, liver, and rib meat. By evening they had four large travois heavily laden with choice cuts of meat, organs, and fat. Although it was a huge amount of meat, enough to feed the Nerea for a moon, the group was disappointed to have to leave so much behind. Reluctantly, the men left for Etseh shortly before midday after feasting one more time.

Chapter Sixteen

"It came," Avi whispered to Nuri as they left the overhang complex together to gather firewood. "My menses came, and I'll have to sleep in the Red Hearth over the next few days. I'm only allowed to gather firewood and can't even bring water to our hearth."

"Does it hurt?" Nuri asked.

"Only a little, but I'm bleeding a lot, and it's messy. I'm using cottonwood seed and moss tied into place with a skin, fur side up. I have to wash often, but only way downstream at the women's site."

"At least Ono and the others will stay away for sure."

"I guess there are some benefits," Avi acknowledged with a small smile.

"I'm not looking forward to mine. But you're a woman now and will be placed with a mate. Me too, I guess, soon. It's nearly a full moon. That's when it seems to happen as it did for you. It's exciting, but I'm very worried about which man I'll be mated to. It's amazing to me we'll probably both have babies next year."

"I want a good man, a good hunter, who's respected but not a huge man like Ordu," Avi said. "I'm afraid it would break me in half to bear his child."

"Yeah, Tabar's baby almost broke Alta in half from what I hear."

"Uh huh," Avi agreed. "She's still recovering in the Red Hearth, and there are two other women there as well. I guess we'll all be together tonight. Jelli's there and watches over the baby—Zaila—as if she were her own."

The girls had gathered a large batch of firewood and headed back. They dropped off the wood and Avi excused herself to go wash up downstream. Nuri was lost in contemplation as she went out for more wood. Her thoughts were on Moctu and Jabil. She knew both the young men liked her and wondered if one of them would end up as her mate. Jabil was a little older, bigger and stronger than Moctu, but she enjoyed being with Moctu more. Her thoughts faded as she heard a call from the northern scout that the hunting party had been sighted. This was earlier than expected, and she hoped it meant they'd been successful. It could also mean that someone had been injured or killed.

Soon word was back that the hunters were bringing back mammoth meat. Nuri knew that meant a lot of meat and that there'd be feasting this evening. It also meant another group of mostly women would be sent out immediately to travel to the kill site and, over a period of days, help butcher and carry home the remaining meat. With the salt expedition group still gone, and Alta, Avi and the two other women in the Red Hearth, Nuri expected that she'd be assigned to the outgoing group.

With the help of people streaming out to meet them, the hunters soon got their four heavily loaded travois back to Etseh, and they were showing off large piles of rich meat and fat and telling the story of what had happened. The crowd was soon buzzing with the news of the indirect encounter with the Pale Ones.

"No return party will be sent," said Ordu. "It's too dangerous, and too many men would be needed to guard the group. Also, we left no guards to watch over the carcass, and in the three days it would take to get back to it, the Pale Ones, wolves, hyenas or vultures would strip much of the remaining meat from it."

The hunters were exhausted from three days of hard travel after staying up that first night stripping meat from the mammoth carcass. After listening to the "Song of the Tribe" around the group fire, the men ate while conducting a brief-er-than-usual meeting. Most of the talk centered on what was to be done about the Pale Ones. Ordu, sounding drained and worried, said there would be a meeting of the Tribal elders soon to discuss that and other topics. One by one, the men departed the fire circle to be with their mates and sleep.

The next morning when Nuri awoke, she felt a wetness between her legs and found blood covering her thighs. Her menses had come.

Chapter Seventeen

"We have much to talk about," Ordu said to the three other elders after giving a long, impassioned prayer to the Spirits for wisdom and guidance. Although Ordu had more power, it was constrained by these men, with whom he had to gain consensus on major decisions.

Samar, Ono, and Tabar nodded solemnly in agreement. The four men, all able hunters, but among the oldest of the tribe, sat around a small fire in a shadowed hearth.

Ordu continued, "Our game is getting ever scarcer. The women must forage farther and farther for nuts and berries as well as for firewood. Rats have become numerous, damaging some of our dried meat reserves. The Pale Ones challenge us from the north taking game we've stalked for days. So, we must consider a move, a move for all the Nerea." There was silence as the men contemplated the momentousness of the statement. All knew the difficulties and worsening inadequacies of Etseh, but it was home and still dear to them in many ways. A move was a huge undertaking and fraught with its own difficulties and uncertainties.

"Where would you have us consider moving? We can't go much farther north toward the big ice. If the Spirits were to take the sacred fire from us, the whole tribe would freeze in the winter. Are you thinking of the overhang we saw to the northeast closer to where the mammoth was killed?" Samar asked. "That's near Lion People territory, and we could have difficulty with them."

"There are several choices already, each with its own problems. We need to do more scouting. I think we should undertake another trip north very soon for hunting and for scouting both the Pale Ones and for potential living sites. We'll need to evaluate every option more fully," Ordu said. "Moving the tribe is not a step to be taken with little thought or planning. While we're thinking on that, there are several other decisions to discuss. It's time for Seetu and Sokum to have manhood rites. When should those be held?"

"I still think of them as the skinny boys who helped Moctu fight off the wolves," said Samar while pulling on his dark beard. "But I guess time has passed and they are of the age."

Before anyone could comment further, Ordu moved on to a different topic. "Probably the most pressing decisions to be made concern the girls. Let's focus on that today. Both Avi and Nuri have recently become women and should be placed with mates."

"I'd like either or both of them in my night furs," said Samar smiling.

"Our decision should be based on tribal harmony," said Ordu, ignoring the comment. "What pairings are the best in that regard?" The men reflected quietly on the matter for several moments. Tabar broke the silence, saying, "The young men of the tribe are at an age where a woman is especially important to them."

"Does that age ever end?" Samar joked.

"Probably not," Tabar grinned, "but young men are more unstable and hot-headed, and women can be a calming influence."

"I've been worried about the fighting and the tempers of Jabil, Jondu, and Moctu—especially that of Jabil," said Ordu, singling out his nephew.

"A woman would almost certainly calm him somewhat,"

said Ono. "I know he favors Nuri," he continued, "and he's perhaps our best young hunter."

"I agree with all of that," said Ordu. "I just don't want to reward his bad recent behavior by awarding him a woman right now. We should have promised Nuri to him after the bear hunt last year, but we can't give him a mate right now," Ordu finished.

"He'll be upset at not getting a mate, and especially if Nuri goes to Moctu," Ono cautioned.

"Maybe we can reach a determination for Avi first," said Tabar.

"Yes, good idea," said Ordu. "There are bad feelings between Avi's family and yours, Ono," he stated, looking at him squarely. "Avi's father, Petral, has twice come to me, once about your... indiscretion, and once about Jondu. He's very angry with both of you. I've been thinking we should give Avi to Jondu to soften his anger and to cement your families more strongly, but we'd need your assurance that you'll keep your hands off her," he finished, looking at Ono reproachfully. This was a rather severe rebuke, and all were quiet as Ono formed his response.

"I won't intrude in my son's relationship if he's given Avi," he finally said a little weakly, not meeting the other men's eyes.

"Then that one is settled, yes?" Ordu asked. The others nodded. "And I feel strongly that we should give Nuri to Moctu," he went on. "Jabil needs to realize that there are repercussions for unacceptable conduct."

Ordu's force of personality was strong and the others nodded their agreement.

"Good," he said. "As for the possible move, and the manhood rites, we'll continue to think on those. About the move, we will know more after another scouting trip north. There's also the possibility that the tribe could split again with part moving and part staying at Etseh, but with the uncertainties concerning the Pale Ones, I don't favor that."

Chapter Eighteen

It rained off and on for three days, slowing, but not stopping the salt production effort. Finding relatively dry wood to burn was becoming more of a struggle, and Jabil and Jondu had to range ever farther from their camp.

"After this, I hope to never again collect another piece of firewood," Jondu said wearily, as they headed back toward the fires with another load. They were both completely soaked, and their arms and legs bore dozens of scratches from their efforts.

"We're nearing the end," said Jabil. "We already have more salt than the group from last year. We'll be headed back to Etseh soon."

The next day the rain stopped, and it was decided that no more seawater was needed. Shortly thereafter, the last boiled-down residues were scraped into the collection skin, and the muddy and tired group broke camp and began the trip home. The storm runoff had turned creeks into streams and streams into rivers, and some of the crossings were treacherous. Two men were assigned to carrying the salt skin at all times, so that if one stepped in a hole or was washed downstream, the other could secure the precious salt.

Jondu had been told to scout for the best crossing sites, and to be the first to lead the group into the fast-flowing waters, to check for deep holes or especially fast currents. The two guards carried the salt, Jabil brought up the rear, and the women fended for themselves in-between. The men carried their weapons, and everyone carried packs with food and personal items such as tools and sleeping furs. One of the women carried a heavy skin full of large shells which Nereans used as bowls. The women had fashioned a small rope to which they all clung. If one of them slipped, she could maintain her hold on the rope and the others, with better footing, could pull her back to safety.

On the afternoon of the second day of travel, as they got into more rugged country, the group had come to a particularly fast-moving stream, and they waited while Jondu scouted for the least dangerous place to cross. It wasn't a wide stream—Jabil could easily throw a stone across it, but the water gushed across an uneven bottom with occasional jutting rocks and heavy, partially submerged plant debris.

"I recommend we camp here for the evening and ask the Spirits to calm the water during the night, making crossing safer for us tomorrow morning," Jondu said. The group was spent and no one relished the idea of tackling the stream as it was, so they agreed and bivouacked right where they were. In the morning the stream had indeed receded somewhat, and after more scouting, Jondu found a suitable crossing site.

The group was midway across when Leuna, the younger of Samar's two mates, slipped and cried out, desperately clinging to the rope and trying to regain her feet. The other women held the rope and tried to pull her back until Poza, Nabu's mate, also lost her footing. The three remaining women, fearful of being pulled into the torrent themselves, released the rope and held on to one another. The two released women screamed in terror as they were swept downstream by the cold, roiling water. Jabil knew that the guards carrying the salt could do nothing to help, and he saw that Jondu was in midstream also struggling in the deep water. Only a third of the way across himself, Jabil charged back toward the southern bank from which the group had started. He almost immediately lost his footing and got swept downstream, but using his powerful arms, he managed to keep his face up and his feet in front of him to push away from rocks and submerged timbers. Each time he came near a rock or timber, he used it to help push himself toward the shore. His feet finally found traction, and he was able to stumble and splash to the southern bank.

Jabil jettisoned his pack and weapons and bolted through the brush racing downstream, pausing as he came upon Poza who'd pulled herself safely onto a sloped boulder and debris pile in midstream. She called to him and motioned that Leuna had been washed farther downstream. He commenced running again, tearing through the tangle of brush and vines that clogged the embankment. He was out of breath when he saw her partially trapped under a timber that projected from the rushing water not too far from shore. She was stuck in branches and debris fighting not to be pulled farther under as the water surged past her. He vaulted onto a downed tree that angled into the river, ran along it a short way, and plunged into the water toward Leuna. The rush of the turbulent water propelled him rapidly toward her, and he could begin to feel the water flowing under the obstruction, trying to suck him down as well.

As he neared her, she saw him and let out a guttural, choked scream of terror. The water pressed him against the timber, and it took all his strength to pull himself upward more onto the timber than below it. The water had pulled Leuna farther under and was surging over her head now, allowing her to get breaths only sporadically. With difficulty, he edged toward her, and as he got close, she flailed at him with her left arm. He was able to grab her wrist, and he pulled with all his power and was gratified to see her face break the water. Her eyes wild, she croaked out a primal half-scream, half-cough before being pulled under again. Jabil pulled her a little farther out and toward him, and he felt her left hand grab his arm in a death grip. Her face broke the water once more, and she coughed violently, letting out sounds he'd never heard before.

Her face stayed above water this time and, as her horror-stricken eyes pleaded with his, she coughed and rasped out, "Don't let me go!"

"I've got you," he said, but then was pulled farther down himself by a surge of water.

Jondu and one of the guards had come down the far side of the stream and were watching and calling to them, but could do nothing to help. The cold water and extreme exertion was taking its toll, and Jabil felt himself tiring rapidly. With all the strength he had left, he pulled on Leuna's wrist and felt her come farther up out of the water but no closer to him. Pulling frantically herself, she was able to scramble higher onto the timber. She was still stuck, but being higher out of the water and able to catch her breath, she could discern that her side wrap was what was caught. Her pack was gone, already swept away.

"My… my clothes are caught," she gasped out to Jabil. "Just don't let me go." She tried to loosen the ties but could only fumble at it briefly before the rushing water threatened to suck her down again. Working together, with Jabil pulling her upward, and her twisting, she was able to get out of the garment, and they made some progress toward the riverbank.

Jondu and the guard cheered and continued to call out encouragement. Closer to shore, the water wasn't so swift and powerful, and they moved more easily. Both were shaking and their teeth chattered violently. They climbed out of the water, and Jabil waved and called to Jondu that they were both all right. Jondu loudly thanked the Spirits and called out that he and the other guards would bring Poza to safety. Jabil and Leuna turned away finally collapsing just past the band of brush on the embankment, very cold and utterly spent.

It was late afternoon when Jabil awoke and found that in the fog of exhaustion, he and Leuna had huddled for warmth.

She was still asleep with her back pressed against him, the river having stripped off most of her clothes. He appreciated her warmth and pulled her a little closer to him. The increased warmth added to a happy glow that infused him. They were safe, and he'd saved Leuna's life. As he reflected on what had happened, he began to realize how pretty Leuna was. He knew her well but had never really thought about her as a woman. She was nearly his age, and they'd played together growing up. She'd become Samar's second mate less than two years ago, and she had yet to have a baby which was unusual. Ever more aware of her warmth, the curve of her hips and her fresh smell, he found he was becoming aroused.

This wouldn't do. She was Samar's mate, and it was forbidden. Then he remembered Samar and Ordu at the group fire, rebuking him in front of all the other hunters. Anger welled up inside him at the memory.

Instead of going on the northern hunting trip, he was on this stupid effort doing women's work because of Ordu and Samar. They had humiliated him. And he was, after all, Jabil, killer of cave bears.

Chapter Nineteen

Leuna stirred next to Jabil. She turned to him and looked into his eyes, momentarily wondering where she was. As the earlier events came back to her, she trembled, and her eyes welled with tears.

"I… almost died. I was choking. It was so horrible." Her voice cracked with emotion, and she paused, reliving the memory. She began trembling again, and he pulled her closer. She seemed to melt into him.

"Then you came. You saved my life," she continued. Jabil said nothing and they lay together contentedly for a while. The added warmth and closeness, and her words of praise aroused him further. "You risked your life for me. I can never repay you enough."

Jabil sensed that Leuna, too, was becoming aroused. He said, "I can think of a way," and he pressed his hardness into her leg.

She pushed him away, but without much conviction, saying, "No, that would be wrong. Samar wouldn't approve."

"Samar doesn't have to know about it," Jabil said with a thin smile, pressing himself against her even more.

"Jabil… it would… it would be wrong," she went on.

Jabil's hand had worked down from the curve of her hip to her naked thighs and his fingers explored her more fully. She arched away from him, but when he moved against her again, she didn't retreat.

His fingers explored her again, and this time she didn't resist, other than to murmur, "No Jabil, it's... it's wrong."

He found her wet, and knowing she was aroused, it thrilled and inflamed him. He fumbled his still-soaked covering off and rolled between Leuna's legs, rigid with desire. One push and he was deep inside her, and she gave up any pretense of resistance. Her heat, her beauty, her youth all excited him more than ever before. It had been almost a year since he'd taken a woman, and he didn't last long. He drove into her with powerful thrusts and she responded, pushing into him. He climaxed violently and continued pounding into her, even as the exquisite feeling ebbed.

They lay in satisfied silence for a while, enjoying the warmth and nearness of each other. Leuna propped herself on one elbow and gently stroked Jabil's chest.

"I've never lain with any man but Samar. Have you taken other women?"

"Only Motela," he said referring to a *rejected woman*. She'd been an older woman who'd never had children other than two stillborns. Her mate had gone out hunting, never came back and was presumed dead. Because of her age and unattractiveness (she'd lost many of her front teeth) and because she had a reputation for laziness, no man wanted her for a mate. She became a rejected woman, mostly scorned by the tribe. Any man could take her whenever he wanted, but thereafter, he would owe her a day's food or the equivalent.

Most rejected women didn't last long unless they had direct family to care for them, and Motela had died of sickness during the past winter. Reflecting on Motela and her fate, Leuna shuddered a little and snuggled closer to Jabil. Becoming rejected was every woman's greatest fear—worse even than cave lions or wolves. The unspoken threat of it probably caused women to work a little harder and be a little nicer to the men than they would otherwise. In a very real sense, their lives depended on it. And women with few children, or worse, no children at all, like Leuna, worried about it more than others. She shuddered again, but her thoughts gradually turned back to Jabil.

"You were very… powerful. You're so strong," she said, her hand moving from his chest to the bulge of his bicep. "It's hard to believe I almost died today, and I would have if not for you." She smiled at him, and he stared for a moment into her large, dark eyes. He was again struck by how pretty she was. He kissed her, and gently pushed her back down while he climbed atop her again.

* * * *

"Jabil! Leuna!" They were awakened in the early evening by Jondu calling their names. Jabil clothed himself quickly and stood up calling back greetings to Jondu.

Jondu yelled, "We've been getting worried about you two. We've cut long saplings and can form a human rope to help you cross the stream. It worked well for Poza."

"No, please! I can't cross that stream right now," Leuna whispered up to Jabil.

"Thank you Jondu, my friend," Jabil called back to him. "It's late, and we're still very tired. It'll be better to cross in the morning when the stream has receded even more."

"But you won't have fire tonight," Jondu worried.

"I have my weapons, and we'll be all right for one night without fire," Jabil responded.

Jondu nodded, waved and left.

Jabil said to Leuna, "I'm really hungry. I'll go get my gear that I left upstream." He soon returned with his weapons and pack, which he opened and inspected. He saw the spearhead of the Pale Ones and quickly hid it farther down inside his pack. The sleeping furs were tightly wrapped and surprisingly dry, and he draped them around them both. They shared most of Jabil's remaining dried meat, made love once more, and slept soundly in each other's arms until the morning sun came streaming through the thin forest canopy.

"Jabil! Leuna! Are you awake? We need you to cross so we can make progress toward Etseh today," Jondu yelled. Jabil had wanted to make love with Leuna again this morning but had overslept.

He looked into her big, dark eyes, and said, "My feelings are strong for you, Leuna, but we can tell no one of our... *activities*."

"Yes, I agree. Samar must not find out."

"*No one* can find out," he stressed.

The crossing was relatively easy using the long saplings and with the help of Jondu and the guards. As they trekked toward Etseh, Jabil and Leuna walked apart, lost in their own thoughts and memories.

Chapter Twenty

"Moctu, I have some good news for you," Tabar said as he returned to their hearth. Moctu looked up with interest as he tied thin sinew strands to secure a flint point onto a shaft. He'd mixed melted pine resin with charcoal and put it into a notch he'd carved at the top of the shaft, and he was just finishing the tie-off.

"I like conversations that start that way," he replied smiling.

"First, I want to thank you deeply for your blood sacrifice that saved Zaila. You know I would have endured it myself if I'd been here, but you did it nobly as the man you are. You have my gratitude."

Moctu was humbled by the respect Tabar showed him. "You honor me, Tabar. But I… I was just worried about my… about Mother Alta and her baby—my sister—Zaila," Moctu stammered out with some embarrassment.

"I hope you're all healed?"

"It's a lot better. It doesn't bother me much anymore."

"Well, I have some news that I think will please you," said Tabar, smiling broadly.

"You have my full interest and attention."

"Well, as you're aware—in fact, the whole tribe knows now that Avi and Nuri have reached womanhood. The elders have met with Ordu and with their counsel, he's decided on mates for the two of them," Tabar said, pausing a little and enjoying the suspense he was creating.

"Yes, and what? What was decided?" Moctu asked, his heart pounding.

"I think you liked them both, right?"

"Yes, yes, they're both fine young women," Moctu said quickly, trying to speed up the discussion. But he found himself thinking only of Nuri.

"Well, you can't have them both!" Tabar joked.

"Tabar, may the Spirits take you right now if you don't give me the news," Moctu exclaimed.

"All right, all right," said Tabar laughing. "You're to be mated to… Nuri."

Moctu raised both fists above his head as he closed his eyes and breathed out a "Yes!" Tabar grinned broadly at his happiness and patted him on the back.

"She's a wonderful young woman and you two are a good match. The ceremony will be in one moon, after her next menses."

Moctu's mind was racing, and he barely heard Tabar. He was to have Nuri as his mate. A glow had come over him—he hadn't realized just how much he'd wanted this. He visualized her eyes, her smile, and her hair. She was to be his! He became aware that Tabar was still talking.

Tabar said, "And Avi is to be mated with Jondu."

Moctu flashed on his last encounter with Jondu, and Jabil also came to mind. Jabil wouldn't be pleased to lose Nuri, he thought, especially to him. But those two were both away on the Gatza.

He dismissed those thoughts and refocused on Nuri. She was to be his!

Chapter Twenty-One

The caribou kills and the mammoth meat had allowed the Nerea to eat well for most of the past moon. They dried much of the meat to save it for the future, but they didn't have nearly enough to last through the winter. Ordu named the members of a new hunting party, which would swing far to the north looking for game while at the same time scouting to better evaluate the threat posed by the Pale Ones. The group would include Moctu, and his friends Palo and Nabu, but again left out Jabil and Jondu. Moctu was elated to be going and realized he'd probably have his mating ceremony with Nuri as soon as he got back. He smiled inwardly—the Spirits were favoring him. He held his wolf totem and said a prayer of thanks for his good fortune.

Word had gotten out, and the other men began congratulating and sometimes kidding him on being awarded Nuri for his mate.

"You'd better start building up your strength," Samar joked. "She looks like she has the stamina of a young lioness."

Palo offered his congratulations. "She's a prize and this couldn't happen to a more deserving man."

Alta, too, had both congratulated and teased him, saying she'd seen how "love-struck and tongue-tied he was around her."

A call came down from a scout on a hill to the south

that the salt expedition group was in sight. Family and friends streamed southward to meet and welcome the returning group. There was near-pandemonium as members of each group tried to tell their news first. Jondu was told about being awarded Avi for a mate, and Jabil overheard Samar tell Leuna, as they embraced, about Nuri being awarded to Moctu. Jabil and Leuna locked eyes briefly, and Leuna could see the hurt seem to radiate from his entire being. Was all that pain for Nuri, or was any of it because Samar now had her in his arms?

Despite his recent liaison with Leuna, it was the news of Nuri that disturbed and outraged Jabil. The only thing that prevented his anger from boiling over right then were the stories being told by members of his group of his strength and bravery in the rescue of Leuna. Pride overpowered anger for the moment, but the wash of mixed emotions had his mind racing. He liked Leuna, but she was Samar's—and she wasn't Nuri. Nuri was his favorite. She should be his—and to have her go to Moctu was almost too much to bear.

Then Jabil heard about being excluded from the upcoming hunting trip, and it was too much. He wanted to break something, hurt someone—Moctu would do nicely. He needed to be alone to gather his thoughts and regain his composure. Some in the crowd, as they described his heroism, were surprised when Jabil stormed away, but Ono knew exactly what had disturbed him. He'd warned Ordu of this. Leuna, too, still in Samar's embrace, watched the angry departure and was convinced that she knew the reason for it.

Jabil passed by the hearths at Etseh, moving rapidly northwest, ignoring those who waved and called greetings to him. He climbed up the slope and came to a group of boulders that provided a partial enclosure. Sitting down on the ground, he leaned against the largest boulder and fought to recover his self-control and sort out his emotions. He was overwhelmed by anger, incensed with Ordu for punishing him like this—first, giving Nuri to Moctu and second, rubbing his face in the dirt by not including him on the hunt. This was now the second time he'd been excluded from an important hunt. Such public humiliation! He was Jabil, probably the best hunter in the tribe—cave bear killer. He was Jabil, rescuer of drowning women. The more he thought about the injustice of it, the more he seethed with fury. Ordu would pay for this. He'd gone too far. Jabil envisioned sticking a spear into his gut and watching with some pleasure as he died slowly in great agony. Moctu as well. Killing Moctu would solve many problems too, but everyone would know who'd done it.

Time went by, and his fury waned. Despondency set in.

I'm not to get Nuri, he thought morosely. He'd so often envisioned her as his mate, and now he was left with no one. I'm not even given Avi. She goes to Jondu instead. He's my friend, but what has he done to deserve this favor? He's not the hunter that I am. Has he killed a cave bear? He isn't the leader that I am. He follows me. Yet he's given Avi. He thought again of Leuna and his night with her. It had been wonderful, but she was Samar's, and he could never have her. Samar would be grateful that he'd saved Leuna's life. And Samar was an elder—probably Ordu's closest advisor. The thought clicked.

I wonder if I can change Ordu's decisions with Samar's support. Not likely, but it's worth a try. That's all I have left to do. When Samar thanks me—and I know he will—I'll enlist his support. Then I'll try to get Ordu to change his decisions. I must have Nuri, and Moctu—that stinking hyena—may the Spirits take him if he touches her.

Chapter Twenty-Two

It was a warm, bright morning, and Jabil eyed Samar as he approached Jabil's family hearth.

"Greetings, Jabil," Samar called as he got within hailing distance.

"Hello, Samar. Welcome to our hearth."

"Are you rested from the Gatza?"

"I'm rested enough to hunt," Jabil said pointedly.

"Yes, um… I'm sorry to hear that you're not on the hunt with us," Samar replied, not liking the direction this conversation had immediately taken. Jabil felt a surge of anger knowing Samar had probably played a role in the decision, but he held his temper and suggested Samar have a seat nearby.

Samar remained standing, saying, "I can't stay long. I wanted to formally thank you for saving Leuna's life. Your actions took courage, and I wanted to pay you this tribute." As he spoke, he gently laid two beautiful, large spearheads on the rock ledge near Jabil. Samar was the best flint worker in the tribe, and Jabil yearned to pick up the superbly crafted spear points.

Instead, he faked a yawn and said, "I appreciate this gesture, Samar, but nothing is needed." After a short pause, he added, "I was surprised by all the news when I returned. Are the decisions about the mating ceremonies and the hunt completely final? Or could they be revisited?" Samar immediately knew what Jabil wanted, and he was silent for a long time as he considered a response.

"I doubt the mating ceremonies could be *revisited*. But the hunting party could benefit from your courage and skill. I'll speak with Ordu about it if you'd like."

"Yes, I'd appreciate that, Samar. I plan to speak with Ordu myself, later today. If you could see him before I do, that would be a great tribute to me." Jabil lifted the spear points, returning them to Samar. "Once again, thank you for this gift, but your kind words are enough."

As Samar left, Jabil smiled thinly, reflecting that Leuna had already paid him Samar's tribute. He'd allow Samar time to speak with Ordu, and then he'd approach Ordu, himself, this afternoon. He was confident about getting to participate in the hunt, but he still ached over the likely loss of Nuri to Moctu. He wasn't going to let that happen.

It was late afternoon when Jabil neared Ordu's hearth, and he heard a child's happy shriek and Ordu's laughter. He passed a hanging skin that served as a wall and could see Ordu on his back holding his youngest son, Zori, high above him with one hand. Zori, who'd been born four summers past, squealed with delight.

Jabil called out, "Hello, esteemed Ordu. Do you have time to hear from me Uncle?"

"Greetings, Jabil. Please come in," Ordu replied, setting his son down and getting up.

"Zori grows bigger every day."

"Yes, he's going to be a big one," Ordu said, smiling at the boy who was already running out of the hearth. "The salt trip was extremely successful, and you played a significant role," Ordu started.

"Thank you, Uncle."

"And Samar has recently spoken to me and offered his gratitude for your saving Leuna's life. I'm very pleased with you."

Jabil looked down at the ground. After a pause, he quietly asked, "Pleased enough to rescind the mating ceremony of Nuri?"

Ordu was ready for this question and said, "I can't do that. But I invite you to join in the upcoming hunt."

"Thank you for that, Uncle, but isn't there anything I can do to change your mind about Nuri? She's very important to me," Jabil said, looking into Ordu's eyes. It was difficult to read Ordu's face behind the thick brown beard, but Jabil thought he saw the features soften a little.

But then Ordu stiffened and said, "That decision's been made and is final. If you continue to conduct yourself as you did on the salt trip, you'll have any of the next girls who reach womanhood or your first choice at the tribal conclave."

An overwhelming mix of anger and despair overtook Jabil, but he concealed it as best he could. "Thank you, Uncle for considering the matter."

As Jabil walked away, his mind raced with wild plans to stop the impending mating ceremony. It must not happen. Most of his plans revolved around Moctu's death, and he schemed for ways to make that occur, musing on possibilities for undetectable murder. They'd both be on the hunting trip, and there'd likely be numerous opportunities for an "accident." He should have done this long ago, when any suspicion generated would have been much less. He smiled tightly. There were still ways to make this work.

Chapter Twenty-Three

It rained for two days, and on the second, the ground briefly trembled. Jelli threw bones, and her readings indicated that dire misfortune was likely on the trip. She advised Ordu that the Spirits were unhappy and favored a delay of the hunt. He still favored leaving as soon as the rain let up, but Samar and Ono counseled holding off until Jelli foresaw a better outlook.

The men met nightly around the main fire, and Jabil and Jondu steered much of the conversation to the threat from the Pale Ones.

"We all know that the misfortune Jelli sees stems from the Pale Ones," Jabil said in a loud voice. "The People Eaters—they not only take our game, but now they prevent us from even hunting for it. And we cower in our shelters, waiting for them to allow us to hunt," he continued scornfully. The men murmured in angry agreement. "Are we little girls who run scared from rabbits? We are hunters and warriors of the Nerea—or at least we used to be." Jabil could see that he had most of the men following him, angry at the inaction against the Pale Ones. Only Ordu, Samar, and Tabar seemed unswayed.

He was about to continue when Ordu waved his hand. Ordu stood and the murmuring stopped. He said, "No one here is afraid of the Pale Ones." He looked directly at Jabil. "Where is this threat? So, they've killed one mammoth, from which we benefited. Should we stop hunting game and become hunters of the Pale Ones? That'll bring us nothing but hunger during the long winter." The men seemed calmer now, and several nodded in agreement. Ordu paused, thinking to himself, then said, "I can see that further delay is unwise. We leave tomorrow."

* * * *

A bright and nearly cloudless morning greeted the men as they prepared to depart. The rain had stopped and a rainbow briefly appeared, which most thought was a good omen. Moctu had gotten little sleep during the night as he'd excitedly checked and rechecked his weapons and gear. Holding his wolf totem, he said a silent prayer to the Spirits, ate a last bite of cold stew and went to meet his stepfather, Tabar, who'd already left for the muster area on the northwest side of Etseh.

The men set a fast pace, and by noon they were already nearly a day's walk north of Etseh. They saw no large game, but their spirits were high as they edged northeastward along a stream swollen by the recent rains. The men rounded a wooded bend in the stream, and they heard an urgent call from Nabu whom they could now see returning at a run after being sent ahead to scout for game.

"A single rhinoceros bull not far ahead. A big one," he said grinning while pointing to the hill from which he'd just come. This was very good fortune. If they could make a kill this close to Etseh, they could send the two boys, Seetu and Sokum, back to Etseh to bring a slaughter party back to the kill site, and they could then continue northward looking for more game. A rhino offered a huge amount of meat, weighing nearly half as much as a mammoth, and an early kill would be a good omen for the hunt, dispelling the warnings of Jelli. As the men advanced, Nabu described the area surrounding the rhino and offered suggestions on how to make the kill. It was decided that Samar, Ordu, and Nabu would make the initial approach after Tabar, Jabil, and Moctu flanked the bull and approached it from the far direction.

The rhino was soon in view, and it looked to be healthy and well-fed. It was indeed a big one, easily outweighing two hands of Nerea's largest hunters. Its front horn was huge, nearly the length of a man, and it had a smaller second horn behind the first. It was still as Nabu had described, grazing on grass on a flat, low hill near the stream. The three flanking hunters kept low and tried to stay out of sight as they moved into position to the northeast. The bull noticed them but paid little attention.

Once they were in place, Ordu, Samar, and Nabu advanced toward the rhino, each with a long shaft in their atlatls and their larger spears close at hand. As they got within range, the rhino lowered its head and charged. The beast was deceptively fast for its great bulk and was halfway to them before they had much chance to react. Ordu made a half-hearted throw which missed, then broke and ran. Samar and Nabu had already realized that any delay could be deadly and were slightly ahead of Ordu. The men split, running different ways, confusing the near-sighted rhino which slowed to a stop. It turned and trotted back to the area it had been grazing.

The other three had moved closer with Jabil and Moctu seemingly competing for who would get the closest and who would get the first hit. "Let's go in a little slower and all throw our first shafts together," Tabar encouraged. As the three got within a fallen tree-length away, the rhino became increasingly agitated, snorting and head-bobbing. It was considered an honor to make the first wound, and Moctu wasn't surprised to see Jabil ignore Tabar's suggestion and begin his throwing motion. Moctu didn't see Jabil's shaft hit but knew it had, based on the animal's violent reaction and bellow. He and Tabar released their own shafts as the beast turned to charge them, his shaft taking it in the groin, just in front of the haunch. Because the animal had turned so quickly, Tabar's shaft glanced off his armored back. The men broke and ran, splitting up, hoping the rhino would again be confused by the maneuver. But it had focused on Jabil and was closing the distance between them quickly. Moctu saw the imminent danger and sprang toward the beast yelling loudly and waving his hands.

Although they had poor eyesight, rhinos could hear well. It was just moments from goring and trampling Jabil, but it slowed quickly and turned to view the new threat. The sight of the immense, hideous beast now targeting him shocked Moctu to his core, and he began backing up furiously. The rhino turned his flank to Jabil, and charged toward Moctu, closing the gap rapidly. Seeing that he was no longer in danger, Jabil stopped and threw another shaft at it, which buried itself into its neck. From the other side, Ordu, Samar, and Nabu also had good shots, so shafts began to stab into the beast from all directions. None of the early hits were mortal wounds because the rhino had mats of woolly hair and armor as thick as the length of a man's little finger. The beast was confused and hurt and stopped its pursuit of Moctu. Since the rhino was no longer charging, the hunters could get closer and throw their shafts with more force and accuracy. It finally turned away, took a few steps, and collapsed on its right side, snapping shafts, and driving some in deeper. The men cheered and approached warily. The rhino attempted unsuccessfully to stand again, and Samar, from close range, threw his large spear into its soft underbelly. It appeared to be a mortal blow, as the animal gasped, shuddered, and lay still.

Over the next few moments, the men chattered excitedly amongst themselves about whether the beast was dead. No one got close to it other than Nabu and Ordu, who each threw their large spears into the chest area between its front legs. Neither penetration brought movement or sound from the rhino. The men were now convinced that it was dead and began to congratulate themselves and slap each other on the back. A mix of relief and joy swept over them, and the few uninvolved hunters including Sokum and Seetu joined them in an impromptu celebration. Ordu asked Samar to start a fire nearby and directed Sokum and Seetu to go back to Etseh to bring back helpers to butcher and carry the meat.

Ordu seemed buoyant, and for the first time in many moons, happy and relaxed. The enormous amount of rhino meat would do much to feed his tribe through the long winter, and they had salt to help better preserve the meat. There would be no starving time this winter. The men began the grueling work of gutting, cleaning and preparing the carcass for butchering. As the men worked diligently through the afternoon, they recounted the events of the day, and Jabil gained evermore credit for the kill. He'd made the first wound, and the hunters counted a total of four of his shafts in the carcass as they gradually retrieved as many of their shafts and points as possible. Jabil was awarded the head of the beast, which included the delicacies of the tongue, eyes, and brain, as well as several other choice cuts. Jabil brimmed with pride and began calling the beast *his rhino*. He was less pleased to hear the men murmur agreement when Palo recounted how Moctu had saved Jabil's life by diverting the animal's attention as it charged him. To Jabil, Moctu wasn't even a man; he was the boy who was to get Nuri instead of him.

Conversations with these themes continued through the evening as the men sat around the fire retelling and reliving the rhino kill.

Near the end of the evening, hoping to put something of an end to the matter, Jabil stood and said, "Moctu, I offer my gratitude for your bravery. You *may* have saved my life today." He tried not to emphasize the *may* too much in the sentence, but it was clear that he doubted being saved.

Moctu replied in kind, saying, "Jabil, you're welcome. I was just trying to save *one* of our best hunters." He placed the emphasis on the *one*.

Most of the hunters picked up on both the nuances and

grinned, even chuckled under their breath. But, as Jabil had hoped, the subject was dropped, and the hunters planned for the next day.

After feasting the next morning, the hunters moved out, leaving Seetu, Sokum, and a large crew of mostly women still butchering and processing the carcass. Heading north, the hunting party made good progress, and two days later were at the foothills of the Alpeetans.

Chapter Twenty-Four

"You seem happy," said Avi, smiling, as she approached Nuri who was humming as she worked on weaving a reed basket.

"I am happy. It's a relief to know which man will be my mate, and the Spirits have been good to me—it's as if I got to pick my favorite from the whole tribe."

"Yes," Avi said. "The waiting and not knowing what man you'll be paired with was the hardest part. I could have done much worse. At least I know that Jondu likes me. He's *visited* me twice since the announcement. And he's gotten an oath from his father, Ono, that he won't try to *visit* me. Jondu's tall and strong, and he's a good young hunter. I, too, am fortunate." She sounded a little like she was trying to convince herself.

"I'm glad you're pleased, Avi, and you're right—we both could have done so much worse. And now we'll both have our mating ceremonies together, and in a year we'll probably be raising our babies together. That thought also makes me happy because you've always been like a sister to me. It's perfect."

"I feel the same way about you," said Avi, gratified by Nuri's warm comment.

Nuri rummaged in some skins and woven materials at the corner of the hearth.

"Here, I want you to have this to wear at the ceremony," she said, handing Avi a tunic made of soft, light-gray caribou hide alternating in vertical stripes with darker hide, with sleeves of even softer, cream-colored chamois, laced together with thin leather strips. Along the neckline, Nuri had attached small carved rings of white mammoth ivory, each about the diameter of a little finger. The garment was strikingly lovely.

"I was going to wear it, but I want my sister-friend to have it."

Avi stared at the fine tunic and her eyes brimmed with tears.

"Oh Nuri, this is beautiful. How did you learn to make something this nice?" she exclaimed. "But I couldn't. This is for you to wear. Not to give to me."

"Oh, I have some similar, leftover materials that I'll use to make another one before the ceremony," Nuri said, shrugging off the praise.

A tear ran down Avi's cheek, and she hugged Nuri. "You're my best friend, and I'll always hold you in my heart. I'm so glad I have you to talk to and share things with."

"And I feel the same," Nuri said. "A moon from now, after the ceremony, we'll have our mates to care for, but we'll always be best friends."

A cool breeze blew in, and there was a distant but loud peal of thunder from the west. Avi's eyes met Nuri's.

"Is that a bad omen—to happen while we're talking of our mating ceremonies?" asked Avi nervously.

"I think it's a good omen," said Nuri, but a small chill went down her spine.

Chapter Twenty-Five

It was distinctly colder in the foothills, and the men traded their sandals for shoes made of thick hide stuffed with dried grass for warmth. Most also added soft hide leggings, which covered the thigh and calf and strapped to their belts and shoes. They'd seen no large game, but had crossed tracks of deer and horses, so they scanned the surrounding area with increased focus. They also searched for evidence of the Pale Ones. This was the area where the earlier scouting party, nearly two moons ago, had found the most indications of their presence. The men carefully watched the hills for smoke from fires, because they knew the Pale Ones, like them, had to keep one going to have fire for the harsh winter. No one could survive a winter in this country without fire. Even though they saw no smoke, Jabil continually reminded the men of the threat from the People Eaters and their likely proximity.

The hunters worked their way westward, following the deer tracks which they lost in a thick wood late on the afternoon of the fourth day since the rhino kill. Ordu decided they'd make camp on a nearby low hill that overlooked a small lake which might attract game, especially during the evening or morning times. Most of the men went down to the lake to drink, wash up, and look for small edibles like fish, turtles, or frogs.

Samar had a fire going, and the hunters gradually gave up

on catching dinner and joined the circle around it. Like most of the men, Moctu had been unsuccessful in catching any food for dinner, so he resorted to the dried meat he'd brought along. For the first few nights, the men had continued to feast on rhino meat, but the fresh meat was gone and all were eating dried meat now. Moctu's thoughts kept returning to Nuri.

He was to be mated to Nuri in less than a moon!

Lost in such thoughts, Moctu heard Samar joke, "Look at Moctu daydreaming about Nuri again."

Most of the men laughed, and Moctu flushed with embarrassment. Across the fire, Jabil felt his breath taken away with the reminder of it. For most of the trip, he'd been able to focus on hunting and the Pale Ones and stay away from thoughts of Nuri with Moctu. But now the image scorched his mind, and he seethed with renewed hatred of Moctu. He had to come up with a way to stop the ceremony, and time was running out. This hunt represented his best chance for altering the situation. He had to get Moctu alone for an "accident."

That evening the men checked their weapons and worked on their kit, mending shoes in many cases and repairing torn clothing, especially leggings, in others. Jabil was searching for a thin leather strap when he found the spearhead of the Pale Ones at the base of his pack. He quickly and furtively examined it, again noting the odd craftsmanship and the thick, broken shaft, then carefully replaced it and sat back on a log engrossed in thought, a new plan forming.

Dusk had fallen, and the men began settling down to sleep. Ordu had posted two guards, Nabu and Tabar. Jabil studied the layout of the camp and where the guards were, but he couldn't see where Moctu had ended up. Feigning the need to relieve himself, he stretched and walked through the camp, trying to memorize where everyone had bedded down and where the various weapons, packs, and tools were lying. He saw that Moctu had chosen a spot on the outside edge of the campsite not too far from Samar. Samar was a notoriously sound sleeper, so his plan might work. Retracing his steps, Jabil bedded down after first securing the spearhead that he hid under some furs. He also found a fist-sized cobble that he placed near the concealing fur. Jabil had to concentrate on controlling his breathing because of his agitation and excitement. It wasn't long before he heard deep breathing and snoring from the sleeping men. They'd traveled far that day, and all were tired and would undoubtedly sleep well. With the Spirits' help, one or both the guards would also fall asleep or be less than alert. There was no chance of Jabil falling asleep. He was keyed up and forcing himself to wait for the rest of them to be in deep sleep.

The fire was low, and the moon was high but only a fingernail crescent. The stars were bright and provided most of the light. He noticed the Warrior Stars directly overhead and took it as a good omen. Rising to his knees, he placed the spearhead under his arm and took the cobble in his right hand. In the dim light, he studied what he could see of the camp layout once more and silently rose to his feet. This was really happening! With the Spirits' help, after tonight Moctu would be dead, he'd have Nuri, and the Nerea would be focusing on the real threat, the Pale Ones. The plan was so perfect, it was certainly being directed by the Spirits. Jabil crept stealthily through the camp, focusing most on Tabar, the closest guard.

He would crush Moctu's skull with the rock, then ram the spear into his belly. If he were discovered, he could claim that he'd seen one of the People Eaters, and he came to help. Otherwise, he would creep back to his furs, and "discover" the attack in the morning like the rest of the group.

Just then, Ordu spoke to him, and he froze. He didn't understand what Ordu had said. He slowly turned to face the place where Ordu was lying, and he waited to hear the question: "What are you doing, Jabil?"

He could barely make out Ordu, who was still lying down about a man's length away from the embers of the fire.

He waited for Ordu to speak again, but he was silent. Then Ordu murmured softly, and Jabil realized he'd been talking in his sleep. Relief swept over Jabil, and he paused wet with sweat and trembling slightly.

Was that an omen? Were the Spirits telling him to wait? No—nothing had changed. Jabil soundlessly moved closer to Moctu. He had to traverse an area between Samar and Moctu to get close to Moctu's head, but they were far enough apart that there was little chance of waking Samar. His nerves had calmed, and he clutched the heavy cobble tighter. He was about to kneel close to Moctu's head when a wolf howled, and several in the camp stirred, including Moctu.

Jabil knew the wolf was Moctu's totem. Was the Wolf Spirit trying to warn him? He knelt and gripped the cobble firmly, moving it higher into striking position. Two wolves now howled together, and the camp stirred again. His breath caught, and he paused. Anxiety ballooned inside him, and his thoughts became frenetic.

The Wolf Spirits were too strong—the time wasn't good. He'd be discovered, he thought. It wouldn't go well. There would be better times for this before the hunt was over. And with that last thought, he pulled the rock down and quickly retreated to his furs, not as worried about making noise. The wolves quit howling, and Jabil was furious with himself for not carrying out the plan. Had he lost courage, or was he being wise to wait for a better opportunity? He savagely pulled at his hair in frustration. He'd been so close. But the time would come, he vowed to himself.

Chapter Twenty-Six

Moctu awoke to a muted morning light. The sun was up, but it had not yet crested the eastern hills. He hadn't slept well, troubled by unsettling dreams. He struggled to remember but could recall nothing of them. He was left with a vague but encompassing sense of unease. The fire had been rekindled, however, and the camp began to bustle with activity. Soon the sun peered over the hills, and the day seemed to brighten with promise.

Ordu called the hunters together and expressed his disappointment that they'd encountered no large game since the rhino. Additionally, they'd seen no evidence of the Pale Ones, so they knew no more about them than when they started. He told the men that they would break into two groups of four hunters each to cover more ground to either find game or learn of the Pale Ones' activities, size and strength. Maybe both. One group would follow the large canyon north, the other would head west along the foothills. When either group located game or ran into trouble of any kind, they were to build a fire from their skull embers and then pile it with green wood and leaves to give off smoke and alert the other group to come.

"Finding game is our top priority. Our trip started out well with the rhino kill, but we've seen no more animals," Ordu said. "We can't spend a half a moon here in the north and then go back to Etseh empty-handed. We must find more game. I don't like splitting the group when we're in territory that's likely inhabited by the Pale Ones, but we can cover twice as much area this way. But each group must be even more alert and careful about the Pale Ones than before."

He divided the groups, with Nabu leading a fast-moving group to the west, which was a significant honor for him, and Ordu leading the group to the north. Jabil was placed with Nabu's group and Moctu, Samar, and Tabar with Ordu. Jabil's hopes had initially swelled, as he imagined many more opportunities to orchestrate Moctu's demise in a smaller group. However, these deflated quickly with the continued announcement that he and Moctu were placed in different groups. Frustration swept over him, and he again regretted his inaction of the night before. He had to be in the group with Moctu.

He took a half step toward Ordu and said, "Honorable Ordu, may I make a request?" Ordu nodded, and Jabil continued. "Yesterday I twisted my ankle, and I'm not sure I can keep up with Nabu's fast-moving group. Wouldn't it be better for Tabar to switch with me so that Nabu's group has his added experience?"

Ordu considered this for a moment and said, "Yes, a switch can be made to accommodate you." Jabil's heart leapt with renewed optimism, but swooned as Ordu continued, "Moctu will switch with you."

Moctu shrugged—he was happy with either group. He always learned things from the older men, but Nabu's group had more chance to find game because they would move faster.

Jabil bit his lip but saw no further possibilities to change Ordu's plan. He couldn't fully hide his dejection, which Samar noticed and joked, "Don't worry, Jabil. We aren't as bad and slow as you've heard."

The men laughed, and the group broke up to organize into their smaller units before departing. Jabil's mind raced, recalibrating and searching for new, workable plans. The two groups would likely be apart for a quarter moon, and time was running out before he would be attending a ceremony in Etseh in which Nuri'd be given to Moctu. He couldn't let that happen.

* * * *

It had been three days since the split, and Ordu's group had still seen no large game. The lack of smoke on the horizon suggested Nabu's group was faring similarly. Ordu had led his group far up the valley, which had turned northeastward, so they were diverging farther and faster from Nabu's group than before. They were on the southeastern side of the broad canyon and stopped to look across to the far side. The elevation was high enough here that even though it was late summer, there were still tendrils of ice in nearly every ravine coming off the main glaciers. Most of the hillsides were either barren of trees or had broad treeless swaths which marked previous advances of the alpine glacier during colder times. It was on one of these swaths that Jabil perceived movement and excitedly pointed to a cave bear traversing it toward a rocky area.

It would take some time to descend one side of the valley and ascend the other, and the odds of being able to locate the bear once it made it to the rocks was slim, but it was the best opportunity the hunters had been afforded, and they headed out immediately at a fast pace. As the men descended, they watched the bear progress to the rocks, and soon they could no longer see it. They had to ford a small but icy cold stream at the base of the valley, and they were breathing hard as they neared the rocks. The older men paused to catch their breath, but Jabil hastened forward.

"Slow down, Jabil. Be careful of your twisted ankle,"

Ordu directed. "We'll hunt for the bear as a team, not one on one."

Jabil pretended not to hear and scrambled over some boulders and disappeared.

"Jabil," Ordu called, but there was no response.

"Jabil!" Samar yelled much louder. It would have been hard not to hear his booming call even across the valley.

But Jabil was excited and didn't want to stop, so he again ignored the call. The cave bear was his totem—and he had an affinity with them, a kind of kinship. He wanted to again prove that he, Jabil, of the cave bear totem, was the best cave bear hunter in the tribe. He could find and follow them because he was a kindred spirit, and this one wasn't going to get away. The old men were too slow, and at their pace, they'd surely lose the bear. He'd call for their help once he located the bear again.

But the bear was gone. It had vanished and tracking it over the rocky slope proved impossible even for one of the cave bear totem. The older men had clamored over the rocks and were now visible to Jabil, as he was to them. From a distance, he shrugged, indicating the bear was lost. He moved back toward them, and as he got closer, he could see that Ordu was irate.

"You young, blustering fool!" Ordu said loudly as he got nearer. "You arrogant... you arrogant little..." Ordu shook his head and turned away to better control his temper.

Jabil had expected perhaps a little reproach for ignoring their calls but expected it to be tempered with recognition of his energy and enthusiasm. His pursuit had been their best chance of not losing the bear. He was stunned at the unwarranted level of Ordu's anger and rebuke.

"But Uncle, our best chance for finding—"

He was cut off by Samar. "Didn't you hear us call? Why'd you ignore your uncle's call? And my call?" Samar spit to the side, a sign of great disdain.

Jabil was reeling with what was, to him, an inordinate overreaction. He felt his anger and resentment rising. They were scolding him as if he were a boy. He was Jabil, killer of cave bears, not some child to be berated by tired old men.

In a louder voice, he began, "Our best chance to not lose the—"

But he was again cut off, this time by Ordu. "We are a *team* of hunters," said Ordu through clenched teeth. "We don't charge off recklessly, one at a time, to chase cave bears."

Jabil was seething now, and nearly shouted, "I wasn't chasing the bear. I was trying not to lose it!"

"If you like danger so much, I'll give you danger. I'll send you home alone if you ever ignore my call again," said Ordu.

Jabil couldn't stop himself, and yelled, "And I'll gladly go!" That seemed to clinch it.

"So tomorrow at first light you'll leave for Etseh, and we'll deal with you when we get back," Ordu said, his voice a low growl.

It was clear there would be no more hunting this day. As if mimicking the mood of the group, heavy, dark clouds began to blow in from the west. No one spoke as Ordu led the party downslope to a small hill overlooking the stream where they'd make camp. Each man was absorbed in his own thoughts, sorting out what had just happened. Jabil's anger had subsided, and he now regretted his final outburst. He'd have to trek back alone to Etseh in shame and await his punishment when the hunters returned. The whole tribe would hear of this, and he'd be humiliated.

He'd gone from hero to disgrace in less than a moon, he thought miserably. And for such a little thing. It wasn't fair. It seemed like Ordu looked for ways to fault him at every opportunity.

Jabil was shaken by a sudden realization. Since he was being sent back to Etseh early, he'd have no chance to get rid of Moctu, and he'd soon be watching Nuri's mating ceremony to him. A wave of desperation swept over him, and he felt light-headed. The desperate jealousy soon gave way to anger, and he again bristled with the unfairness of what Ordu had done to him. Right now he hated his uncle and wished Ordu were dead.

They'd gone a long way today, and the men were extremely tired. Although they'd seen no evidence of the Pale Ones, Ordu directed that each of them would stand guard for a portion of the night to ensure the night watch stayed awake and alert. Tabar would stand first guard, to be relieved by Jabil, then Samar, followed by Ordu. There was almost no conversation around the small fire, where they had a quick, light dinner of mostly dried caribou meat, thereafter retiring to their sleeping furs. Tabar selected a rocky area for his guard station. It had some boulders on which to sit, and he could see up and down the east-west valley.

Samar was soon snoring, and Ordu's deep breathing indicated he was asleep too. Jabil was wide awake, unable to sleep, his mind awash with a mix of worry, regret, and anger. He brooded over a litany of wild plans, including him taking Nuri by force as soon as he returned to Etseh, and leaving with her, Jondu, and Avi to start a new tribe. But the hunters of Etseh, especially Moctu, would try to track them down, and even if they could initially elude the searchers, he and Jondu would always be looking over their shoulders, expecting pursuit. Maybe he could leave in the morning and try to meet up with the other party and kill Moctu before they reunited with Ordu's group. No, that would never work. It was hopeless. He was to be humiliated upon his return, then humiliated again as Moctu took *his* mate. That image filled him with rage. All this over a stupid disagreement with three old men who couldn't keep up with him.

He hated them all right now. Especially his uncle. Family was supposed to provide ties and even privileges, and yet it seemed to work against him time after time. A distant roll of thunder broke the quiet. He wished a lightning strike would kill all three of the old men. That would solve most of his problems. There would be a new leader, and perhaps he could convince him to call off the mating ceremony. Perhaps Ono, Jondu's father would take over the tribe—or even his own father, Alfer, who was, after all, Ordu's brother. But that was unlikely because Alfer wasn't a good hunter, nor was he well-respected. It would take a good hunter to be leader, and the best hunters were on this trip. He and Moctu were the best young hunters, perhaps even the best hunters now.

"Oh, Spirits!" he whispered. Even the remote possibility of Moctu as tribe leader galled him. "May You take me if Moctu becomes the tribe leader."

He thought it was even possible that he could become leader. That was a powerful image. There were less than four hands of hunters in the tribe, and lately they'd broken into roughly equal sides on major issues such as the threat from the Pale Ones. Several of the men besides Ono and Alfer had sided with his and Jondu's arguments that the Pale Ones needed to be dealt with. Unconsciously, his hands counted out the numbers under his furs. Thunder pealed again, still distant, but getting closer. Maybe the Spirits were coming to help him with a lightning bolt.

Wouldn't that be a sign, he thought. Then he'd know the Spirits favored him. Not likely though. But if Ordu's side lost three members to a lightning strike, the other side, his side, would have increased standing and power, and they could finally deal with the stinking People Eaters.

A revelation overwhelmed his thoughts. A solution… its simplicity both excited him and repulsed him. He knew what he had to do and it had to be tonight.

Chapter Twenty-Seven

Jabil's pulse raced as he made his plan. As he plotted, he continually had second thoughts.

Was he really going to do this? Could he actually kill these three men? Three men whom he'd known his whole life. And one of them his uncle? And each time, he came up with the same answer. He had to. It was his only option. The only option that could work anyway. If this plan didn't work, he was ruined, but he was ruined either way.

Each time his determination would waver, he tried to recall their disagreement that afternoon and the way they scolded him and planned to punish him. These were the men responsible for giving Nuri to Moctu, he reflected, his anger rising. He could do this. He had to.

He would take out Tabar, the guard, first. I could club him or hit him with a large rock—maybe at the shift change. But it had to be quiet, so it didn't wake the others. The approaching storm might help, unless the thunder woke them all or had them sleeping particularly lightly, or it rained. That last thought worried him. He had to move soon. After Tabar, he would club Ordu, and finally Samar, who slept the most soundly. Earlier, he'd moved some rocks away as he made a place to bed down, and now he groped for an appropriately sized cobble.

He found one that was perfect. One hit with it and Tabar

would go down without a fight—or a sound. Thunder boomed again, and he knew he had to act now. He couldn't risk rain waking up the sleeping men. He would tell Tabar that he couldn't sleep and that he'd stand guard. He came to his knees clutching the rock and once again wondered was he really going to do this? But the answer was the same. He draped a light skin over his hand holding the rock and quietly moved toward Tabar. The stars still showed over the eastern sky and gave a modest light.

"Tabar, I can't sleep so I'll take this watch," he said softly as he approached, not wanting to startle him. Jabil was close enough to make out that Tabar was awake, but he looked sleepy.

"All right, that's good because I'm having trouble staying awake."

Tabar turned as he got up from the boulder he'd been sitting on, and Jabil thought this was it. Hit him now! But his arm only flinched. He couldn't do it, he admitted. He would be leaving for Etseh tomorrow, and he'd face his humiliation. He'd watch Moctu be mated to Nuri. He'd have to endure... Before he realized it, his arm was swinging, and he heard a 'thunk' like a woman beating the dust from a thick hide with a stout branch. Tabar crumpled at his feet, making almost no sound. He felt Tabar's head, finding a large depression where the rock had fractured his skull. His hand came away wet.

One down, Jabil thought, and no turning back now. He peered over the boulder and could make out the still sleeping forms of Ordu and Samar. There was no movement or sound, other than Samar's snoring. Jabil gradually made his way toward Ordu. This was going to be the toughest one. His uncle. He'd been a good uncle. A man who'd swung him round and round in the air as a child. He'd probably learned more about hunting from Ordu than any man in the tribe. His father wasn't much of a hunter and had taught him little.

There was no turning back. It had to be completed. He

tried to focus on the reprimands he'd recently gotten from Ordu. This was the man who'd assigned Nuri to Moctu instead of him. He might still get Nuri, he thought. He clutched the rock tightly and knelt by Ordu.

As he raised the rock, Ordu opened his eyes! The sleep cleared almost instantaneously from his eyes as they met Jabil's. There was a moment of recognition, and the rock came down, crushing his head in. The resultant 'thunk' seemed loud enough to Jabil to wake someone sleeping on the next hill. But Samar snored on. Jabil moved toward him clutching the rock which was now slippery with blood and clumps of what had to be brain matter. He moved toward Samar, numb now, and feeling as if he were under water.

Moments later he could barely recall that he'd knelt before Samar and brought the rock down on the side of his head. Jabil was sitting on a small boulder to the side of the camp, shivering, still holding the killing rock. It was done. He'd killed them all.

Chapter Twenty-Eight

A light rain began to fall, rousing Jabil from sleep. It was still dark. Horrible thoughts and images came to him, and he wondered briefly if he had dreamed them. But no, they were real. He'd really killed the three men. Part of him still couldn't believe it, so he got up and went to where Ordu lay and knelt beside him. Even in the dim light, the massive damage to Ordu's head was apparent, and it was clear he was dead. Jabil became light-headed and nauseous, filled with regret, shame, and now, worry.

He'd be blamed for the murders unless he carefully altered the evidence and built a strong case for a different narrative. Jabil had already considered this briefly before the… *incident* and had crafted an alternate storyline. They'd been overrun by the Pale Ones and he'd managed to get away. The vile People Eaters. This would serve the double purpose of taking suspicion away from him and putting it on the Pale Ones which would further his argument that they needed to be driven off or, better yet, exterminated.

Jabil started making a mental list of what evidence needed to be contrived or manipulated. He'd leave the Pale Ones' spearhead and broken shaft that he'd found with Jondu. It would need to be discarded or lost before getting back to Etseh, or else Jondu would know what had happened. He wasn't sure whether Jondu would expose him or not, but he didn't want to take the chance. If Jondu heard about a broken spear shaft left by the Pale Ones, he might be suspicious, but he'd be less so than if he saw the exact spearhead that he and Jabil had found, cast as a killing weapon.

He needed to leave some diffuse tracks which could be construed as having been left by the Pale Ones, and hardest of all, he needed to figure out a good story as to why he hadn't met the same fate as the other hunters. But he had some time to think through all the aspects of this and to get it right. Even if he built the signal fire now, it would be days before Nabu's group got here.

The fire! Jabil thought with panic. The rain was coming ever stronger, and he worked feverishly to stoke the fire and build it stronger. He couldn't let it go out—he had to be able to signal the other group. As an additional safeguard, he went to Samar's body and retrieved the wolf skull that lay nearby, which Samar used to nurture the embers through bad weather. Jabil found that the fresh maple leaves inside contained charcoal that had gone out. Retrieving a viable ember from the fire, he wrapped it loosely in the maple leaves and replaced it into the skull. That done, he felt confident that he'd still have fire even after a heavy rain.

And a heavy rain did come, a cold, slanting rain that stung his face. He sheltered under a skin beneath a nearby tree, but even so, he was drenched by the time morning dawned. It was still raining, and the growing light displayed the gruesome murder scene ever more clearly. He was cold, wet, and miserable, but the rain was probably a blessing. If he worked quickly, he thought he could substantially bolster his story. Strapping small portions of hide to his feet, he walked up and down the hill multiple times in different areas. Each time he walked up, he rotated the hide to a new surface, sometimes placing a small stick under the base strap. With some luck and continued rain to obscure the tracks, this would appear to be the tracks of several different men all wearing footgear unlike that of Etseh hunters.

Jabil was out of breath when he finished making the tracks. He sat under the tree thinking about the other evidence he needed to create. By midmorning, the rain stopped. He rebuilt the fire and threw the muddy skins he'd worn onto it. He retrieved the spearhead of the Pale Ones from his pack and looked at it again. It was very different from anything the Nerea made, and it got him thinking about when he first learned to knap flint under Samar's expert tutelage. Regret threatened to flood in, but he forced himself to stay on task. He tried to envision their camp being overrun by the Pale Ones. Who would the creatures spear first?

Kneeling by Samar, Jabil pushed the spearhead hard against the woven fabric on the corpse's midsection, but it didn't penetrate deeply enough. He would need to thrust it. Retrieving his spear, he poised himself over Samar's body, plunged the spear into the corpse, and then worked to carefully extract it. The incision complete, he again knelt by the body and pushed the Pale Ones' spearhead into the gash. He punctured something inside that discharged foul-smelling gas.

Jabil needed to light the signal fire soon. It could take two days or more for Nabu's group to reach him. Here he was alone in territory inhabited by the People Eaters. He knew he'd better stay alert and sleep lightly—and keep his weapons close.

Jabil settled back against a rock and considered what he had left to do, what kinds of questions Nabu's group would have, and what his story would be. He let his mind imagine the scene. Before the Pale Ones attacked they would have watched and studied his group, and they would have coveted some of their weapons and gear. For instance, Samar and Ordu both carried finely crafted spears and knives that Samar had fashioned, and Nerean footgear was obviously superior to that of the Pale Ones. The People Eaters would have taken some of these items for their own use but more likely as trophies of war. By midday, he had a plan—and a story that would hold up to questions and scrutiny from the other hunters. If he played this right, he could end up a hero, furthering his chances for advancement toward a leadership role in the tribe.

He added wet wood and leaves to the fire and built it to a level where it was churning out massive clouds of smoke. He still had a lot of work to do. He needed to make some of their best weapons and gear disappear, which would ostensibly be the equipment taken by the Pale Ones. He collected all Tabar's weaponry and valuable possessions, including his spear, knife, tunic, pack, and shoes. He reluctantly added in Samar's fine spear. He went to Ordu's body next and covered his head with a skin so that he didn't have to see his face. He added in Ordu's ornate spear and some other weaponry and personal items, placing all the collected equipment on a large fur.

Drawing up the fur around the items, he hoisted them on his back and set out eastward, away from the direction Nabu's group would be traveling. He walked until he found what he was looking for—some rocks under which he could hide the weaponry and personal items so they'd never be found. After hiding the gear, he returned to camp, rebuilt the fire, and began to build a large travois. He rolled Samar over so that the broken end of the Pale Ones' spear was jammed into the mud, obscuring the fact that the break had happened long ago. While arranging Samar's corpse, it occurred to him that Leuna was now a widow, and he might have her as a mate as well as Nuri. But Nuri was to be first—he wanted her more than anything—and securing her as his mate would take both luck and skillful manipulation.

Jabil was moving the other two bodies when he had a sudden vision of Ordu's eyes opening just before he'd killed him. The look of shock and betrayal in Ordu's eyes filled him with remorse, and overcome with weakness, he struggled to catch his breath. Although he quickly forced the vision from his mind, it left him feeling exhausted and nauseous. He worried about these feelings overwhelming him after Nabu's group returned, and how he'd explain them, and he had a sudden insight. He could weave the symptoms into his story and blame them on a sickness. Jabil spent the rest of the day working to fashion a travois on which to carry the bodies back to Etseh.

Keeping the fire built high was a priority, and it continued to pour out torrents of dark gray smoke. The fire would keep away any threatening beasts such as lions or wolves. But as dusk approached, he was considerably disturbed by being alone in this territory occupied by the Pale Ones. They too would no doubt have seen the smoke. Besides the fear he felt, it irritated him that he had to worry about the Pale Ones. He gathered his weapons near him, placed them at the ready, and was somewhat comforted. Jabil slept little that night, partly due to his worries about an attack, but also because he had sporadic, fitful visions of the murders. Had he really done this? He felt disconnected from reality, as if he'd been placed in a nightmarish dream world.

Finishing the travois the next day, he loaded Ordu's and Tabar's bodies onto it, after which he covered them with skins partly to keep the flies off, but mostly so that he didn't have to see them. All through the day, he speculated on questions he might be asked, and he developed smooth answers embellished with contrived details that would make the story more believable. He considered what details he could have seen in the murky firelight and what sounds he would have heard in the confusion of an attack. He tried to recall exactly how Moctu had described the Pale Ones so that he could incorporate credible descriptions into his account. He remembered how strong and powerful Moctu had said they were—how hairy, and that some of it was red hair. He covered Samar but didn't load his body onto the travois because he wanted Nabu's group to see the spear when they turned Samar over.

That would have more impact. As long as they arrived soon, he could say that loading Samar's body was the next thing he planned to do.

He still worried about a real attack from the Pale Ones, and he carefully surveyed the surrounding area for any sign of them but saw nothing. Jabil had built up such a powerful, detailed, and believable story in his mind that even he was beginning to actually worry the People Eaters were an imminent threat. It was probably just nervousness, but he maintained a careful watch anyway. The visions kept returning, but they were getting less frequent. The roaring fire seemed to help, and proximity to its heat and light inexplicably soothed his conscience. He again slept little, as his mind churned with jumbled ideas and memories. For the first time since the murders, he clutched his cave bear totem and offered up a prayer.

"Oh, Cave Bear Spirit, please keep me safe and give me strength and shrewdness over these next days. And for Ordu, Samar, and Tabar, I call on their totem Spirits, the Lion, Mammoth, and Caribou, to grant me forgiveness for... for what happened here."

Chapter Twenty-Nine

It was late morning the next day when he heard a shout from the west. He recognized Nabu's voice and yelled back a somber greeting. He went out to meet their group wearing and carrying extra weaponry.

He called to them saying, "I have bad news, the worst news. We've been attacked by the Pale Ones and all are dead except me."

Nabu, who'd been smiling, was stunned by the news and fell to his knees.

Moctu, Palo, and the older man were also shocked, and Moctu asked, "Tabar, my father, Tabar—is he, too, among the dead?"

Jabil nodded sadly and turned to escort them to the camp. As they followed, questions and comments were called out. "Ordu is dead? No, no this can't be. And Samar? No. No, I don't believe it."

The men were soon in the camp surveying the scene of carnage. Moctu pulled away the skins from the travois exposing the gray and already stinking corpses of Ordu and Tabar. He fell to his knees and sobbed audibly. Palo patted his shoulder and seemed close to tears as well. Nabu went to Samar's corpse, still on the ground, uncovered it, and rolled it over. As Jabil had expected, there was an exclamation of dismay and indignation from the men regarding the jutting spear, which increased when Nabu pulled it from Samar's body. The near chaos and tumult gradually died down, and Jabil found himself telling portions of his story in segments in response to questions directed at him.

After a while, he started over from the beginning.

"It was early nightfall. Tabar was on guard, and I couldn't sleep due to the hitz." Hitz was the term the Nerea used for severe diarrhea, which was considered extremely unclean, and to be kept away from group settings. "I'd gone downstream to relieve and cleanse myself, and fortunately, I'd taken my weapons. We'd earlier seen tracks we thought might have been left by the Pale Ones, so we were trying to stay extra vigilant. I'm not sure exactly what happened, except that I heard yelling and other noises as the vile People Eaters overran our camp. I believe they first killed Tabar, who was on guard, and then rushed Ordu and Samar who'd been sleeping. I heard the commotion and ran back uphill in time to see brave Ordu throw his spear at one of the Pale Ones and Samar be impaled and clubbed to death while arising from sleep," Jabil's voice cracked, and he looked down. "It was a red-haired monster." Some of the men nodded as this matched their image of the creatures.

"The Pale Ones... they have great strength and agility. One of Ordu's attackers dodged his spear throw, which broke its tip and bounced off that boulder there," he pointed at a nearby boulder. "The great beast picked it up and snapped it in two across his knee as if it were thin kindling. His arms were huge. One of their warriors stopped stripping Samar's body and clubbed Ordu's head with a rock-tipped cudgel. I had hurried and was close enough now to throw a shaft at the red-haired beast. He was still holding the broken spear when the atlatl shaft took him in the shoulder. The cowardly savage bellowed in pain and turned and ran. The two other beasts saw him run, and they, too, broke and ran for the forest carrying off much of our gear and weaponry. I chased them and threw two more shafts, but it was dark, and I didn't hit them." He dropped his head in the direction of Ordu's and Tabar's bodies. "I… I couldn't save them," he said dejectedly and sobbed.

One of the hunters patted his back and said, "You did all you could."

Palo said, "At least you wounded one of them. I hope he dies a slow death."

Moctu had listened but couldn't focus. He was almost reeling, numb with anguish. He'd lost another father. This was going to kill Alta. She'd been so happy.

And Ordu, he thought. Who would be their leader now? Perhaps Ono? He was the most likely, but he didn't really command great respect. Samar would certainly have taken over as leader, but… he was gone now too. Their best flint napper and fire keeper. And always quick with a joke or funny comment. They'd lost three of the Nerea's finest men.

Nabu told Jabil that his group had seen twin wisps of smoke in the morning when they were still two days to the west. The smoke most likely came from an encampment of the Pale Ones, and they'd moved toward it to scout and investigate it further, when they saw the gray smoke from Jabil's fire.

The newly arrived hunters, all proficient trackers, scouted the surrounding area noting the odd footprints and trying to determine for themselves exactly what had transpired. Everything seemed to corroborate Jabil's account. The footprints led to the creek and then were lost completely. They conjectured that the Pale Ones probably waded up or downstream and then came out on a rocky surface leaving no trail. The lack of a trail frustrated the men, and their intense anger toward the Pale Ones was palpable.

"We will avenge these murders," Nabu raged, loud enough that the creatures might hear. "I can't believe Ordu is dead—and Samar—and Tabar!" And then he asked aloud the question on all their minds, "Who will be our leader?"

Moctu, as well, was feeling rage toward the Pale Ones. He'd misjudged them. They were indeed vicious and apparently as great a threat as Jabil and Jondu had warned.

The grief-stricken men spent the rest of the morning securing Samar's body to the travois and readying themselves for the bitter trip back to Etseh. All were dejected and disconsolate. Instead of triumphantly returning with massive loads of fresh meat, they were bringing the decaying remains of the finest men of the tribe. There would be great wailing and heartbreak on this homecoming.

"Jelli was right," Nabu said. "She warned us of grave misfortune before this trip."

Even as gloomy as they were, the men made good progress and were soon well into the lowlands. There was little conversation. The men were absorbed in their own thoughts, sometimes distraught, sometimes angry. All seemed to want to get this trip over with, to bring the horrible news back to Nerea, to share the grief, and to make plans for revenge. Jabil had secured the bloody spearhead taken from Samar's body, and he was able to dispose of it behind a rock at one of their resting spots. He didn't want Jondu to see and recognize it.

At night around the campfire, they asked Jabil more questions, and he was glad he'd imagined the scene in detail. The visions of the murders came to him less frequently, but they still had the power to stagger him. The one that came the most often was of Ordu opening his eyes a heartbeat before Jabil crushed his skull. When the visions unsettled him, he blamed his gasping weakness on his recent illness, and it often elicited consolation from the men.

"Even suffering, you were able to drive off the attackers. You were brave Jabil. I just wish you'd killed them all," said Palo.

The thought flashed through Jabil's conflicted mind that he had killed them all, which made him both smile tightly at the irony and feel deep guilt at the same time.

Another of the men said, "You and Jondu tried to warn us. I wish we and the elders had listened to you." Mentioning the elders was dangerously close to disparaging the dead and drew looks of rebuke from the others. But most of the men were having similar thoughts. If Ordu and the elders had only listened to Jabil and Jondu, this wouldn't have happened.

As the evening progressed, even Moctu found himself praising Jabil, saying, "You did what you could to save my father, and Ordu and Samar. I... we all appreciate that."

Three days later, in the afternoon, the men hauled their gruesome travois load into the familiar highlands near Etseh and were soon hailed by a Nerean lookout. Word of their return quickly got back to Etseh, and mates, relatives, and friends streamed out to meet the approaching hunters. As Nereans learned what had happened, bedlam ensued. Cries and hysterical shrieks of anguish surrounded the newly arrived hunters as the people viewed the three bodies. Alta was one of the first to meet the group and was so staggered that she fell backwards, still holding Zaila, and was fortunately caught by the people behind her. She sat on the ground, tightly holding Zaila, moaning and wailing, in direct view of Tabar's body. Ordu's two mates also shrieked and collapsed, one of them beating the ground and pulling out clumps of her own hair. Samar's older mate was constrained as she attempted to throw herself on Samar's bloated body. Moctu's eyes welled up as he knelt beside Alta, holding her and stroking the crying baby Zaila. The other hunters likewise tried to console friends and mates. Jabil found himself holding Leuna, who sobbed loudly. For some in the group, grief gradually waned and enraged questions followed.

"How did this happen? Who did this?"

All the hunters began fielding the questions with short answers like, "The Pale Ones," but gradually they looked to Jabil to answer the group's questions in more detail. Jabil also answered the rapid-fire questions with short answers until they slowed, and as more people arrived from Etseh, he started from the beginning. He was careful to tell the story exactly as he had before and was gratified to see that the people felt he acted honorably and with great courage. Jondu was in the crowd and listening, so Jabil judiciously excluded mention of the broken spearhead. As he related the story, the people's grief turned quickly to outrage, and there were many cries for an immediate mission of revenge. The clamor was periodically renewed as new arrivals from Etseh swelled the crowd until nearly all the tribe was there.

Jabil was encouraged to recount the full story again, and it once more elicited cries for revenge. Over the rest of the afternoon, as the story was told and retold by the hunters, Jondu once heard mention of the broken spearhead taken from Samar's body. His mind flashed on the spearhead that he and Jabil had found during the Gatza effort, and he momentarily wondered, Could that…? No, that was unthinkable. He discarded the thought.

Some of the group recalled Jelli's warning and her credibility soared to new heights. Other people reminded the crowd that Jabil and Jondu had continually warned of the dangers of the Pale Ones and that the elders should have acted. Although this feeling was widespread, open discussion was suppressed by most so as not to disparage the dead, all of whom were elders.

After some time, the travois bearing the bodies was moved to the far side of Etseh, where the bodies would be buried. The only remaining elder, Ono, as acting leader, called an emergency Council of Warriors, and all the men including the tired hunters sat to determine what to do next. There was no "Song of the Tribe" or opening proceedings.

Ono started by saying, "We've suffered a grievous blow. Three of our best men are gone—all of them great hunters and… and wonderful friends." His voice broke as he croaked out the last words. "We underestimated and misjudged the menace of the Pale Ones. Three things we must do now," he continued in a somber monotone. "We must bury our dead with honors, we must hold a Council of Warriors to determine a new leader, and we must decide how best to strike back at these beasts who attacked us." The last comment provoked an uproar of supporting shouts.

"Tomorrow we'll bury the dead," he went on. "Three days from now we will reconvene to decide a new leader by a vote of all warriors of the tribe. Men wanting the role can stand and ask for their support." He paused for a long time, and then said, "Because I was partly at fault for underestimating the threat we faced from the Pale Ones," he paused again. "I will not be under consideration for leader," he said finally. This comment caused some consternation because most had considered him to be the likely replacement. When the furor subsided, he went on, "I'm firm in that decision. The elders failed to recognize the threat." He stressed the word *elders*. "Maybe it's time for younger leadership." The men saw him cast his gaze on his son, Jondu. "It was some of the young men who perceived the danger that these savages posed."

Chapter Thirty

Ono and the crowd patiently waited for the sun to be directly overhead. The three graves had been dug yesterday evening, side by side, and the three bodies had been reverently placed in them this morning. The corpses were placed upright, knees drawn in. Before burial, they'd get one more full view of the sun, as well as a dusting of sacred red ocher by Jelli. All the while, she chanted prayers to the Spirits while Nindai played wistful tones on his flute. Tabar's semi-naked body had been redressed so that all the dead men now were clothed in loincloths and tunics. Each had his atlatl and two shafts, and each had their totems—Ordu the lion, Samar the mammoth, and Tabar the caribou.

Jelli and Nindai called on these Spirits to welcome their relations back into the Spirit world. The assembled crowd was more awed by Jelli than ever, because her powers were undeniable. Horrible repercussions had come from not heeding her recent warnings to the hunters.

If they'd only listened to her, most had thought of late. Tears streaked many of the faces of the women in the crowd while the men fought to control their sorrow. Moctu was numb, completely drained of emotion. Last night he'd tried to comfort his mother as she was convulsed with grief. At one point she'd asked him why the Spirits hated her so much that they did this to her twice. He had no answer.

The sun reached its zenith, and Ono spoke, intoning the Spirits to accept these good men back into their world. His message was short and subdued except for the ending in which he promised the dead men that they'd be avenged. The melancholy crowd, silent to that point, loudly and stridently confirmed this vow. The assembled group was swept with a new wave of grief and pity as Zori, Ordu's youngest boy, was sent to throw some yellow flowers onto his father's grave. The confused boy bravely and solemnly did as he'd been instructed, but then hurried back to clutch his mother's leg. The men were buried with dirt and rock, and the bulk of the crowd dispersed leaving the five widows and close relatives to continue their mourning. Alta prostrated herself on Tabar's grave, trying to stay close, quiet now except for low moaning muted by her near exhaustion. Moctu fought back tears as he held Zaila and knelt beside his mother at the grave. The other widows mourned their dead mates in much the same way as they, too, were consoled by their relatives.

The next day, the question of who was to be the next leader consumed the people, and the behind-the-scenes maneuvering began in earnest. Moctu was surprised to see Avi's father, Petral, nearing their hearth.

"Welcome, Petral," said Moctu. "Come in."

"Hello, Moctu," said Petral. "I've come to pay my respects to you and Mother Alta. Tabar was a very good man. I… we'll all miss him greatly."

"Thank you, Petral. Those are kind words. Mother has taken the baby to the stream to wash her. Nuri's with her. I'll tell her of your coming and your kind thoughts."

"Yes, please do. Um… that's not the only reason I've come to see you today," said Petral lowering his voice. The hanging skins that made up the walls of the hearth didn't stop much noise, and there were always people nearby.

Petral came closer to Moctu and said, "I'll speak candidly to you. I don't want Avi to be mated with Jondu. That whole family is filth, and I don't want to be associated with them. I was very disappointed when Ordu declared that Jondu would mate Avi, but now that he's no longer here and no longer leader, I'd like to change things."

Moctu hadn't considered that the mating ceremonies could be called off because of the recent events and was suddenly anxious about losing Nuri. Petral saw this recognition dawn on Moctu and touched his arm.

"I know you favor Nuri, but I wish to make a deal with you. With the deaths, there are a lot of women now needing mates, seven in total. Five widows and Nuri and Avi. Additionally, a new leader will be chosen in two days. It's clear that Ono won't be that leader, thank the Spirits, but he favors and promotes his son Jondu, and we can't let that happen. Both of them are scum. You may not know that both forced themselves on Avi long before she reached womanhood. It was filthy and outrageous behavior. They could have hurt her; in fact Ono did hurt her." He paused, then said, "I know you want Nuri, but I know you also like Avi. And she likes you. If you promise to take Avi instead, I'll support *you* for leader." He smiled as he said the last words and pointed to Moctu's chest.

Moctu was confounded by this offer. Growing up, he considered and sometimes dreamed of being leader of the tribe. He, too, had discerned Ono's not-so-subtle attempted elevation of his son toward the leadership. And when Ono had said that the tribe needed younger leadership, he'd briefly considered himself for the position. But he was too young, and there were more qualified men like Nabu that he'd like to support. And he didn't want to give up Nuri, even to be leader.

"Petral, you honor me with this proposal. But I think I'm too young to be leader."

"I was afraid you'd say that," said Petral. "Look, the tribe is wishful for a young leader, one who is wise, brave, and an excellent hunter. You're all those things." He paused. "Is it that you're infatuated with Nuri? I know young men often get captivated by one girl and can see nothing beyond her."

He thought he saw in Moctu's eyes that he was right.

"All right, here is my final offer. I'll support you for leader. When you become leader, take Nuri for your mate. Sure, sure, fine. But also take Avi as your second. Promise this, and I will support you for leader. I think you can get it. How can you not accept that proposal?"

Moctu was dumbfounded by this offer and overwhelmed by the vision of it. He'd be getting three wonderful rewards, three treasures from this deal, and he was absorbed contemplating it for a few moments. But then reality set in and he realized its improbability. Petral was desperate to keep his family, and especially Avi, from being joined to Ono's.

"That's a very attractive and tempting offer," Moctu replied. "If I thought it were a likely outcome, I would readily consent. I still think I'm too young to be supported by most of the men, and I think there are better candidates for leader. How about if I supported you, Petral?"

Petral smiled and said, "Believe me, if I thought I'd be supported, I'd want the leadership. Then I could make sure Avi got a good man. A decent and honorable man. But I'm not a good hunter, and the men wouldn't support me."

The two men were quiet for a while, until Petral said, "I didn't hear you say no."

"Let me ask you this," Moctu responded. "If I say no, who will you approach next?"

"See, you are wise," said Petral smiling. "I'll again be open with you. If you say no, I'll approach either Nabu or Jabil. Both are young and excellent hunters. Both are respected by the men of the tribe."

The thought of Jabil as leader shook Moctu. He was sure that Jabil would make his life extremely difficult, probably starting by taking Nuri from him. Until yesterday evening, Moctu had thought Ono, the only remaining elder, would likely be leader, and he'd since been so absorbed in consoling Alta and caring for Zaila that he hadn't given much thought to other outcomes.

Jabil as leader, he thought with alarm. Jondu would be bad enough, but Jabil? Either could very possibly be the next leader and neither was an appealing choice to Moctu. He looked at Petral and said, "I'll work with you to support Nabu. If for some reason he doesn't want the role, then I'll stand at the Council to ask for support to be leader."

Chapter Thirty-One

Jondu and Ono were also maneuvering and scheming, as was Jabil. Jondu and Ono had visited about half of the men in the tribe soliciting their support for Jondu as leader. There was reasonable support, although few of the men had committed firmly. Jabil had visited several of the same men to similar effect. Now, Jondu approached Jabil.

"Hello, Jabil."

"Welcome, Jondu, I think I know why you're here. It seems we've been working at cross-purposes. Come, sit. Maybe we can work together?"

"Yes, well that depends," said Jondu.

"Here's what I suggest," said Jabil. "First, let me say that I think you'd make a good leader." Jondu nodded his head in agreement and appreciation. "I hope you'll agree with me that I, too, would make a good leader," Jabil continued. He waited for a response from Jondu and got an affirmative nod, but less pronounced than the last one. "The Council of Warriors will happen tomorrow evening. I propose that we both rise, separately, and speak, and whichever of us gets the most support, the other of us will thereafter support him strongly. That way, one of us is very likely to become leader. If it's me, I can assure you that you'll have a place of honor. You know you'll be my most trusted elder and my second in command. Plus, I can also assure you that you'll get Avi."

Jondu smiled, thinking he and his father had lined up more support than Jabil. He nodded and said, "Likewise, if it's me, you'll be second in command."

"And you can assure me that I'll get Nuri?"

"Sure, of course," said Jondu.

"Then that's good," said Jabil. "We've been best friends for so long, and I'm glad this episode won't be changing that." The two young men embraced and then parted, each planning a rapid succession of final day visits to attempt to secure more support.

Meanwhile, Moctu and Petral visited Nabu. The formal pleasantries were over, and Petral got right to their reason for the visit.

"Nabu, we want to express our support for you to be our next leader. You're the right age, you have good experience, you're a good hunter, and you're respected by all in the tribe. Will you be speaking at the Council? If so, you can count on our wholehearted support."

"Whew,'" Nabu said, his lips pursing and his brow furrowing. "You… you honor me greatly. Thanks, um… thank you for your words. That you two would ask me this… I'm… stunned." He was lost in thought for a moment. "You've honored me greatly," he said finally. "But I can't do it."

Now Moctu and Petral were stunned. "But why not?" they asked in unison.

"I just can't do it. I… I'm not the right man to lead the tribe. I can't do it," replied Nabu, showing a nervousness that wasn't there before.

Nabu was Moctu's best hope for circumventing leadership by either Jabil or Jondu. He was a good age, he was capable, and he was well-liked by the tribe. Moctu realized he'd have to speak if Nabu didn't, and his chances were poor due to his youth. Although he was a good hunter and well-liked, he was just too young to be leader. Even he thought so. He and Petral pressed Nabu to reconsider, but Nabu was adamant. He would not stand to speak at the Council.

Petral, extremely frustrated, said, "I need to leave and get some... some food." With that, he stormed out of Nabu's hearth.

Nabu looked abashedly at Moctu and said, "I have reasons. I've got reasons why I don't wish to speak."

"Then what are they Nabu? Just tell me," said Moctu. "I swear an oath that I won't speak of this to anyone if that's your wish."

"I'm embarrassed. I'm ashamed to tell you," said Nabu.

Moctu was completely baffled and intrigued. What did Nabu have to be ashamed of? What horrible secret was he hiding? Nabu had never done anything to Moctu's knowledge that was dishonorable.

Nabu saw the mystified look on Moctu's face and in a quiet voice said, "I can't speak to large groups. It terrifies me." Moctu nearly burst out laughing but stifled it. "You did fine leading the men on the hunt recently," he said smiling.

"Uh-huh, I can speak to a few people, that's fine. But the thought of standing at the Council, in front of four hands of warriors... I would rather face a cave bear alone."

Now Moctu did laugh, clapping Nabu on the shoulder. Nabu laughed a little too but remained serious.

"I can't do it," he said simply.

Chapter Thirty-Two

"Are you busy?" Avi called to Nuri as she neared her hearth.

"Never too busy for you," Nuri replied cheerfully.

"The whole tribe is so serious. All the men are busy trying to become leader. Or picking one. Anyway, I'm worried, but mostly, I'll just be glad when the suspense is over."

"Yes," Nuri said distractedly. She was busy working a bone needle through leather, making bridal clothes to replace those she gave Avi. She stopped and looked up at Avi and said, "Yes, Papa's totally absorbed in the activities. I don't like to think about it because so many of the things that could happen seem bad."

"I know, Father has talked to a lot of men and he gets so angry. He's still mad at Ono. I think part of it is that he's trying to forestall the mating ceremony between Jondu and me. I'd pretty much gotten used to the idea of it, but now… now I don't think I want to be Jondu's mate." Her voice broke a little on the last words.

Now Nuri put her sewing down and stood to hug Avi. She could tell Avi was apprehensive and overwrought. She was also nervous about the coming decision on the leadership, and she worried that the results could delay or upend her mating ceremony to Moctu. Just thinking about it, a new wave of anxiety swept over her, and she shivered imperceptibly.

She drew Avi close and said, "We'll get through this.

No matter what. We just have to believe that the Spirits are guiding us, and they know what they're doing." She tried to sound more positive than she was, and continued, "Hey, no matter who we end up with, we've got each other. Nothing can change that."

Avi smiled and said, "I know. It's just hard. It's hard not knowing who my mate will be. Jondu could even end up as leader."

"I know, you'd be mated to the leader," exclaimed Nuri trying to put a favorable spin on it.

"Yes, but... Jondu. He's... I don't know. I guess being mated to the leader wouldn't be all bad," Avi mused. "I know he's attracted to me, that's one thing I suppose."

"I imagine every man in this tribe is attracted to you, Avi," said Nuri laughing. Avi blushed slightly, and Nuri continued, "Your hair is really pretty today."

"Thanks, you think?" Avi replied, pulling her light brown hair back with both hands.

"I know it," said Nuri. "There's not a man in this tribe that wouldn't want you."

"Thanks," said Avi again, feeling better. "But you're the one they really want. You know that, don't you?"

Now it was time for Nuri to blush.

"No, I don't know that," she sputtered.

"Well, it's true," said Avi, smiling and enjoying Nuri's embarrassment. Both girls laughed and hugged again.

"You always put me in a better mood, Avi," said Nuri. "I think we're going to make it through all this. It's... it's going to work out fine." And for a brief moment, she believed it.

Chapter Thirty-Three

The men were subdued as they gathered around the Council fire. Most had worn their finest clothes to the meeting. They would decide something important tonight, something that would impact the tribe's future for years to come. Jondu occasionally whispered with his father, but for the most part, the men were silent. Nearly all were seated when Jabil arrived, bringing the massive cave bear skull with him, which he placed prominently in front of him as he sat down. This action caused a stir among the men, some thinking it was an imaginative stroke of brilliance, some offended by it. Moctu was nervous, realizing the choice for leader had come down to Jondu, Jabil, or himself. His future with the tribe was clouded. If either Jabil or Jondu became leader, they could harass and provoke him at will and would likely do so. Nuri would almost certainly be taken from him.

All the men he'd stand and speak before tonight were older than he was. Would they tolerate being led by a relative youngster? Unlikely. But he had to try. He thought Jabil's ostentatious display of the cave bear skull was crass but probably effective. Mentally, Moctu counted the men who might choose to support him.

He was only sure of Petral and Palo, and probably Nabu. Beyond them, he couldn't really count on anyone else. That made only four. If Sokum and Seetu had taken their manhood rites, they would probably have supported him. If Tabar were there, he'd certainly side with Moctu. But if Tabar were there, he'd probably be the leader. For many reasons Moctu desperately wished that Tabar was with him. Ordu and Samar might have supported him, but they were gone too. He saw Nindai and was sure he could count on his support, but Nindai wasn't a man. He couldn't undergo the manhood rites, and he wasn't allowed to sit at the Council of Warriors.

Nindai chanted the Song of the Tribe and played his flute. The men were on edge, and the familiar tradition seemed to calm them. Ono rose and spoke of the import of the Council of Warriors and the serious implications it had for the tribe's future. He reasserted that the previous elders, himself included, had made crucial mistakes which had severely hurt the tribe. Soberly but firmly, he reiterated that he would not be leader because of his mistake in misjudging the threat of the Pale Ones. Making an undisguised pitch for his son, he reminded the men that Jondu had repeatedly warned of the dangers posed by the Pale Ones. He ended by asking any man who aspired to be leader, or who had anything to say concerning it, to stand and speak.

Jondu rose immediately and said, "Honored men, I ask for your support tonight. The tribe needs a man who knows how to bring meat to our people, and I am one of the best hunters here. The tribe also needs men who see the dangers to our people and who can keep us safe. I was the first to stand in front of you and demand that we drive the vile People Eaters away. My comments were ignored and look what happened."

He paused and looked around the circle. The men were following his words closely, and that buoyed his confidence. "Finally," he said, "I have a close connection to the only remaining elder, an elder who, along with those passed, did many good things." He looked down at his father. "Yes, they made some mistakes, but mostly they guided us with wisdom and bravery." As many of the men cheered in agreement, Jondu put his hands on Ono's shoulders. "I will be keeping Ono as a valued elder, one who brings a wealth of experience. I hope you'll support me." This prompted shouts of acclamation from several in the crowd and raised Jondu's hopes.

Jondu sat, and Jabil was disturbed that the crowd seemed largely won over by his remarks. Seeing this, he was about to stand when Petral rose.

"I have something to say," he said in a loud voice. "I'm not speaking tonight to ask to be your leader. Rather I'm here to help our tribe avoid choosing wrongly." As he said the last words, he looked at Jondu disapprovingly. Jondu glowered back at him. "There are two things you all must know," he continued. "Some of you know one of them and some the other, but very few of you know both. Yes, Jondu advised us about the threat of the Pale Ones and that turned out to be correct. But he and his father Ono are *not* suitable to lead. They are not good people. They're hyenas, men that do unseemly things."

The crowd had been attentive before, but now there was dead silence as the men listened in hushed consternation.

"Both of these *fine* men," Petral continued, "have separately cornered and attacked my young daughter when she was alone. Each forced themselves on her well before she reached womanhood. It was inappropriate. It was wrong. It could have hurt her. In fact, it did hurt her." He said the last words through clenched teeth. Petral was seething now at the memory. Jabil watched the man in fascination and growing optimism regarding his chances.

Petral went on, "Neither of these men is suitable to lead the tribe. I would never support them, and I hope you won't either." He sat, still fuming. Jondu looked around worriedly at the assembled men, and Ono stared at the ground.

Jabil looked at Moctu, and Moctu returned his gaze. Moctu motioned for Jabil to speak next, but Jabil mirrored him, encouraging Moctu to speak. Neither wanted to go next;

both wanted to finish. An awkward moment passed, during which most of the assembled men inexplicably looked toward Moctu.

He finally rose and said in a strong voice that belied his nervousness, "I speak tonight to ask your support to be your next leader. I'll keep this short. Yes, I'm young, but I've proved many times that I'm an excellent hunter. I'll be able to keep the tribe well fed. The tribe's well-being will always be my highest priority, and we'll maintain its safety. I've had contact with the Pale Ones which few can say, and I know some of their methods and abilities. This may prove valuable over the next moons. We will avenge Ordu, Samar, and my father, Tabar!" he said emphatically. This statement elicited shouts of support from several of the men.

"I'll work hard to be the best and fairest leader I can be. I ask for your support." Moctu sat down and saw Petral smile at him. Jabil moved to stand, but Petral stood first.

"I earlier had some negative things to say. Now, I'll say only positive things. Moctu is a good young man, and all the comments he made are true. He'll make a great leader. I support him fully." Petral sat and both Jabil and Jondu scowled at him.

Jabil again began to stand but Palo stood first.

"Moctu has been too modest. He hasn't reminded you of his leadership during the attack by the wolves. I was there. I saw his leadership and bravery under grueling and dangerous conditions, and that was almost three summers ago. He was a man then and has grown even stronger and more mature since. He single-handedly killed two wolves and helped us drive a host of them off. He saved the meat for the tribe, and he saved *our lives*—the boys accompanying him. He'll make an excellent leader and I support him fully."

Several of the men were nodding as Palo sat. Moctu's eyes met Palo's, and he smiled at him in thanks.

Nabu stood nervously and said, "And he saved Jabil's

life during the rhino hunt." He quickly sat and looked at the ground. Moctu wondered at the courage it had taken for him to stand and speak, and he felt very honored and grateful.

There was a pause, and Jabil finally stood.

"It's clear that the tribe has talented men from whom to choose their leader." He nodded graciously at Jondu then Moctu. "I, too, have come tonight to ask for your support," Jabil continued smoothly. "I'm an excellent and brave hunter," he beckoned to the cave bear skull. "My cave bear alone fed the tribe with rich meat and fat for a moon. More recently, I made the first hit on the enormous rhino that feeds the tribe even now. Shortly before that, I'd just gotten back from the Gatza, which was extremely successful. We brought back more salt than ever before. During the trip back from the Gatza, I saved a woman's life—that of our dear Leuna, mate to Samar, may he rest with the Spirits. She'd no longer be with us, she would have drowned if not for me.

"I'll keep the tribe safe. For many moons, I've stood nearly alone, warning of the menace posed by the Pale Ones. Only now do we fully recognize the danger from the People Eaters. Only after losing three of our best." He paused for a moment and saw that most of the men were hanging on his words. "Moctu has said that he's one of the few who have had 'contact' with the Pale Ones. Well, I'm the only other besides him, and I'm the only one who has hurt the beasts!" There were raucous cheers from many in the Council at his last remark.

"I can promise you that if you make me your leader, with your help, we'll track these beasts down and punish them for killing Ordu... Samar... Tabar." As Jabil paused between each name, he saw that he was having a powerful impact by reminding the men of their fallen comrades. "We'll exterminate them." The cheering was even louder now, and Jabil felt confident enough to sit.

The cheering quickly died down, and there was an interval where Ono waited for anyone else to speak. Alfer, Jabil's father, rose and retold the story of the cave bear hunt, emphasizing Jabil's role and reminding them of Jabil's prowess as a hunter. Alfer also reminded the men that Jabil's courage and efforts had probably saved the three fallen men from being eaten by the Pale Ones. He sat and Ono waited for others to speak. None did, so he rose and began to explain the next proceedings.

"We'll now see who has the most support. We'll ask supporters of each of these men," he motioned at Jondu, Moctu, and Jabil, "to stand when I call their names. To become leader, one of them needs at least half of the men to support him. By my count, that means nine supporters. I'll call the names in the same order these men stood." Ono sat and waited for quiet. Then he said, "Jondu, please stand." Jondu stood, and Ono continued. "Now will his supporters stand." He said this last comment with enthusiasm while standing himself. Jabil smiled as he thought he saw Ono's jaw drop open when only two other men stood, making only four in total. Petral caught Moctu's eyes and smiled broadly at him. Ono continued to stand while attempting to catch the eyes of several of the men who'd earlier indicated they would support Jondu. Those men steadfastly looked into the fire or at the ground.

After an awkward lull, Ono sat and seemed disinclined to continue.

He stared at Moctu and finally said, "Moctu, please stand." Moctu stood and Ono said, "Will supporters of Moctu now stand."

Palo and Petral stood immediately, followed by Nabu, then two more, the fathers of Nuri and Seetu. That made only six, more than Jondu, but not enough. Moctu saw that Jabil was smiling, but he looked preoccupied, trying to do the relevant math in his head. The call was made for Jabil to stand, and then his supporters. A total of seven men stood, so none of the three had gotten to the needed nine supporters. Jabil saw

Jondu whispering into his father's ear and smiled, convinced that he knew what Jondu was saying. He watched Ono frown and realized he was right. Ono looked over at him, and Jabil smiled and shrugged slightly. Ono frowned again and nodded and announced that Jondu was withdrawing.

Jondu stood and said, "I confirm that I'm now withdrawing. I thank my supporters and ask that they now support Jabil." Although not unexpected, this still came as a blow to Moctu.

Apprehension surged through him. I've lost and Jabil will be leader. Oh Spirits, what are you thinking? I'll lose Nuri.

Jabil smiled broadly as Jondu made his statement. He rearranged the cave bear skull in front of him and leaned back against the rock behind him and toyed with his thin braid. Ono called for Moctu to stand and then for his supporters. Including Moctu, eight men stood. "I've gained two," Moctu thought, "but not enough!" Despair swamped his senses, and he barely heard the proceedings as Jabil was called next and he stood along with eight other men. He'd gotten to nine.

It's over, Moctu thought as his head sagged in utter dejection. He could barely breathe as he contemplated the ramifications of this evening. Several men, including Alfer, Jabil's father, cheered and clapped the new leader on the back.

"Jabil is our new leader," Ono said in a somber voice. "This Council is over."

Chapter Thirty-Four

Jabil couldn't believe how his fortunes had changed. Less than half a moon ago, he was going to be humiliated and scorned. Now he led the tribe. He was thrilled, nearly intoxicated with the power and the potential of his new position. He still occasionally had visions, horrible visions that would leave him weak and gasping. These were getting less frequent, but some of them seemed, individually, more troublesome than before. The worst of the grisly memories came at night when the darkness seemed to exacerbate them. Some of these episodes would leave him drenched in sweat and whimpering. To those around him, he blamed a recurrence of the hitz sickness he had during the night of the attack. All those who saw him suffer during these times had great sympathy for him.

Jabil lost no time in cementing his victory. Within the first two days, he'd asked Ono, Jondu and Nabu to be elders, and they agreed. He talked with them the next day to decide the disposition of the seven women who had no mates. They decided that the standard of the *Mourning Moon* would be followed, and that the five widows would be placed with mates shortly thereafter. Their children would, of course, go along with them, a considerable new responsibility for the stepfathers.

Moctu was sure Alta wouldn't be ready for a new mate in one moon. Most ominous to Moctu was their decision to cancel the earlier planned mating ceremonies so that they could be reevaluated. Privately, Jabil assured Jondu that he would still get Avi, but he wanted the pair of girls reconsidered together. Soon, when he changed the disposition of Nuri from Moctu to himself, it would seem less precipitous. He also planned to take Leuna, but he needed to think through the timing on that more carefully.

Support was strong for an initiative against the Pale Ones, and it was always the most-discussed topic at the main fire each evening. Jondu, especially, railed against them, but Jabil remained uncharacteristically quiet. Now in Ordu's shoes, Jabil realized how many men it would take to mount a successful expedition against the Pale Ones and how few men that would leave to protect Etseh. His tentativeness caused Jondu to approach and question him as he left the fire one evening.

"Jabil, this isn't like you. Why do we wait? All we do is meet and discuss, meet and discuss. There's no action. I thought we wanted the same thing—to exterminate the Pale Ones."

"It's not that simple, Jondu. We need more men, more warriors. I don't want to leave Etseh almost unguarded while we chase their shadows."

"Then let's get more men. Hold Seetu's and Sokum's manhood rites immediately, and we'll have two more warriors."

"Yes, that would help," said Jabil. "I've been planning that. I thought we'd do that after the women were assigned, but maybe we should move the rites up in time."

The next day, in a discussion with the elders, Jabil announced that the rites would start in two days.

"We need more warriors, so we'll hold manhood rites for Seetu and Sokum," he paused, "and Moctu."

Nabu's jaw dropped in consternation and Ono muttered, "No, no, no." Even Jondu was surprised.

"You can't do that!" Nabu said loudly. "Moctu has already been given manhood status. His handprint is on the Wall of Warriors. This is wrong. It overturns what Ordu and the previous elders did."

Ono said, "I agree. It's wrong and will be viewed poorly by the tribe."

"Haven't all the other men in the tribe undergone manhood rites?" asked Jabil. "Why should there be exceptions?"

"I agree with Jabil," said Jondu.

"Of course you do!" said Ono savagely to his son. "Neither of you like Moctu, and now you abuse him at your earliest opportunity."

"I've made my decision," said Jabil. "It can be disregarded if you all oppose it."

"I favor it," said Jondu. Ono rolled his eyes in disdain.

* * * *

Nabu approached Moctu that afternoon.

"Moctu, I'm afraid I have some unfortunate news."

"There has been too much of that lately," said Moctu, smiling grimly. "But tell me, what is it?" He felt his pulse rise as he knew what Nabu would tell him—he was losing Nuri to Jabil. Moctu almost laughed at what Nabu said.

"You have to take manhood rites."

Although manhood rites were tortuous ordeals, and this was bad news, it wasn't the horrible news he'd been expecting. He barely heard as Nabu continued, "Jabil says there are to be no exceptions. The rites will start in a couple of days with the induced vomiting then the three days of fasting."

Moctu was lost in thought. The news about Nuri would come soon after the manhood rites. How could he stop him from taking her? How could he stop Jabil?

Nabu droned on repeating what every adolescent boy knew. "After the fasting, there'll be the two sessions of whipping and then the cutting and piercing."

Nerean boys were taught that they needed to vomit and suffer blood loss from being whipped and from cuts on their tongue, head, and hands to cleanse them of any remaining female influences left in them from their mothers. They couldn't cry out or show any sign of weakness. All this was done to prove their courage and to gain the favor and approval of the Spirits. If a boy couldn't complete the rites successfully, he'd suffer the consequences for the rest of his life, and never be recognized as a real man.

"You're taking this better than I thought you would," Nabu said. "Actually better than I did when Jabil announced it to the elders. I… I want you to know that I opposed it, as did Ono. Both of us recognize, as will the rest of the tribe I think, that Jabil is just using his new position to abuse you. I only hope he doesn't try to… seriously harm you."

Nabu left him, and as Moctu began to focus on the manhood rites rather than the impending loss of Nuri, his relative relief was clouded with new worries.

"Wonder if Jabil plans to kill me so he can get Nuri that way," he murmured.

Chapter Thirty-Five

"I think I'm carrying your child," Leuna whispered to Jabil as she encountered him on the trail to the creek. Jabil was surprised, but not displeased. He looked around to be sure no one saw them talking.

"Why do you think it's mine and not Samar's?"

"Samar's seed was never powerful in me. I couldn't get pregnant from him. One moon after our… after lying with you, I'm obviously with child. Your seed is very strong. My mother and Jelli are the only ones that know I'm with child, but they think it's Samar's."

Jabil smiled and said, "My first child. So, my first child will always be known as *Samar's child*," he said chuckling. "Well, so be it. Sometime following the Mourning Moon, you'll be mated to me, and I'll raise *Samar's child* as if he were my own."

"Oh, I'm so relieved. I was hoping you'd say that," said Leuna. "Although I miss Samar greatly, I miss… I miss being with you, Jabil. I didn't want to be given as a mate to someone else."

"I miss being with you too," said Jabil, growing aroused just thinking about it. "Maybe we can meet in the west woods while you're gathering firewood?"

"You're the leader now, but it would be… um… you'd be dishonored if we're discovered," she responded. "We'd both be dishonored."

"The west woods are vast, and there are places where no one would find us," he responded, shrugging off her worries and growing more excited by the thought.

"I think it's a bad idea. It's too dangerous. If we just wait a little while, there'll be no risk."

"Risk is part of the fun. It makes it even better, more exciting," Jabil replied huskily.

"Well, you're both leader and my future mate, so I'll do as you tell me. But I really think it's better to wait."

"Then I'll meet you in the west woods shortly after noon," said Jabil.

Throughout the rest of the morning, Leuna kept a close eye on the sun. Although she was worried about being discovered, she was thrilled that Jabil wanted her as a mate. Leuna knew, everyone knew, that he wanted Nuri most of all, but he wanted her too. She didn't mind being a second mate, especially to the leader. Her heart was beating fast as she took her skin for gathering firewood and strode toward the west woods.

As she entered the woods, Jabil called to her from behind a giant oak. "Over here. I've been waiting for you."

Leuna felt happy, almost giddy as she walked over to him and he embraced her. She hadn't been this happy in a long time. There had been so much sadness lately that this feeling inside her was a welcome change.

"You're right, this is kind of exciting," she said giggling. She stayed close by his side, holding his arm as they moved farther into the woods, both feeling exhilarated with anticipation. She babbled with elation, telling him how happy she'd make him and how many strong sons she'd give him.

Nuri and Avi were gathering firewood when they heard movement and soft voices nearby in the forest. They'd taken to gathering wood together ever since they reached womanhood, thinking that as a twosome, they were safer from Jondu and other aggressive men. Thinking it might be Jondu or other men, they were immediately quiet, concentrating on the sounds. They soon made out a woman's voice and relaxed somewhat.

Nuri whispered, "It sounds like Leuna. And she sounds... happy?" She whispered the last statement as a question, because everyone knew that Leuna had been devoted to Nuri's uncle, Samar, and was devastated by his death.

"There's a man with her," Avi whispered back. They could both make out the pair as they crouched behind the clump of thick beech and oak foliage. Jabil and Leuna passed within an easy stone's throw of the hidden pair.

"Why is Jabil with her?" Avi hissed.

"Not sure, but they look like they're a couple, holding each other like that."

"But..." Avi said perplexed.

"I know, I know," said Nuri, her curiosity growing. As the couple moved farther into the woods, the girls followed silently. It soon became evident what their purpose was. Jabil and Leuna stopped, and Jabil peered carefully around, listening intently. At one point, Nuri bit her lip as his gaze lingered on the bush behind which the girls had hidden. But his mind was captivated by Leuna. As he began undressing her, Avi gasped audibly, and Nuri worried that Jabil would hear. But he was absorbed in his activity and continued single-mindedly. It became clear that Leuna was there willingly and knew what was to happen. The couple sank to the leafy ground and mostly out of sight.

"This is just wrong. It's despicable," Avi fumed. "Samar's only been gone a matter of days."

Nuri and Avi were close enough to hear the sounds of lovemaking and remained where they were, spellbound. They could make out much but not all of what was said after the couple finished their amorous activity.

They heard Jabil say, "I've missed that. I've missed you." Nuri and Avi looked at each other shocked.

"I've missed you too," replied Leuna. The next words were muffled, and all they could make out was talk of a baby.

"Is Leuna pregnant?" Nuri whispered. "Is it Samar's? Or is it... maybe Jabil's?"

Leuna giggled and said, "No, we need to get back... and I need to gather some firewood."

"After the Gatza, I told myself I'd never gather another stick of firewood, but I'll help you," Jabil said.

Leuna said something and giggled again and Jabil responded, "Better stop that if we're going to get back." Soon they were up and had clothed themselves, and began to gather wood. Leuna moved in their direction, and Nuri realized they were likely to be discovered if they stayed where they were. She placed a finger over her lips and motioned to Avi the direction they should move. They carefully and gradually backed away, putting some distance between themselves and the couple.

"I don't believe it!" said Avi in a shocked whisper when they were a safe distance away. "It's... it's..."

"I know," said Nuri. "It's contemptible. I'm not surprised about Jabil, but I've always liked Leuna, and I thought she was devoted to Samar."

"My father will be repulsed by this," said Avi. "The whole tribe will be."

"Avi, please don't tell anyone yet. We need to think through all this first. Promise me that you won't say anything to anyone for a while."

"Hmm. I don't know... it's so... slimy. Don't you think people should know?"

"Maybe. But a lot of things are going to happen over this next moon," said Nuri. "Things that concern you and me greatly, about which we have no control. Well, maybe that's changed a little now," she concluded, her jaw clenched.

Chapter Thirty-Six

"What are you doing?" Jondu asked Jabil as he saw him working on a leather whip.

"The fasting is almost over, and I've heard that Moctu isn't suffering much… isn't that worried about the manhood rites. I'm preparing a whip that will definitely get his attention," replied Jabil smiling.

Jondu whistled and frowned as he watched Jabil push a wicked looking hawthorn barb into a knot at the end of the whip, concealing most of it. He held up the end of the whip for Jondu to see. On close inspection, Jondu could see the tips of thorns that protruded from most of the knotted ends of the whip.

"This whip will get him worrying," Jabil chuckled. "By the time I'm finished with him, he'll cry like a little girl and show the tribe what a disgrace he really is."

"You could kill him with that thing if you're not careful."

"Wouldn't that be tragic," Jabil said with a wry smile.

"Well, I don't like him either, but don't overdo it."

"Let me ask you this," Jabil replied. "Would you want him in your hunting party? I'm sure he plans to retaliate against us at some point."

Jondu shook his head.

"Then if he's not in your hunting party, do you want him back here at Etseh around the women? I don't want to have to worry about that."

Jondu shrugged and nodded. "I understand that. But we've had way too much death around here. Don't overdo it, Jabil. Got to keep our focus. We still need every possible warrior to rid ourselves of the Pale Ones."

Jondu's comments about "too much death" initiated an immediate flashback for Jabil to the bloody camp scene. He shuddered, as he saw Ordu's eyes opening in recognition the instant before his death. Sweat beaded on his forehead and he felt dizzy. He set the whip aside and fought to catch his breath. Jondu realized what was happening and tried to comfort him.

"Easy there my friend. I didn't mean to remind you of the bad times. You were very brave, and we will soon rid ourselves of the beasts that attacked us." He patted Jabil's back.

Meanwhile, in the Manhood Hearth, Moctu's tongue was thick, and his mouth felt wooden. He, Seetu and Sokum hadn't eaten or drunk for three days. To ensure compliance, Ono was there with them in the Hearth which was at the extreme end of Etseh, as far from the Red Hearth as possible. Under Ono's watchful presence, each of the young men had thrust a smooth, carved stick down their throat until they vomited. They each did this three times. That was three days ago, and Moctu could still smell the vomit. He could taste nothing as his mouth and throat were too dry. He remembered Nindai telling him that water was the essence of life, even more so than fire.

"All people need water," Nindai had said. "Lots of it. Especially the sick ones. No one can live even half a moon without water."

The boys had spent most of the three days quietly in the hearth, trying to conserve their dwindling energy. Conversation, which was limited on the first day, was now non-existent. None of the boys had complained during the ordeal, but Sokum had moaned in his sleep. They dreaded the next two days when they'd be whipped by the elders in front of any of the tribe who wanted to view the torment. Usually, there was great interest in the rites, and none of them doubted that many from the tribe would be there to watch the event.

The young men weren't allowed to cry out during the whippings. To do so was to shame yourself and your totem Spirit. They'd been told that the worst part was the night after the first whipping when the anticipation of the next day's whipping was too much to bear for some. Even so, all of them looked forward to that evening because they were, at that point, finally allowed to drink water. They were so thirsty! After the whippings came ceremonial tongue-piercing and bloodletting from the forehead and hands. Immediately thereafter, the boys' faces and arms were painted with Spirit paint to encourage the Spirits to guide them to prey. Finally, they were each given an atlatl with one shaft, and they were then on their own until they brought back enough meat to feed one hand of men for a day. That usually meant killing a deer or several smaller animals. This often took days, sometimes a half moon. The task had become more arduous as game became less abundant in recent years. Most boys managed the undertaking and most survived, but four summers before, hyenas had taken one boy on his second night out. He'd still been close enough that his screams were heard in Etseh. Hunters had left immediately to attempt to find and rescue him, but they discovered only remnants of his body.

Moctu was light-headed as the boys made their way toward the large boulders they'd lean into while they were whipped.

So thirsty, he thought. What I wouldn't do for a drink of water! At one point, he could see the nearby creek, and the urge to go drink from it almost overwhelmed him. Seetu and Sokum were holding up well, and he found he was proud of them, as an older brother would be proud to see his younger brothers excel. He could see Nabu, Jondu, and Jabil, all grim-faced, in position with their whips. A sizable crowd had gathered, and he saw Nuri standing next to Alta. Zaila wasn't with her.

Be strong, he kept telling himself. It was unlikely that he'd get Nabu, Jabil would see to that. So, he steeled himself to show no emotion when either Jondu or Jabil lined up to whip him. It was Jabil. As he lined up near Moctu, his grim expression broke and he smiled a little.

"I'll be gentle," he joked. Moctu said nothing but turned his back to him and placed his hands on the boulder. He clenched his teeth hard on a thick piece of leather he'd brought.

I will not cry out. Please, Wolf Spirit, give me courage and strength, he prayed silently. Jabil will do anything to break me. Help me to show no weakness to him. Let me be strong for Nuri, for Mother, for my friends.

The first strike took his breath away. The intensity of the pain was more than anything he'd experienced. Worse than the Odel-emit. Worse than his fight with Jabil and Jondu. He ground his teeth into the leather strip. The next strike came, and his knees nearly buckled. There was something wrong. Sure, whippings were supposed to hurt, but this was something entirely different. The pain was excruciating.

Please, Wolf Spirit! I won't make it through this, he pleaded in his mind. But each strike seemed to increase the pain to new, unbelievable levels. The crowd had begun to murmur, and in his peripheral vision, he could see some pointing at him. He wondered if they'd seen his knees almost buckle. I can't break. I won't. Oh, Spirits! he thought as the next burst of pain washed over him. Jabil is trying to kill me! Spirits help me.

A voice came through his pain-blurred mind, "You will do this. You're going to make it." It was Tabar!

Another voice, less clear, echoed the thought. "You are my son. You're going to get through this." It was his father, Jona! Both of his fathers were there to support him. His body seemed to go numb, and the pain, while still there, still as intense, just didn't seem to register anymore.

It was as if he were viewing his body from the outside. He was one of the crowd. He could see his back was a bloody mess, much bloodier than either Seetu's or Sokum's. Blood had soaked the back of his loin cloth. It ran in small rivulets down his legs. That's what the crowd was pointing at. Now he could make out Nuri's and Alta's shrieks to stop the assault. Nabu had stopped whipping Seetu and was staring apprehensively at Jabil who continued to flail at the bloody mess. His face, arms, and clothes were splattered with blood, but he kept whipping.

Petral stepped forward followed by a limping Nindai.

"This one has been whipped enough," Petral shouted loud enough for the whole crowd to hear.

Nindai grabbed Jabil's arm which was poised for another strike. The crowd rumbled its agreement, and Jabil saw no advantage to continuing. He quickly placed the bloody whip out of view under a nearby skin and acted concerned for Moctu.

"Poor boy—his skin appears weaker than the other boys'," he said loudly. "Apparently, there was more female influence left in him and it's bleeding out." Jabil was annoyed that Nuri was one of the people supporting a dazed Moctu as Nindai led him to a place in the shade where he could care for his wounds. The group stopped as Alta offered him a skin of water which he gratefully accepted and drank from deeply.

The pain had returned in full force. It had never really left him, rather, it seemed that he'd returned to it. But Nuri was near him now, and he'd made it through the ordeal without breaking. He hadn't cried out. He was aware his loin cloth was soaked with blood, but that seemed to upset others around him more than it did him.

Later, when Moctu awoke, he could recall little of what had happened after the whipping. He was now in the Manhood Hearth, lying on his stomach on thick furs and Nindai was kneeling next to him. He didn't remember walking to the Hearth. Vaguely, he recalled kneeling in the shade with Nindai applying a poultice to his wounds and Nuri stroking his forehead.

He moved slightly and pain surged through him. His back was on fire.

"Ah, you're awake," said Nindai. "Try to lie still. Your back is torn up and you've lost a lot of blood." Nindai seemed business-like as he chanted and hummed prayers over Moctu while continuing to mix another poultice. He was puzzled about the wounds on Moctu's back which were unlike any whipping marks he'd ever seen. Many of the wounds had deep punctures at the uppermost parts of the lacerations. Very peculiar. Inwardly, he worried that Moctu would die if he underwent another whipping tomorrow.

Chapter Thirty-Seven

Nuri swallowed hard as she approached Jabil's hearth. This was a big gamble, and she might just make the situation worse than it was. One thing she knew for sure. If Moctu was whipped again tomorrow, he'd die. It was that simple. She'd seen how close he came today, and it had totally unnerved her. Jabil had been merciless and would have whipped him to death if he hadn't been stopped by some of the men in the crowd. Nuri knew she had to convince Jabil not to whip Moctu tomorrow. Today she was far overstepping the bounds of propriety, but she had a little leverage, and she needed to use it now.

Unrelated women seldom approached a leader. It was considered inappropriate, above their status. Especially one-on-one.

Mustering her courage, she called out as she neared the hearth, "Hello, Esteemed Jabil. May I please talk with you?" A surprised Jabil appeared at the entrance and seemed happy to see her.

"Hello, Nuri. The hearth is occupied. Let's get away from here." They wound past a few more hearths and reached an uninhabited area on the north end of Etseh. They left the coolness and shade of the overhang and reached an isolated spot where the bright afternoon sun beat down on them both. Nuri felt perspiration bead on her forehead and temples.

"Thank you for taking the time to hear me, Jabil," Nuri started, disconcerted by the quaver in her voice.

"Oh Nuri, no need to be so formal. We've been friends for a long time," replied Jabil. He was thinking through her possible reasons for approaching him, and he was sure it concerned Moctu.

"Thank you," she repeated and then paused. She wished she weren't so nervous! "I come today to ask your forbearance. I respectfully ask that Moctu not be whipped tomorrow as scheduled. I think it could kill him."

"Yes," Jabil responded feigning sorrow. "I was sorry to see that his skin appears thin and weak. He had large amounts of the female influence left within him." His comment irritated Nuri, but she held her emotions in check.

"Nonetheless, he's a valuable member of the tribe and another whipping will likely kill him."

"What would you have me do?" asked Jabil shrugging his shoulders. "The manhood rites are the same for everyone. There can be no exceptions. He has to attend the whipping tomorrow or be deemed not a man." Jabil was barely able to stifle a smile after this last comment.

"The rules for the manhood rites are just traditions," she said. "Must they always be followed? Even when someone could be critically hurt?"Jabil was impressed with Nuri's poise and eloquence. He briefly eyed her lustrous, dark hair and the delicious curve of her hip.

"Traditions are what maintain the tribe's stability," he moralized. "They're followed for the tribe's benefit. I don't think we can alter traditions without trouble." He was enjoying this. He wondered how far she would go—would she beg for his life? If so, what should he ask for in return?

"How about the tradition of the Mourning Moon?" Nuri asked with mock innocence. It took a moment for the question to register with Jabil.

"Um," he said, somewhat staggered and buying time.

Where had that come from? "What do you mean by that?" he asked, probing for what, exactly, she knew.

"If you search your heart, you probably know what I mean," Nuri replied cryptically, not giving him much. She enjoyed seeing his arrogance turn to nervous uncertainty.

Jabil wondered if she had seen him with Leuna. That could be real trouble. He had to know what Nuri knew. "What are you saying? Why should the manhood rites not continue?" he finally said sternly, trying to regain his authority.

"If the tradition of the Mourning Moon can be broken, especially after our *leader* announces that it will be followed, then it seems that the manhood rites could be altered to potentially save a life of a valued tribe member."

His face and voice hardened measurably, and he said, "I don't know what you think you've seen or heard, but you're mistaken, and your words are inappropriate."

"I know what I've seen and heard," she said with confidence, although she worried her trembling would betray her.

"Whatever you *think* you've seen, if your account is different from mine, who will be believed?" he asked. "One little girl, or the respected leader of the tribe?"

"Other people will share my account."

"Ah, Avi no doubt. You two are always together. Well, I'll change my earlier question. Who will be believed? Two little girls, or the leader of the tribe and Leuna, mate to great Samar? And as leader, I assure you that I can make yours and your friend's life much more difficult."

There was a pause while both considered their precarious positions. Jabil finally threw out an offering.

"If I can get your oath that this will never be spoken of again, never by you or... your friend, I'll make my oath to you that Moctu won't be harmed tomorrow at the last whipping. This I swear to you and call on all the sacred Spirits to enforce."

Relief flooded through Nuri and her trembling was now

evident. She was sure she could convince Avi to remain silent. She took a deep breath to try and calm herself. In as steady a voice as she could muster she said, "I'll be present tomorrow to see that your oath is fulfilled. If you've spoken truly, then I, too, swear by the sacred Spirits that this subject will never be heard by others."

Both smiled, and Jabil said, "You're a very spirited and beautiful girl." He extended his arm to touch her shoulder but she drew away.

"I'll be there tomorrow," she said and turned and left.

Chapter Thirty-Eight

It was late afternoon when Petral and Palo found Jabil talking with Jondu.

"Esteemed Jabil, may we have a word with you?" Petral called out as they approached. He was trying to be polite even though he was still incensed that Jabil had continued to beat Moctu when he was so obviously badly injured. He and Palo, as well as many others, had been stunned by the ferocity of Jabil's administration of the whipping. The other two boys had come through the initial whipping reasonably well. Most whippings raised severe welts and drew some blood, but Jabil's whipping of Moctu had nearly killed him. Jondu eyed Jabil briefly, then excused himself and went to attend to other matters.

"Palo and I are here to ask your restraint in tomorrow's whipping of Moctu," Petral said. "Many in the tribe share our concern."

"As do I," said Jabil with fake sincerity. "I've already decided to have only a symbolic whipping of Moctu tomorrow. He won't even be touched. I'm concerned for his health. He needs to heal. The poor boy didn't do well in today's whipping." Jabil saw that his statements produced immediate relief to the two men as their unease abated and their features softened. Jabil smiled, enjoying playing the concerned leader.

"That's good," said Palo. "We... well, many in the tribe

are very worried."

"I hope you'll tell others in the tribe of my concern and the actions I'm taking to sidestep tradition to aid Moctu," Jabil said.

"Yes, we thank and praise you for this," said Palo.

"We'll tell Mother Alta, and all the others who are as concerned as we are, what you've decided," said Petral. "They'll be extremely pleased to hear of this."

Jabil thought his deal with Nuri was producing benefits he hadn't even counted on. The Spirits were favoring him. They continued to favor him—his life has improved almost daily since… since… he couldn't bring himself to even form the thought. Treading that close to the memory of the killings sent a shiver through him, and his breath caught once again. Palo saw Jabil stagger slightly and grabbed his arm to steady him.

"Are you having another one of your illness attacks?" Palo asked.

"I'll be all right," Jabil croaked as he forced the thoughts away and fought to regain full control. "I have yet to completely shake the illness, but it's getting better. Thanks for your kindness, but I'll be fine." After an awkward moment, Petral and Palo departed again thanking Jabil for his forbearance.

The next morning as the crowd gathered, it seemed that even the Spirits were watching as the sun crested the eastern hills and its soft amber beams streamed through breaks in brilliant scarlet and gold clouds. The assembled group was larger than the day before, and their murmuring increased as the three boys arrived, followed shortly thereafter by Jabil and the elders carrying their whips. Jabil had spent a portion of the previous evening removing the hawthorn barbs from the braided ends of his whip which was still moist with Moctu's blood.

Palo had told Moctu of Jabil's assurances that he

wouldn't be harmed in today's whipping, but Moctu was still worried. He didn't trust Jabil. His back ached wretchedly, and each time he moved it felt as if it were bursting into flame. He knew he couldn't take another beating like yesterday. Besides the incredible back pain, he felt unsteady and light-headed. It seemed that a fog had engulfed his mind, and his thoughts came slowly. Nindai had warned him yesterday afternoon that dangerous fevers could result from severe injuries. Moctu had immediately recalled his father Jona, dying in great pain with high fever after his leg was broken. This morning he could feel that a fever had indeed come, and he was disheartened upon seeing Nindai's worried expression.

Seetu and Sokum were as worried as Moctu. Although their injuries were much less severe, their backs were streaked with welts, and they dreaded today's event. The three boys bravely turned, exposing their backs, and placed their hands on the large boulders for support. The buzz of the crowd got louder, and people pointed toward Moctu, whose badly lacerated back still oozed blood from several areas despite Nindai's ministrations. Jabil took up a position near him and readied his whip. Peripherally, Jabil scanned the crowd and saw almost all of them looking directly at him. He saw Nuri, her gaze fixed on him, her face inscrutable. The time had come. Jabil drew back his whip, as did Jondu and Nabu theirs. Jabil flashed his whip and it cracked. Moctu winced, but quickly realized that he hadn't been hit. Low gasps nearby indicated that Seetu and Sokum had not been as fortunate today. The whippings continued, but Jabil, true to his word, never allowed his whip to touch Moctu.

The final bloodlettings were administered by Nindai, who expertly pierced each of their tongues with a fine bone needle, then made small cuts to their foreheads, near each temple, and to the tops of their hands. Although the cuts weren't deep, each one produced copious flows of blood. Moctu's back hurt so much that he barely noticed the small incisions. His thoughts were muddled, seemingly hiding in the shadows of his mind. Much of the crowd had dispersed, but Moctu's blurry vision came to rest on Alta and Nuri. They looked worried, but they were together, holding hands. That pleased him.

Chapter Thirty-Nine

As the boys got ready to begin the hunt, the final phase of their manhood rites, a group of three men, Petral, Palo, and Nindai, approached Jabil.

"Jabil, Esteemed Jabil, may we speak with you once again?" asked Petral. Jabil nodded at them irritably, and Petral looked back to Nindai as he hobbled up to the gathering.

Nindai spoke first, saying, "Thank you for hearing us. We have a request of you concerning the manhood rites. First, please accept our gratitude for sparing Moctu his second whipping. I'm convinced it would have killed him."

Jabil nodded gravely to the group and said, "Yes, I was worried too."

Nindai continued, "Moctu's back has just begun to heal. He was severely injured, and he has a fever which will worsen if he doesn't rest and recover. We're here to ask that the remaining hunt phase of his manhood rites be delayed until he has healed or that it be canceled entirely. He has already proven his hunting prowess many times over."

Petral and Palo nodded vigorously in agreement, feeling that Nindai had presented their request well. Jabil was ready for the request—he'd been expecting it.

He frowned in mock consideration and said, "Moctu has already received more special treatment than any other boy ever has. I don't think it would be fair to our forefathers, who all went through the rites before us, to grant him further favors." The men's faces fell, but Palo was mad.

"But Moctu's already proven that he's a great hunter," he said loudly. "There's no point in forcing him to do this part of the rites after he's been beaten so savagely that his life's in danger."

Jabil stiffened and through clenched teeth said, "Be careful of your words, Palo. Moctu was whipped as the other boys were. We're not going to give him any more special treatment. All the boys will leave for their hunts immediately."

Moctu, Seetu, and Sokum were each given an atlatl and one shaft and were sent in separate directions—Moctu to the north, Seetu to the west, and Sokum to the south. Moctu waved goodbye to a small group that included Palo, Nuri, Alta, and Zaila, and set off to the north. He didn't feel well. The fiery ache in his back was relentless, and he felt light-headed. It was near midday, and the early clouds had burned off to a bright, clear, blue sky. The sun was high and hot, so Moctu found a clear stream and drank deeply to replenish his water-depleted body. He knew in his current state that his situation was dangerous. He still had a fever and needed food. In addition to killing enough animals, or a large enough single animal to bring back the requisite meat to satisfy the manhood rites, he'd need to feed himself in the interim. He had no fire, no shelter, and not much clothing. Any sudden move such as an atlatl throwing motion would likely split the lightly scabbed skin on his back, reopening wounds.

Moctu had to have food soon, and his best chance was here near the stream. Small and large game came to the stream to drink but mostly during the dark. Frogs and crawfish were plentiful and gave him the best opportunity for immediate food. He moved along the stream until he found a slower-moving ponded area not much more than knee deep. He watched quietly for some moments before spotting a large frog on the bank. Using his atlatl, he threw his one shaft at it but it missed, embedding itself in the muddy bank a finger's width from the frog which jumped immediately away. He didn't throw the shaft using his full throwing motion and it hadn't hurt too much. As he retrieved his shaft, several other frogs jumped into the pool and disappeared. Now, at least in this pool, his best chance for food was to try for some crawfish. Wading into the pond, he raked his fingers into the soft mud, and with an arcing motion, threw large volumes of it onto the nearby bank. The movement caused searing back pain, but it was tolerable. He had to have food.

After each effort, he studied the mud for movement, and on his third effort, he was rewarded with a wiggling, medium-sized crawfish. He grabbed it between the back and tail and quickly broke off its claws between a small stick and the ground. He tore off the head and most of the shell, rinsed it in the stream and ate the little morsel hungrily. Nothing had ever tasted better. Several more dredging efforts produced two more crawfish which he dispatched similarly, saving the remnants, which could prove useful as bait for snares. Moctu would've continued but his back pain was now unbearable, and he became so light-headed that he nearly fainted. Resting on a boulder, he leaned his shoulder against a tree so that his back was untouched. He could feel blood oozing down his back from reopened wounds.

He awoke feeling as if he were falling, and indeed he was. His shoulder had slipped off the tree, and he was falling backward. A quick movement of his right arm stabilized him, but the rapid motion renewed the pain in his back.

Although Moctu was in the shade, his face was hot and his head ached. When he stood, his eyes blurred and he staggered to where he could hold onto a branch.

"Got to kill something, get back to Etseh and end this. Need rest and food. A deer—got to kill a deer or an antelope—and it has to be soon."

Chapter Forty

A quarter moon had passed and none of the boys were back. Friends and relatives were getting increasingly concerned, and there was talk that with game being so scarce the requirements of the manhood hunt needed to be eased. It seemed unrealistic to demand so much meat to be killed and brought back. The more days that passed, the more people felt that the rites were too challenging and unnecessarily dangerous. The worry had been exacerbated when vultures were spotted circling far to the west—the direction that Seetu had gone. A party of hunters was dispatched to investigate and bring back Seetu's remains if his body was found. The good news was that it wasn't Seetu, but the carcass of a caribou. The bad news was that it had been killed by a large cat, probably a cave lion.

A collective shudder had gone through the Nerea when the hunters returned with the news, and near jubilation arose three days later when Seetu returned. He was haggard, exhausted, and happy to be home, proud that he was the first back. Jabil, the elders, and the tribe had winked at his paltry offerings: a goose, a medium-sized snake, and a tortoise, and praised his accomplishment. He was now a man.

Meanwhile, Moctu had moved north following deer tracks that could be found in places along the stream. His fever had worsened, and he felt awful. Two days before, he'd seen three red deer far ahead, across the low valley, but they'd vanished, leaving no trackable trail by the time he got there. He was far into the lowlands, and the snowcapped Alpeetans loomed large to the north. He was becoming more dispirited and less confident.

So far Moctu, "the great hunter," has killed a frog and two hands of crawfish, he thought sardonically. He tried to rally past his throbbing head, his aching back, and his overwhelming hunger. He would get this done. Looking to the sky he said, "Wolf Spirit, please help me—guide me and give me strength."

As evening approached, he was by the stream, studying the landscape, deciding where to camp. Here in the lowlands, if he were too close to the water, the mosquitoes and flies would suck him dry. Too far, and he would be away from drinking water and thirsty game that might show up. He froze. A red deer doe was drinking at the stream upwind of him to the north. She was on the same side of the stream as he was and already almost within range of his atlatl. His heart began to race, his head cleared, and he felt better than he had in days. Fitting his one shaft into the atlatl, with supreme care he gradually moved closer to the doe. He had to get closer. This had to be a kill shot. If he lost his shaft, he was finished. Moctu was close now. Any other time he'd have taken the shot from here, but he had to make this one perfect.

He'd get one tree closer and take the shot. He was nearly in position when a gust of wind caused the doe to look up warily. Moctu launched his shaft as the doe seemed to recognize the threat from his direction. She was just beginning to move when his shaft took her behind the shoulder, higher than he intended, not in the heart, but still probably a mortal wound. She leapt away from him and ran with an ease that dismayed him. Following as fast as he could, he bounded through the undergrowth, trying desperately to keep her in sight. In his weakened state, fatigue set in quickly, but he pressed on resolutely. His head began to throb again, and he thought he could feel wounds reopening on his lacerated back. He'd lost sight of the deer but could hear her ahead as she charged through the reeds and brush.

It would be dark soon, and he had to stay close.

Moctu didn't have his spear or any more shafts, and he wondered how to dispatch the deer when he came upon her. He was breathing hard, and he slowed to look for a good-sized cobble. He bent down to retrieve one, but as he stood back up, his head swam, and he almost fainted. He felt so weak! Although he soon regained his equilibrium, nausea overtook him and he came close to retching. He had to go on. If he didn't catch her tonight, he'd be searching for her tracks and blood trail tomorrow and his chances were much poorer. Taking a deep breath, he surged onward. He could no longer hear the deer, but her trail was still discernable by the disturbed brush.

He awoke groggily, lying on his stomach in complete darkness.

Dung! I must have… I must have passed out. Will I be able to… to track her in the morning? Oh Spirits, I feel like slug scum!

Nothing could be done in the dark. There would be no tracking tonight. He wasn't even sure if he could make it to the stream, which he could hear softly gurgling to his left. Thirst finally forced him to rise, but his head swam once again. His face was hot, and his head pounded, but he staggered to the stream. Kneeling in the mud, he submerged his head in the cool water. He drank deeply and felt a little better, but he was consumed with anxiety about finding the deer tomorrow. Mosquitoes flocked to him, and he gave up trying to keep them away. He lay on his side and tried to remember all he'd been taught about tracking game. Most of his training had come from Tabar and Samar. Samar had been the best tracker in the tribe. He missed them both.

The sun was out when his eyes opened, and Moctu momentarily couldn't figure out where he was or what he was doing. Surging to his feet with the recollection of the doe, he was immediately weak and light-headed and went back to his knees. Moctu ran his hands over his face and worried at the fever he felt. Crawling to the stream, he once more drank his fill. Arising more gradually, he made it up and surveyed the area for the deer trail. He saw the trail he'd been following last evening and moved to it and was pleased to see a blood smear on a fern frond.

He felt awful as he slowly moved through the brush. His back ached, his head pounded, his stomach was queasy, and now he was covered with itchy welts from last night's mosquitoes.

Moctu's dazed mind wandered while he followed the trail intuitively. Diffuse thoughts rambled from Nuri, to Alta and Zaila, to Samar, and back to Nuri. Near a bend in the stream, where it broadened into several shallower, narrower flows between sand bars and marshes, he lost the trail, and his focus, limited as it was, returned. As he struggled to find any evidence of the doe, anxiety set in, and he twice felt as if he would retch.

The doe must have crossed to the other side, he reasoned, so he removed his wolf hide shoes and forded the stream. The cool water felt good, and he was excited to see deer tracks as he got to the far bank. He groggily sat to strap on his shoes and realized one was missing. "Crap! I have to find it," he thought wearily. He waded back in and retraced his passage, but the shoe was gone. His mind was a fog when he got back to the deer tracks on the bank. He sat and considered his predicament. Finally, a workable solution occurred to him. He located two large chert cobbles, and struck them together, shattering one into three pieces. Using the sharp edge from one of the shards, he laboriously hacked a foot-sized pad and two long thin strips from his loincloth, and he tied the pad around his foot to make a crude shoe. This effort would normally have been simple for him, but now it left him exhausted and sweating profusely.

The disappointment of losing the shoe was partially offset by being back on the trail. Moctu was again pleased to see blood spatter, and he pressed on. The doe had moved along the base of a low, rocky hill, and then climbed it. Following the tracks, Moctu was shocked at how weak he felt as he attempted to scale the slope. Near the top, he was overcome by his sick stomach, and he went to his knees and retched. It had been so long since he'd had anything to eat that there was no vomit, just dry heaves. They left him shaky and gasping. He was exhausted, utterly spent.

Chapter Forty-One

Moctu awoke with a sense of tremendous unease feeling movement and hearing unrecognizable sounds. His head and back ached, his arms wouldn't move, and his eyes couldn't seem to focus. Fragments of recollections flickered through his mind.

He'd been tracking... a wounded deer. His mind was foggy. Manhood rites. He'd been whipped. He remembered the pain, such pain! He was now aware of the pain in his back and of the bumping and jerking that was exacerbating it. "Where am I?"

Moctu struggled to suck in the hot, stale air as small beams of light pierced the periphery of his vision, and a sour-smelling weight draped his face. A hide was over his head. He tried to move but couldn't. "What the..." Anxiety swept over him, deepening his sense of apprehension. He must have croaked out his last thoughts because a hideous being with a misshapen head flipped up the hide covering his face and peered at him. The bumping stopped, and several more grotesque faces gawked at him. His eyes focused and he was looking directly into the face of the red-haired beast! The Pale Ones crowded around him, gesticulating, uttering grunts and making unrecognizable sounds. Several prodded at him, one grabbing at his uncovered genitals, another touching his face. They'd taken his footwear and his loincloth, leaving his lower half naked and exposed. His feet were bound, and he was strapped to a travois.

Oh, Spirits! Moctu thought in abject terror. The People Eaters! With the adrenaline kicking in, he was fully awake and mostly lucid now. He squirmed frantically to free his arms. The movements brought nothing but pain. His torso was wrapped in skins and tied securely to the travois. All of the surrounding Pale Ones laughed vigorously, pointing, gesticulating, and making odd sounds. The more agitated he got, the more he tried to move without effect, the more they laughed. They were appallingly ugly, with slanted foreheads, protruding eyebrows, no chins, and bleached-out skin and hair. He could tell one of them was a female by her small, pendulous breasts. Where they didn't have hair, their skin color was light, sickeningly light, almost pink or light tan. A different, larger, red-haired male made a series of loud grunts and the gawkers seemed to lose interest in Moctu. The stinking skin was draped back over his face obscuring his view completely. The front of the travois rose, and the bumping and jerking resumed, and he knew they were taking him with them. In the darkness memories of his boyhood nightmares surfaced. His body trembled violently as he recalled the horrible dreams— Palo's shrieks as he was butchered by the beasts in their dark cave. After Palo, they were coming for him next.

Could this be another nightmare? A jarring bump convinced him it was really happening. He shuddered uncontrollably, completely overwrought with fear. Not a dream. And I'm… to be their next meal!

He awoke confused, wondering where he was. As the horror of his situation flooded back, he realized that he must have passed out because the travois was now flat and motionless. The leather flap over his face was slightly askew, and he could see that it was completely dark except for a large campfire. He struggled with his restraints but could make no progress toward freeing himself. His head swam with the effort, and he recalled how sick he'd felt while chasing the deer. The smell of roasting meat filled his nostrils, and he became aware that he was ravenous with hunger. And thirsty... he was so thirsty. Moctu again tried to free himself, and the effort brought nothing but intense back pain. He must have made a sound because the leather flap was retracted and he was staring into the face of the female creature. More of them gathered around, seemingly fascinated by his appearance, pointing at him and grunting their odd sounds. Although he couldn't understand any of their grunts, he could recognize some meaning from their gestures and tone. He was oddly calmed that, for the moment, both were more demeaning than threatening.

He went in and out of delirium, with each new conscious moment bringing a surge of adrenaline-drenched horror at his predicament. He again passed out only to be revived by feeling his genitals being groped amid loud laughter and grunting. In the dim light, he could see one of the males, one with tan hair and a crooked, broken nose, had grabbed his penis and put a large flint knife to its base hooting with laughter and grunting toward the female. She grunted back disinterestedly, prompting more laughter.

Moctu was now fully conscious and had never been more disturbed and frightened in his life. The creature holding his penis looked at him with unmistakable contempt, spoke several grunts to him and moved the blade even closer, prompting more chuckles and laughter from the crowd. Bound and frozen with fear, Moctu could only stare into the malevolent eyes of his tormentor. Several moments passed with Moctu wondering what would happen. The beast continued to eye him, then, almost casually, uttered a grunt to the crowd and flipped his unharmed penis to the side. The crowd laughed, and Moctu gasped in relief, realizing he'd been holding his breath the whole time.

He became conscious that they were moving again, and

he could see daylight from folds in the skins covering his face.

I must have passed out last night after… he thought groggily, and shivered as he recalled fragments of the events of the past evening. His brain was foggy, but he could remember the People Eater threatening to take his manhood. These animals—these scum—what were they going to do with him?

It was dusk when he next awoke. The female was looking at him and seemed pleased that he was conscious.

Several more Pale Ones were peering at him, and one of them, a young male beast with long, shaggy blond hair, touched his cheek and grunted, pointing at the face of the female, as though asking her, "Why is his skin so dark compared to yours?"

The female grunted to them and made hand gestures. She picked up a gourd, touched Moctu's shoulder with her other hand, drank from the gourd, grunted, "Wog," then put it to his lips as if implying, almost condescendingly, "This is how we drink water from gourds. Now you try." He gratefully put his lips to the vessel and drank, coughing when he couldn't swallow the water fast enough in his prone position. This caused raucous laughter among the small group. Several of them pointed to him and snickered while shaking their heads.

Even in his confused state, he could tell that they were mocking him. The filthy beasts were mocking him!

He was so thirsty. The one gulp of water he'd gotten had been so good! His whole body seemed to scream for more. "Please, more water," he croaked. Laughter and more curious pointing followed. Then Moctu said, "Wog." He saw two of the Pale Ones rotate their heads in consternation. The group quieted measurably, and the female retrieved the gourd and put it to his lips. This time she poured the water more slowly into his mouth, and he drank several gulps before choking and coughing once again. His coughing brought no laughter this time, their earlier derisive grunts and gesticulations replaced by rapt fascination.

Still thirsty, he said, "Wog... wog." This brought further apparent amazement, with rapid grunting and hand movements among the group. There was no laughing, just hushed interest as a larger gourd was slowly lifted to his lips. The female again poured, this time even more slowly, and he drank his fill without choking. He turned his face when he could drink no more, and she quickly stopped pouring. Moctu whispered, "Thanks," and nodded his head while closing his eyes. This gesture seemed to resonate with the group, because when he reopened his eyes, he saw several of them making similar actions. The female was smiling at him.

Chapter Forty-Two

Moctu had been gone for nearly a moon and was presumed dead by most of the tribe. Sokum had returned several days after Seetu, looking even more haggard and drawn. His meat offering had been similarly meager, a rabbit, a beaver, and a large rat. The elders and the tribe, who earlier feared they'd lost all three of the boys, were joyful at his return and accepted his meat offering. Sokum was now a man.

Although Alta, Nuri, and his friends held out hope for Moctu, a sense of creeping bereavement began to envelop the tribe. At the urging of Alta, Nindai, and others, a scouting party had been sent to look for Moctu, but after five days of searching, they returned having found no trace of him. Alta seemed emotionally destroyed, and Nuri looked after Zaila more and more. She'd heard Alta praying to Suge, the Spirit of Evil, to depart from her, to please return Moctu, and to spare Zaila.

Four of the best hunters in the tribe were either dead or missing. The overwhelming sense of loss weighed on the Nereans, with many asking Jelli why the Spirits had turned against them. She could give no satisfactory answers, but she and Nindai undertook sacred Cleansing and Rejuvenation rites for the tribe. They spent most of their time in a shallow cave south of Etseh, chanting, praying, and making small offerings.

The Mourning Moon was nearly over, and Jabil had several discussions with the elders on how to place the widows and their children. There were a lot of children to consider with Ordu's mate and Samar's older mate each still raising three and Alta having her new baby. Jabil was confident that he'd end up with Leuna and felt fortunate that she was childless at present, so he wouldn't be taking on much added responsibility. Although the widows were all pleasant, hard-working, and still physically desirable, most men didn't want so many new dependents, so measures needed to be taken in that regard. It was decided that the orphans would be fed from the general tribal stores, which came not from individual hunting efforts, but from large group hunts such as the recent mammoth and rhino successes. That settled, it was decided that Samar's older widow would go to Nabu, Leuna to Jabil, Ordu's widows to Petral and Lagun, and Alta to Jabil's father, Alfer.

"So when do I get Avi?" Jondu asked Jabil in private.

"I know, I know, you're getting tired of waiting. I've been delaying the announcement to see if Moctu was going to return. If he doesn't, and I guess now we can say he's not going to, it makes things easier with Nuri. I wanted to announce your tie to Avi at the same time as my tie to Nuri."

"Moctu's dead. He's not coming back," said Jondu. "Let's get on with it. Let's go ahead and get this done. Petral is making things difficult between Avi and me, and I'm sick of it."

"Yes, we've probably waited long enough. I think even Nuri has given up on him by now," said Jabil. "Give me a little while longer—I need to do a couple of things," Jabil said as he winked at Jondu. "Soon, Jondu, soon."

Jabil found Leuna kneeling, using long reeds to weave a basket. Intent on her work, she didn't see him approach, and he paused to admire both her work ethic and the graceful curves of her body. She realized someone was there and looked up, smiling broadly when she saw him.

"I didn't know you were there," she said, stopping her work and brushing reed materials from her clothes with one hand while gracefully smoothing her long hair back with the other.

"Yes, I need to talk with you."

"Are you wanting to help me gather firewood again?" she said teasingly.

"Um, yes, it's about that. You didn't say anything about that to anyone, did you?"

Her demeanor changed immediately. "Of course not. It would damage my standing with everyone in the tribe. Why? Does someone know?"

"Well, yes. I think Nuri and Avi saw us."

"Oh no, no. I knew we shouldn't have done that," she cried.

"Now don't get too upset," he interjected. "I've got it under control. I don't think anyone else will ever know."

"Are you sure? How do you know? I thought Avi was looking at me oddly yesterday."

"It's controlled," he said more calmly than he felt. "Just act normally, and this'll all fade away. Just don't say anything to anyone." He abruptly turned and walked away, leaving Leuna lost in thought staring at the ground and nervously biting her lip.

It was midafternoon when Jabil found Nuri alone in her hearth.

"Hello, Nuri," he said, feeling more nervousness than he expected.

"Hello, Jabil," Nuri responded warily, getting to her feet and brushing dust from her knees.

"I wanted to talk with you," he started, but paused, unsure of how to progress. Nuri watched him nervously toy with his braid and quietly waited for him to formulate his thoughts, curious what this concerned. It probably wasn't anything she'd be pleased about. "The elders and I have been discussing… well, we've discussed many things, but one of them was… was your mating ceremony." Nuri's pulse quickened. "You were scheduled to be mated to Moctu, but it appears, sadly, that he won't be coming back."

"I still think he will," said Nuri.

"Nuri, Nuri, he's been gone more than a moon and the search party found no trace of him. We all need to accept that he's not coming back."

"He's going to…" Nuri started, but was cut off by Jabil.

"The elders have decided that you'll be mated to me."

It wasn't unexpected, but it still took Nuri's breath away.

Jabil hurried on. "The ceremony will be soon, to be performed along with the ceremonies of the widows to their new mates, now that the Mourning Moon has passed."

"No, no…" Nuri said in a near whisper.

"Nuri, I'll make you happy. Look, the elders have decided. This is going to happen, and it's going to work out just fine. It's going to be fine." Jabil's last words came out weakly, more as a plea than a statement, and that made him angry at himself. And a little angry at Nuri. He was leader, after all, and she was just a girl. His expression hardened.

"You must ready yourself for the mating ceremony in three days," he said, striking a more dominant tone. Nuri searched her brain for ways to stop this, or at least slow it. She immediately thought to use Jabil's dalliance with Leuna as leverage, but she'd given her oath not to mention that event again. Still, it was her only leverage. A sudden thought came to her.

"What about my Mourning Moon?" she asked.

"You were never mated to Moctu," Jabil countered loudly.

"But I was committed to him, and if he is dead, I should get a Mourning Moon," she said staring squarely at Jabil.

There was a long silence between them. Jabil's thoughts raced. He'd earlier planned to take Nuri from Moctu even if he did come back. But that would have been extremely confrontational with Nuri and Moctu and perhaps many others in the tribe as well. Moctu's death had allowed him to avoid that conflict.

Finally, Jabil said, "If you get your Mourning Moon, after that, will you enter into the mating ceremony with me willingly?"

Nuri's face knitted while she quickly considered.

"Yes," she said softly.

Figures

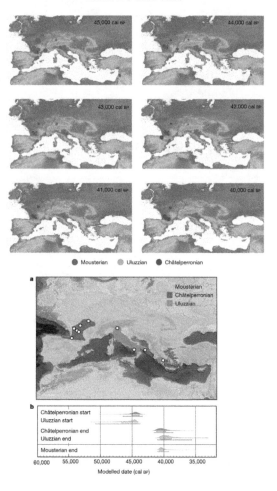

Figure 1 Time slices for western Europe between 45,000 (upper left) and 40,000 (lower right) cal BP showing the gradual replacement of Neanderthal (Mousterian sites in blue) by mixed sites (Chatelperronian in red) and EMH (Uluzzian sites in green). Size of dots represents increasing and decreasing levels of the 95.4% probability ranges. From Higham et al. (2014).

Figure 2 Neanderthal wrongly pictured as a stooped, brutish, ape-like creature, from artist's rendering in 1909, based on Boule's study of some of the first bones discovered, later determined to be arthritic.

Figure 3 Handprints in the Cueva de las Manos, Santa Cruz, Argentina, up to 13,000 years old. Similar hand prints from Sulawesi, Indonesia date to 40,000 years. Interestingly, most are left hand prints and those of women.

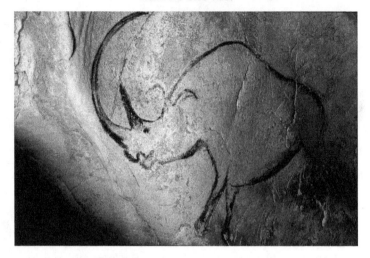

Figure 4 Rhinoceros on a wall of Chauvet Cave in France from 20,000 to 30,000 years ago. Note the two-meter (6.5') front horn.

Figure 5 An illustration of a woolly rhinoceros, based on fossil and other evidence. It was common throughout Europe and northern Asia circa 45,000 years ago.

Figure 6 The oldest musical instrument yet discovered. Paleolithic flute from southern Germany, made from bird bone about 40,000 years ago (Photo from Jose-Manuel Benito).

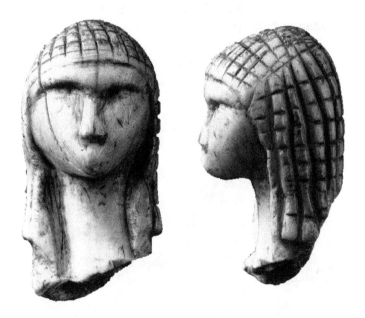

Figure 7 Venus of Brassempouy - One of the earliest known realistic representations of a human face, carved in ivory, circa 25,000 years ago from SW France (Photo by Jean-Gilles Berizzi).

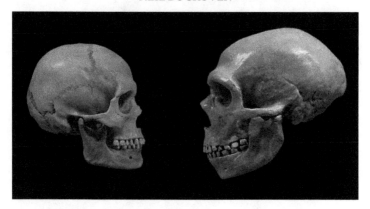

Figure 8 Comparison of Modern Human (left) and Neanderthal (right) skulls from the Cleveland Museum of Natural History (From hairymuseummatt [original photo], DrMikeBaxter-derivative work).

Figure 9 Homotherium – saber-tooth cat of Europe which survived in Eurasia until about 28,000 years ago (Copyright permission from Remie Bakker and Rene Bleuanus).

Figure 10 Adult male buried at Sunghir (east of Moscow) about 28,000 years ago. Along with a nearby grave bearing two handicapped adolescents, more than 13,000 ivory beads were found, which would have taken 10,000 hours to produce. Also found with the adult were 12 pierced fox canines, 25 ivory arm bands, and a schist pendant. None of the three buried were closely related, and at least one may represent a ritual sacrifice (Permission to use photo from Alexandra Buzhilova).

PART TWO

THE MAMMOTH
PEOPLE

Main Characters and Places

- Krog – Name of the Pale One's tribe (means *Mammoth People* in their language)

- Uhda – Rock overhang, main home to Krog

- Rah – Older woman, healer of Krog

- Ef – Young woman of the Krog (called Effie by Moctu)

- Awk – Red-haired man of the Krog (initially called Red-hair by Moctu, later called Hawk)

- Da – Leader of the Krog

- Elka – Baby daughter of Ef (*elkartu* means *unite* in Basque)

Chapter Forty-Three

Moctu was awakened by strong fingers prodding his chest and face. It took him several confused moments to figure out where he was, but once he did, he was alert. Anxiety flooded through his whole being.

The People Eaters! He struggled but his arms and legs were bound tightly. The sharp pain from the exertion once again reminded him of his lacerated back. These are the beasts that killed my father, Ordu, and Samar. They threatened to sever my manhood. But they haven't killed me yet. Are they going to eat me? What? Spirits, what's to happen? Help me, he prayed. Please help me.

It was the female creature again, and there was a younger female with her. The older one peered over his body and put her hand to his forehead and neck. Lifting a gourd, she asked "Wog?"

He was cotton-mouthed, but croaked out, "Yes, wog... wog, please." She smiled faintly and put the gourd to his lips, and he drank several swallows. He closed his eyes, feeling the goodness of the life-giving water. When he opened his eyes, he saw both females had closed their eyes and were nodding. Even within the fog in his brain, he could tell he'd already learned a small piece of their language and customs. A kernel of hope began to grow in him that these beasts weren't going to eat him. At least not right away.

* * * *

Moctu was dreaming fitfully about huge wolves circling him when the younger female woke him. Even in his sleepy confusion, he could make out that she seemed happy, buoyant, and excited. As he became more aware, he noticed she was dressed in better skins than earlier, and she was wearing a white shell necklace and had streaks of red ocher on her cheeks. Although her face seemed slightly misshapen, her eyes were a remarkable, deep blue and she didn't seem as hideous as the other beasts. Smiling, she leaned over him, stuffed some vegetable material into his mouth and quickly raised the small gourd to his lips. He was able to swallow it without choking, and with surprisingly little concern he wondered what she had given him. Was it medicine or poison? As she left, he was already falling asleep again.

He dreamed vivid, wild dreams. The wolves were back for a while, and they seemed to shimmer with colors of silver, black, and gray. They soon dispersed, however, and he felt safer and much happier now snuggling with Nuri in a dark hearth. She had her back to him, and he couldn't seem to talk to her. But it was comforting with her next to him, and he glowed with a warm euphoria, the depths of which he'd never felt before. They were mated, and she was his after all. The Spirits had been good to him. Nuri moved sensually against him, and Moctu could tell in the darkness that she wanted him as much as he wanted her. She reached behind her and took his manhood in her hand and gently stroked it until he was nearly frantic to have her. She took the initiative, and with one languid motion, she thrust herself onto him and the pleasure was indescribably powerful, unspeakably wonderful. Too soon though, the dream faded and was replaced by a series of confusing ones, with wolves curling up next to him. He was in their den! Then Nuri was back, and there was more pleasure and contented happiness.

It was morning now, and Moctu wished to return to his dreams. He could tell he was still feverish, and his thoughts were chaotic, a scrambled mass of fragmented recollections. He remembered being with Nuri, and he tried desperately to hold onto that memory. But it was short-lived, replaced by memories of gawking People Eaters while he was bound and helpless on a travois.

The travois must have been how they brought him here. Moctu's mind cleared slightly, and he began to wonder about his surroundings. He saw the older female off to his side, kneeling and working by a fire-blackened wall. Taking advantage of his less-clouded brain, he surveyed the shelter and watched the female more closely as she ground material on a stone which had a slight hollow. The shelter was a dwelling under a rock overhang, similar to Etseh, but smaller. The rain drip line was tighter which shortened the suitable living space. It had fewer compartments, just a few partial walls of hide draped over several long wooden poles which had been stripped of their branches. The fire pit was little more than a foot across, much smaller and shallower than Nerean hearths which were typically double that size or bigger. He could hear activity nearby, indicating there were more of the beasts out of sight in surrounding areas.

The female was strong with powerful-looking arms and shoulders, but she was shorter than most Nerean women partly because her legs were slightly bowed. She didn't look as dreadful as he recalled. He knew she was older, certainly older than his mother Alta, because she made small groans when she moved her knees and legs as she crouched just as the older women in his tribe did.

After grinding two different vegetable materials into powder, she spit some chewed root matter into the mixture and added some water. She stirred it into a paste and captured the bulk of it on a thin wooden paddle. She stood, made some unintelligible grunts and touched his forehead. He remembered the younger female giving him vegetable material the night before, but this looked different. This was the female who had sat by idly, almost bored, while his manhood was threatened. That memory brought him fully awake.

She attempted to put the paddle to his mouth but he turned his face, resisting, saying, "No," loudly with his teeth clenched.

With practiced hands, she grabbed his nose, plugging it, and when he gasped for breath, she shoved the concoction into his mouth. She switched from plugging his nose to holding his mouth closed while she rubbed his throat, encouraging him to swallow. The mixture was bitter, but he swallowed it and she gave him some "wog" to help wash it down.

What did he just eat? It seemed she was trying to help him, but it could have been ritual poison for all he knew.

When Moctu awoke, he felt better than he had in days. Although he was drenched in sweat, his fever had clearly broken, and his head no longer throbbed. He was thirsty, but most of all, he was ravenously hungry.

"Well, she didn't give me poison," he murmured to himself feeling oddly buoyant. The mood puzzled him. Here he was held captive by the Pale Ones, still bound tightly. He was hungry and thirsty, yet he felt good. It must have been the mixture she'd given him—some powerful medicine! He was so much better. He wasn't sure if it was the medicine or him just finally feeling better, or both, but he had a confidence that everything was going to work out well. Moctu had to force himself to regain some sense of apprehension. After all, these were the beasts who killed his people. He had to stay vigilant. They were probably going to kill and eat him. But his good mood kept bubbling back. "They haven't killed me yet," he murmured cheerfully. "Wog," he called out. "Wog, please."

The younger female he'd seen recently approached with a smile on her face, and she quickly held a gourd to his lips. After he'd drunk his fill, he closed his eyes and nodded, which she reciprocated. Her hair was light, the color of dead grass or straw with a reddish tinge. Her skin was too light, but the bleached pinkness of it didn't bother him as much as before. Oddly, she had tiny spots on her cheeks and nose, but they were much smaller than sickness spots. The streaks of red ocher were gone. He was mesmerized by her eyes, which were strikingly blue, something very rare for Nerean adults. Some Nerean babies were born with blue eyes, but almost all gradually darkened to brown. It was considered a portentous omen when a baby's eyes remained blue or turned green like Avi's.

The female pointed to herself and said, "Ef," and then she pointed to him questioningly. He struggled to move his arms to point to himself, and she held a finger up motioning for him to wait. She quickly left the hearth and was back in short order with the red-haired beast he'd seen originally at the caribou kill. He was wielding a rock-tipped club in one hand and a large flint knife in the other. He seemed suspicious of Moctu, not nearly as friendly as Ef, if that was her name. But he loosened Moctu's bindings and allowed him to stand, which Moctu did falteringly. He was barefooted, still naked from the waist down. Embarrassment swept over him as the young female studied him unabashedly.

Moctu indicated to Red-hair that he needed to relieve himself, and he was guided roughly from the hearth area to the far end of the shelter. Curious eyes gawked at him from the several hearths they passed, and some of the creatures within made raucous, rude-sounding grunts. They left the overhang, and at a broad, flat area he saw one of their women kneeling on a staked-down hide using a carved, caribou leg-bone scraper to remove remnants of flesh and gore. Another worked on a smaller hide, holding it in her teeth while she scraped it with a piece of wood. Once at the designated spot, by sign language, he was shown where to kneel and urinate into a collection skin.

He realized that they must save their urine for use in processing hides just as the Nereans did. As he relieved himself, he was again uncomfortably conscious of the beast's interest in his body and its functioning. On the way back, he found it was getting easier to walk, and he enjoyed stretching his legs and viewing the curious lifestyle of these people or beasts. Their dwelling area seemed more communal and less organized than Etseh. There were more rats.

What are they? Moctu wondered. They had fires, they spoke, and they lived in shelters like those of the Nereans, so they were people. But they brutally slaughtered our men, and they would probably kill him soon, so they were also beasts. That dismal thought finally deflated his mood. His mind flashed on Nuri and then Alta. They'd be so worried and distressed. He remembered how emotionally crushed Alta was at the news of Tabar's death. If she thought he were dead, it could devastate her. He needed to stay focused and watch for his chance to escape.

Chapter Forty-Four

Moctu had to admit that these beasts had cured him of his fever and almost certainly saved his life. Even his back was better. The Pale Ones were primitive, but they had good medicines. The last thing he remembered, he was chasing the wounded deer, and he was so horribly sick that he must have passed out. He would have died out there, but they saved him.

Just then, Ef brought in some hot meat stew in a wooden bowl which she extended to him. It smelled terrific. He didn't care if it was poisoned or not, he was so hungry he'd eat anything. He accepted it gratefully. The two of them went through the "Thank you – you're welcome," ritual, and her eyes lingered on him while he ate the stew with relish.

She pointed to the stew and said, "Muk." Moctu wondered if she were trying to say his name and looked perplexed, shrugging. Using both hands, Ef put her fingers pointing up from the back of her head and said, "Muk" again.

"It's deer stew! Muk very good," he said smiling, nodding and patting his stomach.

Her face showed understanding, and Moctu was stunned when she said, "Muk bur gaw" while patting her stomach. She was trying to learn his language!

They persisted at this verbal exploration, and by the end of the afternoon, Moctu had learned that the deer meat came from the deer he'd wounded which had collapsed and died not far from where the Pale Ones found him. Ef made fluttering circles with her hands in the air, indicating that their party had seen vultures circling in the sky, and they'd gone to investigate. They had found the deer first with the shaft protruding, and him soon thereafter.

Effie, which he started calling her in his thoughts, appeared to be the healer's daughter and her apprentice. Effie was bright and understood Moctu's words and meanings with an intuitive quickness that astonished him. She had trouble pronouncing many Nerean words and he, likewise, had trouble with some of hers. Many of her words weren't much more than hisses and near whistles, and almost half of any conversation involved signing. She laughed when she learned his name was "Moctu" which apparently meant something approximating "deer guts," at which he laughed as well.

Red-hair looked in occasionally, and he had two sharp exchanges with Effie. Although Moctu understood none of it, it was unsettling, and it reinforced that he couldn't let himself become complacent around the Pale Ones. Moctu again found himself extremely conflicted by these people who'd viciously killed his father and friends. He hated them. He absolutely hated them. And yet they'd gone to a lot of trouble to save his life and heal him. And they were treating him pretty well so far.

"How do I deal with that?" he murmured. "Maybe it was a different group of Pale Ones that killed my people."

Effie told him her name meant hawk, or at least some bird of prey, which reminded him again of Nuri, who wore a red hawk feather as her talisman.

Once again, he reminded himself that he had to get away—soon. The older female, the healer, came in, and he learned that her name was Rah. With tortured grunting and sign language, Moctu tried to thank her for healing him and saving his life, ending with the eye closing and nodding custom. Rah smiled, seemingly understanding and appreciating his attempt. She busied herself grinding and mixing more of her medicinal paste, which she again scooped with a wooden paddle and brought to him. This time he accepted it without a struggle, and she beamed at him.

In the evening, Effie brought him more deer stew, which he savored, trying to determine what added ingredients were in it that made it different from what he was used to. Over the course of the afternoon, Effie spoke their word as she individually pointed to a multitude of things from the sun and the clouds to all the items in the hearth area and to each part of their clothes and bodies. In each case, Moctu had given her the equivalent Nerean word. He was again astounded at how fast Effie picked up his language.

He realized with admiration and some embarrassment that she was learning his language faster than he could learn hers. It was only her inability to pronounce some words that slowed her. There were just certain sounds she couldn't pronounce no matter how hard she worked at it.

Her people called themselves the Krog which was similar to their word for mammoth. So the Pale Ones thought of themselves as the Mammoth People. The Mammoth People had saved his life and were… what? He had to admit that they were people, and they were mostly friendly. He smiled when he learned the Krog called Nereans either *the Dark Ones* or *the Others*. As he watched Effie rehearse Nerean words, he found he was growing quite fond of her and her people. For her part, Effie clearly liked Moctu and had told him that his face was "cute like child."

Moctu was convinced that it had to have been a different group of Pale Ones that killed his father.

Red-hair again strode into the hearth and indicated he was there to bind Moctu's legs and hands. Although Moctu planned to escape at his earliest opportunity, the action inexplicably offended him, and it incensed Effie. She and Red-hair had a sharp exchange, whereupon he bypassed her and, with lightning speed, grabbed Moctu's wrists in his powerful hands. When Moctu resisted, he removed one hand long enough to cuff Moctu on the ear, causing him to see stars. Moctu was quickly tied and settled on some furs, and after another sharp exchange with Effie, Red-hair left.

Effie pointed after him and said, "Awk" to Moctu. Moctu couldn't immediately tell if that was his name or an invective. Effie was able to convey that Awk was his name but Moctu sensed that she didn't like him much. Largely by pantomime, and with some apparent chagrin, Effie informed Moctu that with the next sunrise, he'd be expected to carry water and firewood all day until sundown.

So I'm to be a slave, he thought morosely. I guess it's better than being eaten.

Chapter Forty-Five

It had been more than half a moon since Moctu arrived at Uhda, which was what Effie called the rock overhang the Krog used for shelter. Here in the highlands, Moctu could feel the breath of winter's approach in the cold nights and misty mornings. His health had mostly returned, the fever was long gone and his back was healed.

His days were drudgery, an endless series of trips to the forest for firewood or to the stream for water, all under the watchful eye of at least one of the brutes who always carried one of their thick spears. One of his overseers was Sag, the sour, flat-faced, broken-nosed brute who had threatened his manhood shortly after they first captured him. He was by far the most unpleasant of the Krog that Moctu had encountered.

Each evening Moctu was exhausted and could barely concentrate as Effie tried to learn more of his language and he hers. The time with her was the best part of his day, the only tolerable part of a miserable existence. Most of the Pale Ones treated him decently. Only Gut and Sag had beaten him, and even that seemed half-hearted. They thought he was shirking his firewood hauling because he didn't carry nearly the quantity of wood that they could. They pushed and punched him, but he got the sense that they weren't using their full power. Even so, the two of them attacking him together had seemed like the fight with Jabil and Jondu all over again, but with men twice as strong. He quickly conceded and gave up trying to fight back, and they almost as quickly ceased their attack. These men were so powerful, they could have easily killed him. All the Krog men were brawny and robust, much stronger than he was, even now that he was healthy.

Several of them had limps, and both Gut's and Sag's left forearms were misshapen, all probably the results of hunting injuries. He recalled when he first saw them long ago, how they charged in amongst the caribou herd slashing and stabbing with their spears. He'd wondered then why they weren't injured by the powerful animals' antlers and hooves. Now he could see that they sometimes were.

His thoughts often turned to Nuri. She and Alta had probably given up on him by now. That meant Alta was even more disconsolate than when he left, and it meant Jabil probably had Nuri. Each time, it was that thought that energized him. He had to escape, but how? The men watched him during the day, and they tied him each night. He had no food, no weapons, poor footwear, and he didn't know where he was. He knew he should head south, but what if he came to a cliff or box canyon? At night would he fend off wolves and cave lions with a sharpened stick? No matter, he'd try soon.

He had to. He had to get back. He wasn't going to be a slave for the rest of his life.

Moctu had convinced himself that the Krog were not the Pale Ones that had killed his father, Ordu, and Samar. He saw no evidence of the gear and weaponry that Jabil had described the murderous beasts taking that horrible night. Just because one of the killers was red-haired, that didn't mean it had to be Awk or another of the red-haired Krog men. Da, their apparent leader, had red hair. It seemed to be relatively common in these people. These Pale Ones hadn't tried to kill him, rather they saved his life. It had to be a different group.

"Krog kill three Nereans?" Moctu sprang the question on Effie one evening and watched her face carefully. He saw surprise, indignation and… something else in her eyes.

"No," Effie said. "Krog no kill Nereans."

He didn't know exactly why, but he believed her. He'd also asked her about cannibalism.

"Krog eat people?" which he quickly changed to, "Why Krog eat people?"

"Only in hungry-hungry time. Only dead people. No waste food in hungry-hungry time. Krog not like…" she shuddered. "Krog not like the Shiv people to north. Shiv eat people. Live people. Eat Krog. Come, fight, try take women, children." She closed her eyes and mumbled something to herself.

So maybe it was the Shiv who'd killed his people. The Krog only ate their dead, and only in the starving times. That wasn't so bad. He'd been told stories by his grandfather about starving times so bad that Nereans ate their dead.

"Starving times bring out the worst in people," his grandfather had said. "They'll do things they'd never do otherwise. Awful things."

So maybe the Krog weren't that different from his people.

He studied Uhda and the Krog carefully, partly out of curiosity and partly looking for means to escape. The Krog kept to the southeastern end of the long, flat-lying overhang avoiding the western end, no doubt due to the many huge, irregular blocks of ceiling rock that had fallen there. The overhang, which formed where a hard, gray rock overlay a softer, reddish clay-rich layer, was shallower than at Etseh, although there was one area that broadened into a sizable cavity. That area was the nucleus of activity and habitation in the shelter.

There were about six hands of the Krog, mostly females and children, with about two hands of strong, able-bodied males. The females were powerful, too, and any one of them could prove to be a formidable adversary if it came to that.

They were much more sexually open. The males sometimes took a female with little regard for the privacy that Nereans favored. The women were more forward, at times making suggestive gestures and grunts as he passed them, especially during his early days in the camp. It had often seemed to Moctu that they were just trying to shock him.

The Krog's initial fascination with him had dimmed significantly except for Effie, Rah, and Awk. Each of them constantly tried to learn more from him—Effie his language and culture, Rah his knowledge of Nerean medicines and treatments, and Awk his tools and weapons. Effie was key to most of these communications because her ability to speak Nerean was much better than Moctu's competence with Krog. Moctu had discovered that Krog was a simpler language, not as nuanced, with fewer words than Nerean. But Effie seemed to have a natural aptitude for language and soon knew much more Nerean than he knew Krog.

"How you learn Nerean fast-fast, I learn Krog slow?" he asked her.

"Yaw tired-tired we talk," she replied modestly. He'd learned that Krog had no plurals. Instead, the word was said twice. Doublets were also used to express severity, or to indicate a great deal of something. He remembered when he was first captured, he'd asked for *wog* which surprised the Krog, either that he already knew their word, or that he'd learned it so quickly. When Moctu had pleaded for *wog... wog*, he'd unwittingly asked for a great deal of water, which astonished them further.

Moctu had learned much more about medicines from Rah than she had learned from him. At Etseh, Moctu had occasionally heard portions of the *Medicine Song* which Nindai and Jelli chanted every day. It was many times longer than the Song of the Tribe, and Moctu had never learned large sections of it. They chanted it each morning, in part, to keep it memorized, but also as an act of worship to Giz, the Healing Spirit. Moctu found it interesting, but unsurprising, that Rah and Effie, too, daily chanted their litany of medicines and their uses and preparation techniques, the Krog form of the *Medicine Song*. Most of it he couldn't understand, but there was much he learned that he wished he could discuss with Nindai or Jelli.

Awk most wanted to know how Moctu had buried such a small spear so deeply into the deer. He was convinced that it had to do with the atlatl, but Moctu was disinclined to show or explain the weapon's use. Although the Krog probably hadn't killed Nereans, it seemed to Moctu that the atlatl was an advantage that the Nereans should keep for themselves.

When it rained heavily, Moctu wasn't forced to gather wood. On those days, Awk wanted to know more about Nerean flint knapping and tool making. Moctu complied, teaching him techniques to make more specialized tools, including awls and bone needles. Krog clothes were rudimentary, not much more than skins cut and pulled together in places by leather straps. It was a late afternoon at one of these tool-making sessions that Moctu saw something inconceivable. He and Awk were kneeling on crudely woven mats to protect their knees from the sharp stone chips that littered the hard-packed dirt floor. Moctu was in the final stages of showing Awk how to fashion a flint awl that could be used for making better clothing. They were alone in a hearth without fire, and a cold, wet breeze had blown in from the west along with towering dark clouds.

Deep shadows were overtaking the small room when Sag walked in, and Awk immediately broke away to help him with some short sticks and a small flat piece of wood near the tinder pile. They knelt and worked on the wood with flint scrapers for a short while. Sag put a point on a stick that was about the length of his misshapen forearm and about as thick as his little finger, and Awk made a small divot in the flat wood near its edge. With care and precision, he then made a small cut in the side of the wood which connected to the divot. Moctu was fascinated, wondering what the men were doing. They set a flat piece of bark on the ground which had a small mound of shredded, dry plant fibers on it. Awk placed the flat wood upon it and pinned the whole assembly with his foot. Sag took a small kernel of dry pine pitch and crumbled it to dust in his palm with the pointed end of the stick. He stuck the end of the stick into the divot and pushed down on its other end while Awk placed his palms flat on either side of the middle of the stick and began rotating it quickly by moving his hands in opposite directions, back and forth.

The men worked like this for some time, and Awk began to breathe heavily from the exertion. Then it happened. Moctu sucked in his breath when he saw smoke begin to rise from the divot area. Awk saw it too and seemed to pick up his speed which increased the smoke. Shortly thereafter the men abruptly stopped and pulled their stick and wood away. In the bark was a smoking ember which they blew into flame! Moctu was dumbfounded and astonished beyond comprehension. The Pale Ones could make fire from sticks!

Chapter Forty-Six

Nuri bit her lip as the darkness and fog melted away, and she watched the golden rays of sunlight begin to dapple the tops of nearby trees which blossomed into profusions of red and orange. The sight was breathtakingly beautiful, but Nuri wished she could reverse it. Today the sunrise only served to proclaim the reality of her loss. Her Mourning Moon was over, and Jabil would be here to announce that their mating would take place in several days. Officially, Moctu had been dead for a moon, but it was only now, with the morning light, that she fully accepted the fact. Countless times she had fervently and tearfully prayed for his return, but the Spirits had not seen fit to comply.

The widows had been mated a moon ago, and Avi to Jondu shortly thereafter. The thought of Avi temporarily lifted Nuri's mood. Avi had looked stunningly beautiful at her mating ceremony, and she'd seemed happy enough. She'd looked to Nuri and mouthed another heartfelt "thank you" for the gorgeous outfit she wore that Nuri had made and given to her. The tunic, with its alternating soft gray, brown, and cream-colored leathers and neckline of white ivory ringlets was lovely with Avi's light brown hair and dazzling green eyes. Jondu looked both proud and excited to be mating such a beauty.

Some of the widows were faring well with their new mates, but others were not. Alta, who'd been swallowed by a deep depression following Moctu's death, had been savagely beaten by her new mate, Alfer, as he tried to snap her out of it. Badly bruised, she and Zaila had afterward stayed in Nuri's cramped family hearth for two days while Jabil and others tried to remedy the situation. Jabil excoriated his father for the severity of the beating and implored Alta to return. She finally did, largely to relieve the stress on Nuri and her family.

Leuna had been mated to Jabil, so she'd be his first mate and Nuri his second. Leuna seemed elated to be mating Jabil and almost jubilant that she was having a baby. She hadn't been able to conceive for so long, that some had wondered if she were barren. The tribe considered the coming child to be the last semblance of Samar, a miracle of sorts, a baby to be celebrated. Nuri and Avi wanted to embrace this attitude as well, but privately they were convinced the baby would look like Jabil. Leuna's pregnancy imbued her with a healthy, appealing glow and she looked radiant at the ceremony. First mates enjoyed some privileges over the women who were mated later, but that mattered little to Nuri. It was Jabil. She couldn't believe she'd have to live with, to lie with, and to share furs with such a pompous, lying hyena.

"Hello, Jabil, I've been expecting you," Nuri said as he approached.

"Yes, hello, Nuri. Your Mourning Moon is over today, and I've come to once again offer my sympathy for your loss. We all miss Moctu," Jabil said rather unconvincingly.

"Thank you, Jabil."

"You do remember our agreement, I suppose?"

"Yes, Jabil. When is the ceremony to be?" Nuri responded, trying to keep the resignation from her voice.

"It will happen in three days—at midday. As the sun rises to its high point, so too, will our relationship," he said in a clearly practiced pitch. Nuri nodded, and Jabil smiled, pleased with himself and with her acquiescence. "So, I'll see you there," he said buoyantly and turned and left her to her thoughts.

* * * *

"Jabil. Jabil!" Jondu called to him as he returned from visiting Nuri.

"Hello, Jondu," Jabil said cheerfully. "What brings you here? How is Avi doing?"

"She's fine. She's a good mate. But I've come to talk with you about something else, something much more serious. We need to discuss an attack on the Pale Ones. We have to find them and destroy them. I don't know why we've waited so long."

"Yes, yes, I know," Jabil said. "You've made your position, your impatience clear for many days."

"Well, why is there no action? Why do we do nothing? Remember the anger and outrage we felt when it happened? We're well past the second moon since we suffered their barbarism, and nothing has happened. Please. I volunteer to lead the raid. Let's do something."

It had fallen like a cloud over Jabil the moment Jondu asked him to remember the outrage. His breath caught, and the vision of Ordu's wide, shocked eyes flooded his mind again.

Wouldn't he ever get past this? Nausea welled up in him, and a cold sweat broke out over his whole body. He sat suddenly on a nearby boulder to catch his breath and collect himself. Jondu realized what was happening and sat with him, his arm around Jabil's back.

"I'm sorry, Jabil. I'm sorry that the memories attack and weaken you. But they're not going to get better—you won't get better—until we get our revenge. You don't need to come. It would probably be a bad idea for you to lead the raid. But we must act. The snows will fall in the mountains soon, and it'll be too late. Let's do something soon."

Chapter Forty-Seven

It was a cold dawn, and another tedious day of gathering fire-wood loomed for Moctu. In the diffuse light, he eyed Effie as she got up across the small room, and instead of coming to untie him, she stood motionless, holding her stomach. She looked grayer than the dull autumn sky this morning, and he wasn't surprised when she bolted out of the hearth and threw up a short distance away. Rah quickly followed her, and he could hear her patting Effie's back and speaking softly to her.

Moctu wondered if she was sick or pregnant, but he didn't have long to ponder the question before Awk was there, impatient for him to start his work.

Moctu looked on Awk with a different perspective these days. He still found it hard to believe the big red man could make fire from sticks. He yearned to show the process to Palo, Nindai, and everyone back at Etseh. Samar would have been so amazed, so impressed. Moctu found himself missing him even more fiercely than before. This was such an important learning! The fire of the Nereans was carefully maintained with at least one fire in the camp burning strongly day and night without stop. They'd kept the fire going since it was harvested from a grass fire started by a lightning strike years before Moctu was born. It was considered sacred and life-giving. It took an enormous amount of wood to keep it burning.

The knowledge of fire starting only added to his inclination to escape. He had to get back to Nuri, Alta, and his friends. He wanted his life back. He had to escape, and it had to be soon or the snows would come. While loading and carrying firewood, he daydreamed, envisioning making it back to Etseh, and having Jabil demand to see his meat offerings.

"I have no meat offerings," he'd say, and he could easily predict Jabil's response.

"Then you've failed your manhood rites and are not a man."

Jabil would immediately be moving to erase Moctu's handprint from the Wall of Warriors, when he'd retort, "But I've learned how to make fire."

Jabil would scoff and Moctu would let him bluster on for a while before embarrassing him, shocking him and the tribe with this new wonder.

He didn't think he would show them how to do the process initially. He'd just take the key sticks and kindling into a cold hearth and emerge with a fire blazing. They'd be as stunned as he was.

Even if Jabil had taken Nuri for his mate, which was likely by now, Moctu might be able to win her back. The thought was intoxicating.

But how could he escape? He couldn't store food or clothing anywhere that the Krog wouldn't find or that animals wouldn't eat. They fed him meagerly, not letting him build any stores of fat on his body. And they tied him each night. How could he escape that? Moctu had pondered the problem for days with no good answer.

I made it here with essentially no food, and I was feverish with a mangled back. I'm going to have to try to make it back to Etseh with no supplies. It has to be soon or the weather will prevent it. Moctu had seen Da, the nominal Krog leader, a huge, red-haired man who looked closely related to Awk, leave yesterday on a hunt. Of all the Krog men, Da seemed the fiercest to Moctu. He was even bigger and more powerful than

Awk, and his front teeth looked as if they'd been filed into fangs. He had penetrating blue eyes set beneath protruding, hairy brows. The ends of several of his fingers were missing, probably cut off to avoid gangrene from frostbite.

Da and three other Krog men and two of their women had headed north, so this could be his best opportunity. Since he was heading south, there'd be fewer Krog to track him. He vowed that he'd leave in the next two days.

Moctu savored his meat stew that evening, aware that it could be one of his last meals for a while. Effie was across from him and, mostly by signing, he asked her if she felt better. She smiled and nodded, "Yes," but offered no explanation for the morning sickness.

Gradually, an escape plan formed in his mind, not a great plan, but the best one he could devise under the circumstances. He would work the south woods tomorrow morning. Either Awk or Sag would be watching him. Moctu would lead him as far away from Uhda as possible, far out of earshot, and while he was gathering wood, as soon as he was out of sight, he'd make his break. Even though they were powerful, he still thought he could outrun them. Either his Krog guard would have to track him on his own, or Moctu would gain time as he went back to Uhda for help. Moctu swelled with excitement at the thought of escape. The plan just might work. It was his best chance.

Sag was in a foul mood when he untied Moctu the next morning. Moctu couldn't understand his mutterings. Once again Effie had earlier charged out of the hearth to vomit.

She's pregnant, Moctu decided. Mother was sick almost every morning during the early part of her pregnancy with Zaila, he remembered. The thought of them, and the prospect of seeing them soon, filled him with hope and purpose. As he and Sag started out, the morning seemed colder than usual, and there was a thick, gray mist that had settled in the lower parts of the valley. Larks, robins, and sparrows chirped, and not far off, a woodpecker hammered away. Even as he kept to the narrow path, with Sag closely behind, Moctu's crude foot skins were quickly soaked through from the heavily dew-laden grass. Sag seemed bothered by the wetness, and muttered a complaint to himself, but Moctu considered it a good omen.

Today the mist is my friend, he thought excitedly.

When they came to the fork in the path, Moctu found himself holding his breath as he nonchalantly took the path leading to the south woods. He'd gone only a few steps, however, before Sag barked crossly for him to stop. Sag motioned for him to take the path to the west woods, and Moctu's heart sank.

Why doesn't he want me to go to the south woods? Does he suspect my plan?

On the way to the west woods, at another fork in the path, he again was ordered by Sag to change to the fork he'd not chosen. Moctu bit his lip and considered. He's either trying to disrupt any plans I have, or he's just being an obnoxious hyena to bother me. Probably just being grouchy and unpleasant as usual.

Attempting to escape from the west woods, however, meant backtracking toward Uhda before turning south, so he ruefully decided to wait for a better opportunity. In the hearth that evening he was subdued, lost in his thoughts, working his plan from every angle, trying to think of ways to increase his chances. Effie noticed the change in his state and asked if he were feeling bad.

"Tired, tired," he replied to her, and she nodded her head in understanding. "You feel better?" he asked her, and she nodded and smiled. She had a nice smile and a healthy glow, and he realized he'd gotten accustomed to her bleached-out skin and hair.

He pointed to her midsection. "You have baby—yes?" Her blue eyes seemed to sparkle, and she again smiled and nodded her head affirmatively. "Congratulations," he said, reaching over to pat her shoulder. "Who father?"

She shrugged that she didn't know for sure, then pointed to him and, with palms up, shrugged again. Mild consternation swept over him. He knew he was misunderstanding something here and his brow furrowed.

"Me? It might be my baby?" Moctu asked, pointing to himself.

Effie giggled at his confusion and nodded, "Yes."

Chapter Forty-Eight

Maybe the Krog don't understand how babies are made, he speculated. Obviously, Effie's confused. He scrunched his face and looked at her quizzically.

"How baby mine?" he asked, again pointing to himself.

She giggled again and smiling impishly, but a little shyly, she put her outstretched left index finger between two fingers of her right and moved them suggestively.

Moctu was bewildered, totally baffled. "What? No, no," he said, mystified at how she could be so confused about all this.

Then the story came out. It took a lot of signing and pantomiming, and Moctu only followed parts of it, but she was able to tell him about the Krog expedition during which he was found, and some of what happened afterward. Each year, the Krog made a trip to the lower grasslands for hunting, yes, but more importantly, to harvest the *Jin*, some sort of sacred plant or mushroom. Moctu couldn't fully understand what she said about the plant, but eating it seemed to give people a glimpse into the Spirit world. The Krog were on their way back from a successful outing when they saw the vultures, found the deer, and then him. Most of them had wanted to leave him to die, but Rah had ensured he was rescued and cared for.

The day after the group returned, the Krog held a ceremony or festival involving the Jin, an event in which the plants are ingested. During the resultant mystical visions, women are encouraged to have sex with multiple men. For one of her partners, in fact for her first partner, she'd chosen him even though he was still delirious and incapacitated. Moctu vaguely recalled Effie giving him what he thought at the time was some medicine to eat and the vivid dreams that followed.

He frowned. So his dreams of time with Nuri weren't totally a dream, they just weren't with Nuri. And his first sex had been with… a Pale One.

Effie had relations with Sag that night too, so the baby might also be his. She explained that Krog tradition held that the healer, Rah, would decide who the father was based on the features of the baby at the time of birth. The father would, accordingly, be mated to the mother thereafter.

Moctu saw Effie eyeing him closely as she told him this last part. As her words sank in, it dawned on him that he could be mated to Effie, and he would, after that, be responsible for her and the baby. The thought staggered him, and he could tell his reaction greatly disappointed Effie. Her small chin and lower lip extended, she rose to her feet and left the hearth in a rush.

Now, he saw Rah eyeing him enigmatically from across the hearth.

A sense of shame came over him. This woman had saved his life and now he was hurting her daughter's feelings. Deeply conflicted, Moctu rose, and looking at Rah, shrugged in confusion, and pointed to himself then out the door. Rah nodded affirmatively, so he left, following in the direction Effie had gone.

He liked Effie—he liked her a lot. She was his favorite person of the Krog by far. She was smart, pleasant and not unattractive, for a Krog. He just didn't want her as a mate. He couldn't mate her. He was leaving—maybe tomorrow. Hopefully tomorrow. He saw Effie ahead and slowed, not sure what to say to her.

It was growing dark and Awk or Sag would be by soon to ensure he was securely tied and in his sleeping area. He continued to Effie whose back was to him as he approached. He'd never seen a Krog cry and the sight jolted him.

Moctu was surprised that they cried just as Nerean women did. He placed a hand on her shoulder, and she turned to him. She smiled thinly, and wordlessly embraced him. Flustered, he hugged her and patted her back lightly. They remained like that for several moments and broke apart only when they heard Awk barking a question to Rah.

"I need to go back," Moctu said pointing to himself and then the hearth. Effie nodded, and he headed that way, but Effie stayed behind.

Awk seemed to tie him tighter than usual, and it worried him that they might be able to read his thoughts and know his intentions. The hearth fire died to embers, and the meager light melted into the blue-black of night. Moctu was exhausted, but he couldn't sleep. Effie hadn't returned, and he continued to worry about hurting her.

But this didn't change anything. He couldn't let it. He had to escape. He had to get back to Nuri and Alta and his people. He needed to teach them about fire starting. That would change so many things about their lifestyle and save so much work. It would take away the risk of somehow losing the fire during the winter. But he didn't want to hurt Effie. And what if it was his child? It came as a shock to him that he did have some feelings for Effie.

This mental turmoil went on for a long time before Effie finally came back and quietly bedded down in her usual spot across the hearth from him. He thought he should say something to her—but what? He knew that he needed to sleep, because tomorrow he was on the run. He would need every bit of strength and cleverness he had to make it. If he didn't succeed, if they caught him, they'd probably kill him.

He must have fallen asleep, because Sag prodded him

awake. Sag again seemed perturbed and extremely grumpy. After grabbing a little more dried venison than usual, but not so much as to raise suspicion, Moctu followed him toward the woods to begin another grueling day of gathering and carrying firewood.

But this day could be very different, Moctu thought, and adrenaline surged through him. After a short way, Sag held back and let Moctu lead. The morning was again cold, gray and misty, and the grass heavy with dew. Moctu focused on his plan.

We have to go to the south woods. It all hangs on that. When they got to the fork in the path, this time Moctu chose the one leading toward the west woods, and he was gratified to hear Sag bark a command redirecting him to the south woods. You contrary hyena, he smiled inwardly, his excitement growing.

Today's the day! Moctu realized. It was really happening.

Chapter Forty-Nine

Moctu decided he'd make his break early in the day to give himself more daylight to run. The night was not his ally because this was Krog land, and they knew it far better than he did. Nights were also filled with other dangers for travelers who only had sharpened sticks for defense. He walked as far as he could away from Uhda before venturing into the woods for his first load. Protocol was to find a load of wood, bring it to the forest edge, dump it, and go get another load. Once he had a large pile, he'd begin hauling portions of it to Uhda. When the pile was very large, sometimes Sag would enlist Krog women to accompany them back to the site and help him with the transport of the wood.

Sag was watchful while he gathered his first load but got bored by the second. He tinkered with and then began working in earnest on mending a strap that bound his legging to his belt, helping to hold it up. As Moctu moved into the woods for his third load, he decided it was time, and his heart raced. He made wood-gathering noises, by breaking off dry, dead lower limbs, but he left the limbs on the ground and moved deeper into the woods and farther from Sag. Then he saw what he wanted—a small meadow with a trail opening at the far side. Here was the turning point. He would no longer be a slave. He took a deep breath. Oh, great Wolf Spirit, guide me, he prayed to his totem. Please give me strength and good fortune. Help me through this. And with that, he broke into a run.

I'm on my way, he thought excitedly. I'll see Nuri... Alta... Etseh!

He set a moderate pace, running easily but with purpose, and he tried to be as quiet as possible. The path was a game trail and very narrow in spots, occasionally dwindling to next to nothing. In the distance, he heard a yell from Sag, and he unconsciously picked up speed.

My escape's been discovered. Now comes the hard part. We'll see how good at tracking Sag is. He smiled to himself thinking of Sag's consternation. Will he come hard after me, or will he go back for help? Shortly thereafter, Moctu came to a break in the forest caused by a landslide, and he looked back as he got to the other side. He was astonished to see a thin wisp of dark gray smoke rising from far back near the area where he left Sag. Sag is alerting the Krog by a signal fire, he thought, taken aback. How did he make that so fast? Is their fire-starting that fast, or had Sag carried an ember with him?

Moctu picked up his pace and began using all the tricks Tabar and Ordu had taught him about hiding trail sign. He jumped over a large downed tree, walked a short distance in one direction to a thicket, then carefully backed up, staying in the tracks he'd left. He got up on the tree, walked as far along it as possible, and then jumped off, moving in a different direction. At some of the creeks he came to, he waded along the stream and then emerged onto rocky areas to avoid leaving tracks.

It would take me a long time to find and follow that trail, he thought confidently as he completed one of these maneuvers. Moctu finished his small portion of dried deer meat. He'd be living off the land, or starving, for the rest of his trip to Etseh.

It was incredibly rugged country with nothing but ups and downs. He was on another small game trail when he saw the tracks of several antelope.

He wished he had his atlatl. Moctu had gone only a little farther when he saw something that chilled him and made him rethink his escape. Several huge paw prints overlay some of the antelope tracks. "Whoa, those are cat tracks! A big one," he said, whistling softly. From the tracks, it looked like a saber-tooth, a fierce cat with longer front legs than back. It was all claws and teeth, with two giant fang-like incisors that were more like tusks than teeth. His atlatl would be essentially useless against such a beast, and his heavy spear not much better.

Even so, he found himself yearning for his weapons. What he wouldn't do for his spear right now! Although it wouldn't do much good against a saber-tooth, it would sure make him feel better. He stopped and found a suitable sapling which, with some effort, he broke and fashioned into a staff with a sharp point. The effort had taken long enough that he worried the Krog might have closed the gap, so he picked up his pace once again. At the first opening in the brush, he diverged from the trail and the cat tracks, still trying to maintain a southward bearing.

I won't even have a fire any of these nights to keep wolves, saber-tooths, and hyenas away. But if I did, the Krog might be able to see it or smell it and track me. I don't have an ember anyway, to start one with. Wonder if I could start one the way they do with sticks?

The thick brush and the pathetic state of his primitive footwear kept him from running fast, but he continued at a steady pace. I'll try to start a fire with sticks tonight to see if I can do it. Even if I can't have a real campfire, it'll be good to know if I can make one. While he ran, he looked for appropriately dry sticks and thin slabs of wood from splintered, downed trees, and that took his mind off the saber-tooth for a while. By dusk he'd covered a lot of ground, and he'd left misleading trails all along the way, obscuring his tracks. He was confident that even if the Krog were good trackers, they couldn't catch up with him this evening.

Moctu was tired, but he climbed to the top of the hill he'd been skirting to gain a view to the south before the sunset. He hoped to see the lowlands in the distance and thereby be able to better plan tomorrow's route. He was distressed, however, to see nothing but rolling hills in the foreground with higher ice and snowcapped mountains ahead. He was sure he was looking south because the sun was now edging below the mountains to his right. Moctu was too preoccupied to appreciate the brilliant rays of gold and pink that streamed from the remnant sun through the scattered clouds. He concentrated on what would be the best passage through the mountains ahead.

He had to stop soon. He couldn't risk stepping on something in the dark that could hobble him or being ambushed by a large animal. He needed to find a defensible site that was out of the wind. It was getting cold. It was going to be a long night.

The wind was from the west, so he stayed on the east side of the hill, choosing a spot near the top of a landslide scar where a large, lone oak tree stood not far from a pile of boulders that could provide some shelter. The tree had some lower limbs, and he could climb it, so it offered him a means to escape wolves, hyenas, and lions. He wasn't sure about saber-tooths.

Although he didn't plan to have a fire, he was anxious to try his hand at starting one from scratch. Moctu organized the fire-starting items he'd gathered during his day's travel, and prepared the tinder, spindle stick, and flat wood as he'd seen Sag and Awk do.

He added the crushed pine pitch and excitedly thought, all right, let's see if I can do this. Turning the spindle back and forth rapidly, he worked at it until he was sweating and breathing hard but garnered no smoke or fire. He stopped and checked the end of the stick and was pleased to feel that it was indeed very hot. Moctu redoubled his efforts but again had seen no smoke by the time he was tired and out of breath.

It wasn't as simple as it looked in the hearth. He wondered if they used some special wood. Although he was disappointed, he remained confident that he'd one day master it, because he'd seen that it could be done.

It was dark now, and the stars emerged in full glory far outshining the waning crescent moon. He smiled at the thought that he could be in Etseh before the moon died.

A heavy, cold wind blew in, and tendrils of it seemed to brush against and then wrap themselves around Moctu. He wedged himself in the crook of two large boulders, and with his sharpened stick in front of him, he stared up above, recognizing the Warrior Stars directly overhead. He was strangely comforted by the sight. Maybe it was a good omen. As a youth, he'd been told of them by Tabar, and their appearance tonight resurrected warm memories that seemed to heighten his sense of freedom. He hunkered down lower. The boulders blocked most of the wind, but the cold air was still piercing, so he gathered masses of fallen oak leaves and spread them over his legs for warmth.

It seemed to work well, and he was pleased to be relatively warm and comfortable. Far away, he heard a wolf howl, and it was shortly joined by several more. They were distant enough that he wasn't too worried. Moctu imagined, however, how he might defend himself if wolves approached, by thrusting his sharpened stick outward as they lunged at him.

He realized that the wolves would soon be gnawing his bones. After some time, moved by these thoughts, Moctu reluctantly arose from his bed of leaves and went to the tree. After first lodging the stick between two branches, he began climbing the tree but thought better of it and returned to the ground. Remembering his small band's valiant stand against the wolves long ago, he found two large cobbles and balanced them on a thick lower branch. They could come in handy to discourage an attacking animal. One of them thrown downward might even kill a wolf or a leopard if he hit it right.

Satisfied, he climbed up into the lower limbs. The wind was much worse in the tree, and he was quickly chilled, so he put his back against the thick trunk, using it for a windscreen. He hugged one knee to his chest while his other leg dangled over the limb for balance.

It was going to be a long night, Moctu thought miserably, beginning to shiver. He was already cold. He had to keep his thoughts on Nuri, Alta, Palo, and all the others at Etseh. *He would make it back*!

That's when he heard it. His pulse quickened, and he held his breath straining to hear more. His hand moved reflexively to touch the wolf-tooth talisman around his neck, but the Krog had taken it from him long ago. Something was moving below out beyond the rocks he'd been sitting against earlier. It wasn't just noise from a scurrying rat or marmot, it was big, much bigger.

Chapter Fifty

Night had fallen, and Nuri nervously pulled on a thick strand of hair as she looked at the stars above. Tomorrow was her mating ceremony, and she'd be sharing furs with Jabil that night. He was attentive to her recently, but it hadn't changed her view of him as an arrogant, lying weasel.

Avi had stayed by her side the past two days, trying to cheer her while grooming her hair and readying her for the ceremony. She knew this evening would be hard for Nuri.

"I didn't look forward to mating Jondu, but it's worked out pretty well," Avi said trying to encourage her. "I'll bet the same thing happens when you mate Jabil."

"Well, since I don't have a choice, I have to make this work," Nuri replied resolutely. "If the Spirits favor me, I'll have children soon, and I can focus on them."

"Jondu leaves tomorrow with a group to hunt to the north," Avi said, "but I'd guess that Jabil isn't going, right?"

"Yes, Jabil plans to stay and spend time with me," Nuri said with a barely perceptible shudder.

"During the hunt, Jondu is hoping to find evidence of the Pale Ones so an attack can be planned," Avi continued. "He's upset that nothing has happened, and Ordu, Samar, and Tabar remain unavenged. On that, I agree with him."

"Me too, I guess. It's still hard to believe they're all gone. I especially miss my uncle Samar. He was always so funny, and his work was incomparable. I still have the little toy hatchet that he gave me, of black flint with tiny white snowflakes in it. It's beautiful."

"Yes, I miss them too. Speaking of that, how is Mother Alta doing?"

"I'm worried about her. She wasn't recovered from Tabar's death when Moctu disappeared. And Alfer thinks the secret to her revival is to beat her."

"I think Jondu will beat me if I stay with you any later the evening before he leaves for a hunt," Avi joked. "I'd better be leaving. Are you going to be all right?"

"Yes, I'll be fine. Thanks for being such a good friend, Avi. It's been a real comfort having you around these past few days."

"You will always be my sister-friend," Avi said hugging her. "And this will all work out well—you'll see."

Chapter Fifty-One

Moctu moved the rocks up one branch, and climbed higher himself, and readied his stick, pointing downward.

What was it? If it were wolves or hyenas, he was safe. If it were a leopard or a saber-tooth, he needed to worry. Leopards were good climbers, and saber-tooths could probably climb too. His question was soon answered when the still-distant wolf howls were followed by a nearby massive roar that echoed through the hills and seemed to say, "Stay away. This one's mine." The roar was followed by several more throaty rumblings, the last of which was much closer to the tree than the first.

Moctu's heart seemed to bulge into his throat. His body was frozen, and he could barely breathe. He could hear his pulse throb in his ears. Between the beats, he heard the huge cat move even closer, and his immobility finally melted away. In a near-frenzy, forgetting the rocks, he scrambled even higher in the tree and positioned himself leaning against one limb while standing on another. With trembling hands, he again pointed his stick downward.

He strained his eyes to see through the murky darkness but could only see brief motion as the animal circled the tree. He could tell it was big. Was it the beast whose prints he'd seen today? Had it tracked him? Could he keep a saber-tooth away? His teeth began to chatter, and he gritted them tightly.

Oh, Spirits help me. Give me wisdom and courage. Jona, Tabar, please be with me, and give me courage. Or I'll be with you tonight. Although he'd thought the last part sarcastically, it oddly seemed to calm him. "I will show bravery to my fathers," he whispered fiercely. "I will show bravery to my fathers!" he said louder. He kept repeating the line and found that it freed him to think.

Even when the terrible beast reared up and clawed the tree, Moctu repeated, "I will show bravery," clenching his teeth. It was indeed a monstrous cat, and Moctu was shocked by the sight of it's long fangs. It roared again, and it scrabbled part way up the tree, getting a paw over the first limb, but falling back, its front claws carving off long clumps of bark. Moctu was appalled to see that the cat's claws were as long as his fingers. It was massive, easily the weight of three men, and its size precluded it from being an agile climber. It tried again, this time leaping first before digging its claws into the tree, and it managed to get to the first limb. With its hind feet on the limb, it seemed to uncoil upward toward him, its two front paws coming within an arm's length of Moctu. Fear welled up inside him, but Moctu kept repeating the words that gave him strength, and he thrust down hard with the sharpened stick. The beast let out an angry screech and then lunged upward with its right paw. Its wicked claws were extended fully and sliced the bark a hand's breadth below Moctu's feet.

Moctu again struck downward with the stick, hitting the huge cat in the shoulder but doing little damage. The saber-tooth shrieked in violent fury and made another lunge. "I will show bravery!" he continued repeating. Remembering Sokum and the wolves, he thought, I can't let the beast grab my stick. He kept stabbing downward with it, eliciting screeching growls and quick counter moves.

It was so fast and strong! The cat swung a lightning-quick paw, hitting his stick and almost dislodging it from Moctu's hand. Moctu recognized that if it grabbed the stick in its jaws, it could easily rip it away from him, so he tried to avoid the snarling, gaping mouth. The beast lunged up again and clawed Moctu's left foot deeply almost gaining traction on the limb on which he stood. Pain surged through his foot, and blood ran down through the remnant of his foot wrap and onto the tree limb making his footing slippery. Kicking off the shredded foot skin, Moctu stabbed down violently again just as the huge cat lunged upward. The impact jarred them both, forcing Moctu to grab wildly for a limb as his feet slipped. The saber-tooth also struggled to keep its footing as it fell back to the limb below him.

The growling beast paused in his assault, and Moctu regained his position. The reprieve was short-lived and the powerful cat again reached upward this time springing as it stretched toward him. The claws slashed the bark right next to his bloody foot as he thrust down hard with his stick trying to prevent the beast from gaining purchase on his limb. Worriedly, Moctu looked higher in the tree, but climbing farther up with his stick wasn't an option, because if the cat reached the limb he was currently on, it could easily stretch to the next and dispatch him.

Over and over the beast lunged upward, and each time Moctu stabbed down with his stick. As cold as it was, Moctu was dripping with sweat. The saber-tooth paused briefly collecting itself for another lunge. Moctu sensed that it, too, was tired. With a loud, rasping snarl, the beast surged upward again, and Moctu thrust down with the stick. He once more aimed for its shoulder trying to avoid the creature's cavernous mouth, but the stick glanced off a paw and hit near the mouth just above it on the cat's soft, black nose. The beast fell back, again scrambling furiously not to fall from its limb. It clung to the limb, snarling in pain and angry frustration. It made no further moves toward him while it panted and collected itself.

Hope welled up in Moctu that the cat would leave him

alone, and a primal celebratory urge caused him to howl, "Ar-rrruuuu!" at the top of his lungs while shaking his stick. The saber-tooth seemed convinced. It ignored him and appeared to be looking for a way off the tree. After moving back and forth on its limb several times, it began down the tree head-first, clawing desperately at the bark to hold some of its great weight and slow its descent. In the darkness Moctu couldn't see it well, but about midway down, it seemed to fall and land awkwardly, letting out a grunt of pain. Moctu was jubilant and let out another, "Arrrruuuu!" His sliced foot hurt a lot, but he was relieved, happy, and totally spent. I'm going to live, he thought. Thanks to the Spirits. Thanks to Jona and Tabar.

Chapter Fifty-Two

It was a beautiful morning. The air was cool and fresh, and the wispy clouds high in the indigo blue sky looked like feathers to Nuri. She briefly touched her talisman and smiled grimly, certain that the clouds were a sign that the Hawk Spirit was with her today to give her strength. She added one more groove on the inside of the ivory ringlet and rubbed charcoal into it. Wiping the residue clean, she examined it and was pleased with the tiny wolf engraving. As she rubbed it pensively, an image of Moctu smiling as he ate her stew came to mind.

But Moctu was dead, and today at noon she was to mate Jabil. She shuddered, thinking of the evening and night she would endure. She used to like Jabil even occasionally considering him as a potential mate. But that was before he and Jondu attacked Moctu. That was before seeing him with Leuna and knowing the couple had betrayed Samar. And that was before the whipping. She didn't think she could ever get past that, an episode that probably caused Moctu's death.

"Hello, Nuri." It was Leuna, and as she approached, she extended a bunch of pretty, yellow wildflowers toward Nuri.

"Hello, Leuna. I was just thinking about you. Thank you for the flowers," Nuri said with no trace of the iciness she felt. "Come into the hearth."

"Thank you, Nuri. I've really wanted to talk with you

before… um, before this afternoon. I'd like to… to explain some things."

"If you mean, that you're the first mate, and I'll have to abide by your rules, I'm aware…" Nuri started.

"No, no. Nothing like that. I want to explain about Samar, and um… Jabil."

"You don't have to explain that to me. And I'll keep my oath to remain silent about it," Nuri replied, her eyes cold.

"No, but I want to. To tell you about it… to try to explain. I loved Samar deeply. He was a wonderful man, a wonderful mate. I would never have done something to dishonor him… um, I mean I… I didn't mean to." Nuri started to say something, but Leuna pressed on. "It just happened. I… I almost died. I was moments from death and Jabil saved me. Afterward, I was so tired and so… so thankful to be alive. I was… terribly grateful to Jabil. He risked his life to save me. I knew I could never repay him for what he'd done. And then…" she trailed off.

Nuri was quiet for a long moment, imagining the near drowning and Leuna's feelings afterward. "And then he figured out what he wanted as payment," she finished for Leuna.

Leuna nodded and in a weak voice said, "I resisted, but I kept thinking I'd be dead if not for this man. And then… it… it just happened."

"So, is the baby Samar's or Jabil's?" Nuri asked softly.

"I don't know for sure, but I think it's Jabil's," Leuna said, looking downward. A small sob escaped her, and Nuri moved to put her arm around her.

"You poor girl," she said. "You went through a lot."

"And then, when I became pregnant," Leuna said, her voice breaking, "I was thrilled to finally have a child coming. I'd been so worried I was barren," she continued, her voice still choked with emotion. "It was… it was as if the Spirits had rewarded me for being with Jabil. But then Samar was killed by the Pale Ones, and I knew the Spirits were punishing me."

With this, she broke down completely and sobbed violently into Nuri's chest.

Nuri hugged her and patted her back, but she was too choked up to speak.

After collecting herself, Leuna went on. "And then Jabil... Jabil said he wanted me for his mate, and he was happy about the baby, and then he became leader, and everything seemed... well, it seemed to be getting better."

"And he convinced you to break your Mourning Moon and go to the woods with him," Nuri said, more as a statement than a question.

Leuna nodded. "He was to be my mate, and he was the new leader of the tribe, and I wanted to... I wanted to please him." She hung her head for a moment. After a long pause, she looked at Nuri and said, "I wanted you to know that I meant no disrespect to your uncle. I loved Samar very much, and I didn't want to start... to start my relationship with you on a bad note. Can you forgive me?"

"Oh Leuna, there's no need for that. Of course, I forgive you," Nuri said, touching her face gently. "And I'm glad you explained what happened. The situation had really bothered me, but now I can understand it better. I'm just sorry you had to go through all that."

"Well, I wanted you to know the story and my feelings before the ceremony today. I wanted you to know of the many things I regret," Leuna said. "Thanks for forgiving me. I guess we'll be spending a lot of time together from now on, and I wanted to be... friends. Will that ever be possible?"

"We already are friends," said Nuri hugging her. "Don't worry about that."

She just didn't think she could ever be friends with Leuna's mate—her mate.

Chapter Fifty-Three

The initial elation that Moctu felt after defending himself against the saber-tooth soon faded, and he spent a miserable night in the tree. His foot throbbed, and several times the cold had almost driven him off the tree to bury himself in a blanket of insulating leaves. But each time the thought of the fierce cat had kept him planted firmly in the security of the tree. If the beast was still around, there on the ground, he'd be dead in moments.

As another cold and misty, dew-laden morning dawned, Moctu found himself shivering uncontrollably. He was stiff with fatigue and worried about his foot. He was thirsty and hungry. By feel during the night, and then in the pre-dawn light, Moctu had tried to ascertain how severe the wound was. The foot was swollen, and there were three deep slashes on the side, all of which still oozed blood. Balanced on the tree limb, Moctu had tested putting weight on the foot and found he could do it, but it was painful. The prospect of walking to Etseh on it was disheartening, but he decided to take one day at a time and just make progress. He had to keep moving. If the Krog were still tracking him, their job had gotten a lot easier. But maybe they'd given up and gone back to Uhda.

As the dawn grew brighter and the mist began to clear, Moctu surveyed the area from his perch on the tree. There was no sign of the cat. He could see tracks, but from his height, they were jumbled and unreadable. Fear of capture by the Krog gradually surpassed his fear of the beast, and he finally slipped down the tree, keeping weight off the injured foot where possible. On the ground, he carefully scanned the nearby forest and bushes for any movement, any sign of the saber-tooth. With growing confidence that the cat was gone, he scrutinized the tracks which seemed to indicate it had moved east. He wished it had moved north so the Krog tracking him would have a nice surprise. He smiled at the image that brought to mind.

While examining the tracks, he had come upon the remnant of his footwear which he stopped now to gingerly strap onto the injured foot. Stick in hand and ready to move out, Moctu carefully studied the surrounding area one more time. The thought of the terrible cat could immobilize him if if he focused on its threat. His best chance to make it to Etseh was to leave now. If he waited, the Krog would catch him or kill him for sure. He headed south, hobbling and using the stick for a cane, pleased that the pain was bearable. He had to find water first, and at a stream he drank his fill then soaked his foot in the cool, clear water. The water burned at first, but after a long while it began to numb the whole foot. Although it cleaned the wound and numbed the pain, the sliced flesh reopened, and he oozed more bright red blood. After packing the wound with sphagnum moss and rewrapping the foot more tightly, he set off again.

By noon Moctu was on a hill that would afford him a good view to the south through a pass between the mountains. *If I can just find a break in these trees…* he thought hopefully. All the morning mist had burned off, and the sky was blue and cloudless. He was thrilled when he got to a rocky lookout and could see the lowlands far in the distance beyond the pass.

He finally knew where he was! If he were healthy, he could make it to Etseh in four or five days. His mood fell considerably as he considered his situation. The Krog were probably still chasing him, and it would take double the normal time to Etseh. He'd only had a few blackberries and pine nuts. He looked down at his badly swollen foot. He had to ignore the pain. He would make it to Nuri, to Alta, and all his friends.

He was moving down a scree slope when he heard a wolf howl from the mountain on the east side of the pass. It was answered immediately by a wolf howl from the mountain on the other side of the pass. Something was wrong. It was odd for wolves to howl at midday, Moctu thought. And these howls just sounded… off. Alarm surged through him. It was the Krog and they'd spotted him!

As crippled as he was, he ran for the cover of the trees. Could those really have been wolves? Maybe he was just being jumpy and overreacting? No. Those weren't wolves. The Krog knew Moctu had to use this pass, and they got here before him. They'd been watching for him.

"Slug dung!" he muttered. Why hadn't he stayed better hidden on that scree slope? But it would take them some time to come down the mountains to the pass. It was about a day and a half to the lowlands. Maybe he could get there before them. Moctu ignored the pain in his foot and moved quickly downhill, keeping to the trees. He crossed a saddle through some low beech and chestnut foliage to another, lower hill and paused in the cover of a thicket. His foot was throbbing, each pulse seeming to demand his attention. The foot skin was soaked in blood.

He charged on, crossing a large stream that soaked his foot and added to the pain. The stream ran down toward a U-shaped valley between the mountains. The middle of the valley was occupied by several lakes that lay to the southeast, with marsh and copse between them. Moctu stayed on the edge of the tree line moving ever southward along a narrow game trail, stopping occasionally to watch and listen for pursuers. It was during one of these stops that he heard it—partly a grunt and partly a yell, and definitely Krog, not animal. If they were yelling, they'd recognized that he knew they were here, and they'd given up any semblance of staying hidden. And it hadn't come from far away. He needed to move faster.

Moctu picked up his pace to an ungainly, limping run. His foot felt like it was splitting open each time it hit the ground. He heard another shout nearer now and knew that they were gaining on him. They'd known he was going south, so they hadn't needed to track him. He couldn't outrun them. He needed to lose them somehow. But how? He reached a thick stand of tall brush, and careful not to leave tracks, he left the game trail and broke eastward through the thicket toward the marsh and lakes. He went more slowly now, careful not to make noise in the brush. He heard a shout not far from the place he'd left the trail, and it was quickly answered by another. He continued onward and was pleased when the next shout came from farther south past the place he'd diverged from the trail. They'd missed it, he thought happily. At least for now.

Moctu's hopes dimmed as the shouts indicated his pursuers had quickly realized their error and were backtracking, looking for where he broke off the trail. They were excellent trackers and his ploy hadn't bought him much time. He heard them charge into the brush no longer worried about making noise. He was at the first lake and he could tell the Krog were again gaining on him. They were going to catch him!

On impulse, as he passed some tall reeds, he threw his stick far ahead of him and backtracked carefully in his tracks. He broke off a dry cylindrical reed. Clutching it, he entered the water at a rocky area leaving no tracks. The water was unpleasantly cold, but he plunged in and moved behind a big stand of reeds. He worked on the broken reed until he had a hollow section of it about the length of his foot. He heard thrashing in the brush, and from his hiding spot, he saw Awk race past him. He was followed shortly thereafter by Sag, who wasn't running, but walking slowly, closely examining the trail. Hearing a yell from Awk, Sag quit scanning the trail and with an odd moan, broke into a jog toward the sound of the shout. "Seems like they've found my stick," Moctu whispered and smiled to himself.

The water was so cold—he wasn't going to be able to stand it for long. His only hope was that they moved on soon, and he could get out and double back behind them. It wouldn't be too long before it was dark. That would help. He'd walk all night long if he could just get past them now.

As cold as the water was, it was about as warm as it ever got. In spring, the lakes were mostly snowmelt and too frigid to even wade in for long. By late fall, especially after heavy rains, the lakes were less chilly and could be tolerated for brief swims.

He couldn't take it any longer. Maybe they'd gone far enough ahead for him to double back on them.

Before he could act, however, he heard them returning. It sounded like they were arguing, which for some reason pleased him greatly. He ducked down in the reeds until he was up to his chin. A short way ahead, they stopped and seemed to argue louder. That was probably where he'd stopped walking. They were such good trackers! Sure enough, both began walking back toward his position, scanning the lake carefully. Moctu put the hollow reed to his mouth and ducked completely under the water, breathing through the thin tube. He held on to the reeds to keep from floating up.

He couldn't tell if they were still looking or not—he had to stay underwater as long as he could. He was so cold that he had to bite down hard on the reed to keep his teeth from chattering. He was losing feeling in his extremities and he worried that he'd pass out if he stayed in the water any longer, so he came up slowly and soundlessly. He was relieved to see that the Krog were gone—but where? His face out of the water, he was only slightly less miserable, and he desperately needed to get warmer. Moctu strained to hear any noise and was rewarded with a sound of them down the trail to the west, the direction from which he'd originally come. He eased himself quietly out of the water, but his teeth began chattering so violently that he worried they'd hear him. Moctu put the reed sideways in his mouth and clamped down hard. He decided he'd continue east past the lakes and away from the Krog noise he just heard.

Moctu moved in the direction that he'd thrown his stick hoping that they'd left it. Sure enough, there it was, and he happily picked it up leaning on it heavily. His foot hurt but he had to hurry and get to the far tree line. He had to get some distance from the Krog, or they were certain to catch him. Hoping to avoid making noise, he followed a narrow game trail, the same one the Krog men had been down earlier while looking for him. His confidence growing, he rounded a bend in the trail and came face-to-face with a scowling Awk, his thick spear ready for action.

Chapter Fifty-Four

Nuri lay motionless for fear of waking him. Following the mating ceremony, her first night with Jabil had been everything she expected: painful, repulsive, and emotionally crippling.

The ceremony had been serious and somber. Many in the crowd realized they were there because Moctu was not. Moctu's death permeated the proceeding but wasn't mentioned by Jelli or Nindai who dually presided over the ceremony. Throughout the entire event, Nuri was seen to rub an ivory ringlet on the sleeve of her beautiful gray and cream tunic. Although unsmiling, she looked resplendent, her dark hair flooding over her shoulders, and a woven circlet of tiny, fresh white flowers crowning her head. Jabil was clearly euphoric.

Afterward, he rushed her to his hearth which was empty for the night because he'd sent Leuna to the Red Hearth. Jabil had taken Nuri hungrily, greedily, forcing himself into her almost as soon as they were on the ground. He complained that she wasn't wet like Leuna, and that it was difficult for him. It had hurt Nuri and she bled. When she cried, he slapped her.

He took her again later in the night and it was only slightly better, and she bled some more. Her mother had told Nuri that after the first time, sex was almost as good for the woman as it was for the man, and she'd begin to look forward to it. Nuri didn't think that would ever be the case.

The blackness of night had softened to gray as the sun neared but had yet to crest the eastern mountains. Jabil stirred, and Nuri held her breath. She saw his eyes open and immediately closed hers. It was cold and he got up to add kindling to the remnant embers of the hearth fire. As it blazed up, he exclaimed in dismay and turned to her accusatorially. "Blood! My penis is coated with your female blood! You should have told me about your menses. Get to the Red Hearth! Female blood makes men weak. You've weakened me! I need to wash."

"I'm not having my menses," Nuri retorted angrily. "That blood is from your rough efforts last night."

The blood reminded Jabil of Ordu's death and the horrible, recurrent image sprang to mind. His breath caught and he tasted bile. "Get to the Red Hearth," he croaked. "And send Leuna back."

Nuri got up thinking at least this would save her from another episode with this despicable man, and she left without further comment. Even so, as she walked toward the Red Hearth, she was trembling—angry and humiliated, as mad as she'd ever been.

She found Leuna sleeping alone in the hearth and awoke her saying simply, "Jabil wants you." Leuna looked perplexed and questioned Nuri with her eyes, but Nuri offered no further comment. Once Leuna was gone, Nuri burst into tears, and was angry with herself for allowing Jabil to upset her this much. But it wasn't just Jabil that was upsetting her, she thought as despair welled up inside her. Realization was setting in that she'd just tasted the first part of the rest of her life.

A short while later Alfer called out as he saw Jabil walking down the steps toward the stream. "Ah, Jabil my son. Was your night with Nuri all that you thought it would be for these past many moons?"

"Hello, Father. My night with Nuri was…" Jabil paused searching for the right word.

"Wonderful?" Alfer offered.

"Unsettling."

"Unsettling? What does that mean?"

"I don't want to talk about it right now," Jabil said, moving away.

"You have to maintain your discipline and authority," Alfer called after him. "A new mate needs lots of guidance and scolding," he continued, raising his voice. When Jabil was out of earshot, he muttered, "And a good beating once in a while."

Chapter Fifty-Five

Moctu awoke in the dark grayness of earliest dawn with a throbbing head and a tightness in his chest. Feeling his head, he found a large lump at the back. As his eyes cleared he saw both Awk and Sag glaring at him over a small fire.

At least they hadn't killed him. As he peered at his captors, Sag coughed violently, and leaned over and spit into the fire. Moctu could see, even in the dim light, Sag appeared to be feverish and sick, very sick. His skin was blotchy. He looked like he had *lekuk*, the spotted sickness that Nereans commonly got. But it couldn't be lekuk because he was so ill. Lekuk was mild, just an annoyance, and no one at Etseh ever got that sick.

The murky light of dawn arrived quickly and the Krog men extinguished their fire. They both prompted Moctu roughly with the blunt ends of their spears to get up and start moving. As Moctu arose, he felt the tightness in his chest and found a sore spot below his breastbone. He remembered Awk jamming the blunt end of his spear into his midsection, knocking his wind out, then walloping him as he doubled over.

He hobbled in the direction they pointed, but his foot hurt a great deal, and he could only go slowly. Awk prodded him again, and seeing his stick on the ground, Moctu pointed to his foot and then the stick and then back to his foot.

Awk shook his head "No" and prodded him again. With

Moctu's next step, it felt as if the foot split in half, eliciting profound pain, and almost causing him to fall. Awk clubbed him to the ground, and with Sag pointing his spear at Moctu's chest, Awk knelt and unwrapped Moctu's crude foot wrap to see what the difficulty was. Moctu's foot was badly swollen and bruised, but the three claw marks were still clearly visible. Awk whistled when he saw the three claw marks and with a series of grunts and hand movements, motioned for Sag to look. Sag also let out a note of surprise and pointed to the wound with his crooked arm questioning Moctu with grunts and signs he didn't understand. Awk put his index finger to his mouth, pointing down like a giant incisor and gave a loud hiss and growl, "Hiss-gaw?"

To Moctu, it sounded like a noise that a big cat would make. With his mouth open, and using both index fingers, he pantomimed a saber-tooth face, and both the Krog men said in unison, "Hiss-gaw!" With his hand, Moctu depicted a paw with claws out and showed how he'd received his wound.

Awk and Sag were amazed and chattered at him and between themselves, saying "hiss-gaw" several times. He understood little of it, but it seemed as if they were very impressed.

During their animated chattering, Moctu smiled inwardly and thought, Yeah, that's right. I fought off a hiss-gaw.

They treated him with more respect after that. Awk retrieved his stick and appraised it carefully, as if thinking, this thing held off a hiss-gaw! He broke the sharp end off and then gave the stick to Moctu to use as a cane, which helped him immensely. As he followed the Krog up a winding trail on the side of the eastern mountain, Moctu wondered why they were taking this odd route back to Uhda. Their reasoning became apparent when they stopped at an overlook that gave a wide view of the lowlands to the south. Both Krog men cupped their hands around their eyes and scanned the horizon.

Likely looking for game, Moctu conjectured.

Awk grunted and pointed to the southeast, and Sag reciprocated with a series of grunts. Moctu also shielded his eyes and looked but could see nothing. Sag pointed at Moctu and grunted loudly to Awk. Then Moctu saw Awk sign with fingers to Sag, "Five, maybe six," and he heard Krog words he understood that made his heart race: "Man-man."

He was sure they'd spotted Nereans! Why else would Sag have pointed to him? If only he'd gotten past these two, he would have made it. Maybe he could still get away. Moctu strained his eyes to see what they were seeing, but he could make out nothing that looked like people. The Krog must have better eyesight than Nereans. Then he saw tiny movement far, far into the lowlands. It could be people, he supposed. How did they see them? How did they know how many there were? If those were people, they were at least two days away. For a healthy person.

The Krog seemed to know he'd likely think of escaping again, and they both watched him more closely. After some time studying the Nereans and the surrounding landscape, the two men got up and prodded Moctu into moving downhill, this time north toward Uhda. Moctu's heart fell.

"I was so close," he murmured to himself.

He saw Sag stumble and realized just how sick Sag was. He was bright red after the climb up the hill, and he looked awful now. If it was lekuk, they should give him willow bark, nicroot and lots of water. Yarrow would be good too. The sooner the better. Should he tell them? His chances for escape improved with Sag incapacitated. After some time, Awk began supporting Sag as they walked, and Moctu decided that he couldn't just watch Sag maybe die and not try to help.

"Awk. Awk!" He got Awk's attention and then pantomimed that he could make some medicine to help Sag.

Both watched him and seemed to understand, but Sag shook his head, "No." He heard Awk say Rah's name, and knew they wanted to get back to let Rah treat Sag. With Awk supporting Sag, the men picked up the pace and Moctu struggled to keep up. Twice during the day, Awk stopped and came back to administer painful incentives for Moctu to go faster. After the second time, Moctu hobbled up to where Awk had left Sag sitting on a fallen tree, and he was shocked to see how bad Sag looked. He was coughing nearly continuously and his face was a blotchy gray-red. He worsened throughout the day.

The men made camp on a low hill and Awk built a fire while Sag looked on weakly. Moctu again studied Awk's methodology and paid closer attention to the wood types he used and how Awk positioned himself. He heard Awk say 'hiss-gaw,' and knew he was worried about the saber-tooth. Sag wheezed and moaned faintly. His face had turned a mottled ashen gray. He looked awful.

Sag coughed and wheezed all through the night and was too weak to walk in the morning. Awk carried him on his powerful back while holding both spears under his right arm. About mid-morning, Sag began shaking with seizures and Awk put him gently down on the ground and tried to comfort him, patting him on his shoulders and making soft grunts. Sag's eyes rolled back in his head, and his whole body went stiff. Awk crooned softly, anxiously patting him, distraught that he couldn't help his friend more.

Moctu was deeply moved by the display and wished to help as well. He picked up their water skin and pointed to the creek asking Awk, "Wog?" and then pointing to Sag. Awk nodded and Moctu hurried to the stream to refill the skin. As he returned, Awk let out a mournful wail, a howl of despair and anguish, and even from a distance, Moctu could tell that Sag was dead. Awk's inconsolable grief again moved and unsettled Moctu, leaving him surprised at the level of compassion he felt for his captor.

After some time, Awk composed himself and directed Moctu to ready himself to move out. He wrapped a skin around Sag's upper body and hoisted the corpse to his powerful shoulders. Somberly, the two set out for Uhda, and by nightfall they could see the fires of Uhda still far ahead and tiny but standing in stark contrast to the black sky.

Chapter Fifty-Six

Nearly half the Krog were sick. Gut's mate and their girl child had died. Perhaps worst of all, the Krog healer, Rah, was profoundly ill.

A scout had alerted the camp as Awk and Moctu approached, and a few individuals came out to meet them in the darkness. Effie was among them, looking tired and subdued, but businesslike. She avoided eye contact with Moctu, instead focusing on Sag's body, as Awk continued toward a small fire and gently placed the corpse on the ground. She knelt by it, closely examining the blotchy face and then checking the throat under the ears for nodules. Moctu's first indication that something was very wrong was Effie's lack of consternation at the body. There was no surprise, just sad resignation. This was a man whose baby she might be carrying.

As she talked with Awk, Moctu was able to piece together the gist of the situation. A horrible sickness had settled on the tribe and several had died. When Moctu heard Rah's name mentioned with melancholy tones, he feared she was one. He also heard Gut's name, and several others spoken of in the same tone.

Awk pointed to Moctu, and Effie looked at him briefly with cold, stoic eyes. Her sight was redirected to his foot when Awk pointed to it with signs and unintelligible grunts that included the word *hiss-gaw*. She came and knelt by him, partly unwrapping his foot skin to view the wound. Awk left the two of them, as well as Sag's body, to go check on his family.

"Effie, I'm sorry. I'm… I'm so sorry to hear about Rah," Moctu said, his voice cracking with emotion.

"Rah bur sick," she replied without looking his way.

"So, she's not dead! I thought she was dead. Effie, I can help! I know this disease. Please let me help."

She looked up at him and he could see the pain in her big, expressive eyes. He didn't know if it was for Rah, or because he'd abandoned her and the baby, or for something else entirely.

"Please let me help. I want to help," he repeated. "Rah saved my life."

"How yaw help?" she asked.

"I know how we… I know how Nerean healers treat this disease. I know some things that will help."

Effie stood and covered Sag's body with a skin. "Come," she said. "Help Rah," and she headed at a quick pace toward their hearth.

Rah was coughing violently as Effie and Moctu arrived at the hearth. The night air was brisk and the small fire gave off little heat, but even so, Rah's face was hot and beaded with sweat. Her face looked gray and blotchy, and her eyes were bloodshot and distant, similar to Sag's shortly before he went into convulsions.

This was not good, Moctu thought to himself. She was too far gone. He looked at Effie worriedly and shook his head slightly. Then he took a deep breath and collected his thoughts. "Wog. Wog-wog," he said. "And where is her medicine skin?"

Moctu located some willow bark and dried yarrow stems in Rah's medicine skin but could find no nicroot. Effie returned with the water and Moctu wet a small skin and bared Rah's torso, rubbing her face, neck and chest with the cool water.

"Some fever good. Too much, very bad," he said. "Try to get her to drink some cool water. The more the better." Effie understood and knelt with a small gourd. The water did its job, and lowering the fever revived Rah somewhat, but her racking cough returned and the spasms left her wheezing and weak.

Moctu moved away to grind the willow bark, stew the yarrow stalks, and try, once again, to find the nicroot. She had to have some nicroot in her bag, he thought. But there was none. He ground up the willow bark and made a paste, then used the small paddle to transfer it to Rah's mouth. Rah opened her mouth and accepted the paste willingly, then smiled faintly at him before coughing violently again.

While he was rubbing her with the cool, wet skin, her eyes closed, and she was still. Moctu's pulse rose and he put his ear to her heart and was gratified to hear it still beating. When he looked up, Effie was staring at his face, with a mix of worry and anguish. He smiled at her and nodded his head, indicating Rah was stable for now. Effie clutched him in a hug and hummed oddly, but it was a hopeful-sounding hum, and he hugged her back happily.

Effie pushed slightly away, and with one hand, pointed to the hearth opening. She made several grunts he didn't under-stand, but when she said Gut's name, he realized she wanted him to help there too. He looked again at Rah who seemed stabilized, nodded to Effie, and grabbed the medicine skin.

Gut's mate had died, as had his girl child, but he was so sick, he probably didn't even know it. His adolescent son was extremely sick too, and both were lying nearly comatose in their dark hearth. Their hearth fire had gone out, and the little space was cold and smelled of death. Moctu had seen Gut move slightly as they came into the hearth, but his son re-mained motionless. Effie told Moctu she'd see to the fire and bring some wog to the hearth. Moctu knelt to feel their tem-peratures, needing to first determine if the boy was even alive.

Both were hot, too hot, and Moctu stripped them down, exposing their chests to the cool night air. Effie was soon back, with a gourd of water in one hand and a glowing ember on a small branch in the other.

They spent the entire night visiting the sick and trying to alleviate the high fevers and suffering. During the night, Effie had washed Moctu's foot wound and worked on it while he attended to Gut. She'd mixed and applied a balsam-bark poultice, packed it with sphagnum moss and bound the wound, all while Moctu rubbed a cool, wet skin on Gut's neck and chest.

By dawn they were exhausted, completely spent. A heavy, cold wind had blown in from the west, and instead of mist and fog this morning, the air was clear and there were patches of frost. They revisited Rah and found that she still had the racking cough and her skin remained gray and blotchy. But her fever was reduced. Rah wasn't out of trouble, but she was improved and might make it. After a bout of morning sickness, weary and drained, Effie lay down ostensibly to rest for just a moment and was soon fast asleep. Moctu covered her with a skin, but as the morning light began streaming in, he knew he still had work to do.

He had to find nicroot. Lots of it, he thought. As he headed for the forest he realized no one was watching his movements, no one was guarding him. He could run... and he could make it. At least he'd have a better chance than last time.

But Moctu knew he couldn't leave Rah in such a precarious state. He had to save her. He had to get her some nicroot. Then maybe he'd run.

Chapter Fifty-Seven

The nicroot had helped Rah, but now Effie was sick. Moctu had returned from the forest exultant to have found a large batch of nicroot, only to find Effie feverish and shivering under her furs. The lack of sleep and exhaustion had left her weakened, and the disease appeared to thrive within her. By midday, she was coughing violently and her fever was high, much too high, despite Moctu's efforts to lower it. Although improved, Rah was far too weak to help, so Moctu took on the role of caring for the entire Krog tribe.

It was too much. He focused his main efforts on nursing Effie and Rah back to health, but the disease held on tenaciously within Effie. Her fever was stubbornly high, and her cough worsened keeping her from rest and weakening her with harsh, wracking spasms. A greatly improved Gut brought two desperate parents that Moctu barely recognized to Rah's hearth to ask, then demand, that he help their three children. The mother, a small brown-eyed woman, also had the darkest hair he'd seen among the Krog and he guessed she'd come from a different tribe. Her pleading eyes had finally convinced him. He reluctantly went with them, leaving Effie after she swallowed some willow bark and nicroot paste. Her fever was still too high.

All three children were extremely sick, and there was little he could do for the youngest, an infant boy. Easing the high fevers of the two adolescent twin boys helped them, as did the willow bark and nicroot he administered. They were improved by the late afternoon. He left to check on Effie and Rah and found Rah cooling Effie with a wet skin.

"That's a happy sight," he said with a tired smile.

Even though she didn't understand his words, Rah understood the tone and smiled back weakly.

By nightfall, the infant boy died and Effie had worsened. Gut had returned, wanting Moctu to check on his son and to revisit the grieving couple's two remaining children. Moctu had refused, in order to continue caring for Effie. When Gut had roughly pulled on him, he pushed away and Gut cuffed him, sending him against the rock wall of the hearth. As weak as she was, Rah stood and confronted Gut angrily. Moctu only understood a few of the words and signs, but whatever she said, it worked, and Gut left. Rah immediately began coughing and retired to her furs, depleted of energy.

Effie worsened through the night, becoming delirious, and Moctu found himself frustrated, exhausted, and near despair.

"Please Spirits! Don't take Effie. Please let her live," he whispered to the cold night wind as it buffeted the skin walls of the hearth.

Moctu continued to cool her face and neck with the wet hide, and he wrapped an old caribou skin around himself. Even so, the frigid air seemed intent on sucking the life from him.

As dawn broke Moctu awoke with a start, realizing he'd fallen asleep after two days with no rest. His joints were stiff, and the hearth was so cold that his breath came out in clouds. Two tiny embers were all that was left of the fire. As he got kindling to stoke the fire, he saw that it was snowing. Huge, wet flakes, each nearly the size of a fingernail, were falling in droves. The forest was beautiful, the trees softly blanketed with pure white, while the grasses were still mostly green with almost no accumulation.

Although the scene was breathtakingly lovely, for reasons he couldn't name, Moctu came as close to tears as he had since Tabar's death. But now he had work to do. As he rebuilt the fire, he prayed again to the Spirits.

"Please don't take Effie! Please spare her. Oh Spirits, please… please!" He knelt and touched her face, and again was swept with emotion. Effie's fever had gone down and her face looked less blotchy. "Thank you Spirits. Thank you." As he felt her forehead, her eyes opened, and she smiled faintly. He smiled back broadly.

"It's good to have you back with us."

Her deep blue eyes searched his expression to better understand his words. "How Rah?" she croaked and tried to turn to see for herself.

"Rah good. Much, much better," he answered.

Effie smiled and eased back, closing her eyes. In moments, she was asleep again.

Chapter Fifty-Eight

"I'm sorry, but we saw no evidence of the Pale Ones," Jondu told the men gathered around the main fire. His hunting party had just returned from a disappointing northern trip that found no large game, no sign of Moctu, and no trace of the Pale Ones. Jondu had already recounted the discouraging hunting results, which were foremost on the hunters' minds. Even after the recent mammoth and rhino successes, the food situation was once again problematic, because rodents had ruined some of their dried meat stores.

"If we don't find game soon, we'll be living on rat meat this winter," Alfer said frowning.

"If Jabil agrees, in several days I plan to lead a group south to find game," said Jondu, ignoring the remark. "The snows to the north will preclude good hunting there."

"Yes, that's a good plan," said Jabil, and the hunters murmured their agreement.

It was late, and the tired men began to retreat to the warmth and comfort of their hearths and women. Jondu moved closer to Jabil who remained, thoughtfully staring into the fire.

"So how was it with Nuri?" Jondu asked, eager for details. "Does Leuna get any time with you now?"

"It's not as I expected Jondu. Nuri is cold, distant, and not pleasant to share furs with. I spend most nights with Leuna."

"No. I don't believe it. You were so crazy about Nuri. You would have killed for her! You would…" Jondu stopped as Jabil's eyes closed and he doubled over slightly and gasped. "Another episode?" Jondu muttered to himself, his eyes rolling in mild contempt. They were coming all the time. It was hard to say anything to him—Jondu couldn't even talk about Nuri without him having an attack.

"Easy, my friend. You're having another attack I see. Aren't they getting any better?" he said patting Jabil on his back.

"I'm… I'm all right. I'll be fine," said Jabil, embarrassed, trying to regain his composure. "Go," he said, waving Jondu away. "I'm fine. Go now. Go pleasure Avi. I'm sure she's been lonely these past days. I'll be fine."

With some reluctance, Jondu arose, said good night and left for his hearth. Jabil continued to stare into the fire, trying to let his mind drift away from the earlier thoughts that had disturbed him. But they lingered. He unconsciously pulled on his braid letting his grip gently run down the length of it.

Will these thoughts, these nightmares follow me like a horrible shadow forever? I've got to think of something else. I have to get past this. And I can, he resolved, jutting his jaw. I'm leader of the Nerea—let me focus on that. The tribe needs a good hunt. Maybe I'll go on this next one. I'm probably the best hunter in the tribe. Why should I stay here if we need meat so badly? If the people go hungry this winter, I'll be blamed even though it's not my fault.

A gust of extremely cold air blew past him and he added some wood to the dwindling fire. "It's going to be a long, cold winter," he murmured shaking his head. "Please Spirits," he prayed. "We need meat. Don't let my first winter as leader be a starving time for Etseh."

Chapter Fifty-Nine

Six shallow, oval holes had been dug for the bodies. Four of the dead were children, and their burial holes were heartbreakingly small. The disease had descended swiftly on the Krog, wreaked its death and havoc, and then left just as quickly. Now, although several Krog were still recovering, none were critically ill.

Moctu was treated with much more respect. Most of the tribe recognized that he saved several of their members from nearly certain death. He was no longer bound at night, nor was he guarded during the day. Perhaps the Krog believed that the recent heavy snows made any escape attempt suicidal, and no guarding was necessary.

Both Rah and Effie were fully recovered and planned to attend the burial ceremony. Like the Nerean practice, Krog burials took place when the sun was directly overhead, which was fortunate today as the morning was bitterly cold. Maintaining his position close to the hearth fire, Moctu watched Effie and Rah somberly prepare for the event. They brought out and adorned themselves with attractive shell and ivory necklaces that he had never seen before, and they dressed in their best skins.

People began to stream by their hearth on the way toward the burial site north of Uhda, all apparently wearing their finest apparel and accoutrement. A well-dressed but stricken-looking Gut, who'd lost two of his family, passed slowly by, followed closely by Awk. That's when Moctu saw it.

"It's Tabar's knife! Awk has Tabar's knife!" After a moment of disbelief, Moctu went utterly berserk with rage. He threw himself at Awk's back, grabbing handfuls of his hair and trying to pull him down from behind. Though Awk was much stronger than he was, the intensity and ferocity of Moctu's attack took him by surprise. With a cry, Awk twisted and went to one knee while Moctu, a wad of bloody hair in one hand, wheeled around and kicked Awk in the groin. Awk grunted and doubled over. Moctu kneed him in the side of the face and then was atop him, hitting, clawing, and biting, anything to hurt this beast. He heard Effie screaming as Awk went down under his assault. Lying on his side, with Moctu desperately trying to hurt him, to kill him, Awk threw a blow to Moctu's head that sent him sprawling. Groggily, he got to his knees, but Awk was standing now and kicked him in the side knocking the wind from Moctu and sending him into the wall skins which collapsed upon him.

Continuing to scream, Effie threw herself atop him, while Moctu tried to catch his breath and clear his head. As Moctu struggled to get free of the skins and of Effie's weight, he received another hard kick to the ribs which was only partially absorbed by the skins. The pain was awful. He couldn't breathe or move. It was over. He lay still, gasping for breath, as Awk pulled Effie from over him, removed the skins, and tied his wrists. He was happy to see that Awk's nose was bleeding and that his face was badly scratched near his left eye. A clump of hair was missing at the back of his head, and blood ran from that wound through his hair and down his neck.

"I wish I could have killed him," Moctu fumed. "I will kill him! I'll kill him like the hyena he is."

He was aware of Effie peering questioningly over him chattering and making signs, some of which he understood.

"What happen? Why you do this?" He was pulled upright, and the pain on his left side was immense.

Broken rib, he thought. Maybe several. He caught his breath finally, and he angrily motioned with his bound hands toward Awk's knife in answer to Effie's continued questions. "You're liars—you're all liars! And murderers. That's my father's knife," he shouted savagely. "You killed my father!" Awk, who'd been rubbing his nose and eye, and looking malevolently at Moctu, abruptly changed his demeanor. He touched the knife in comprehension, and nodded solemnly, seeming to understand that a friend or relative of Moctu's had been its owner.

There was a flood of words and signing between Awk and Effie, then she turned to Moctu, pointed at the knife, and said, "Yaw father knife?"

With fury in his eyes, Moctu screamed back, "Yes! It's my father's knife. And you're liars!" He turned toward Awk. "You killed my father, you hyena dung!" He could tell that they both understood him, even Awk, but their reaction wasn't what he expected.

Both shook their heads, "No", and there was another rapid stream of words and signs between them, most of which he didn't understand. Awk looked to Effie and she looked back at Moctu, perplexed as to how to say what they wanted him to know. Awk unstrapped the knife and put it at Moctu's feet.

Moctu tried to kick him and shouted, "I don't want the stinking knife! I want my father, you dung pile!"

"No, no. Krog no kill Nereans," Effie said in a calm, low voice. "Man Nerean kill Nereans."

What is she trying to say? Moctu wondered, some of his anger turning to confusion. He shrugged. It didn't make any sense.

"Krog see man Nerean kill Nereans," she said, looking into his eyes. Her giant, blue eyes were searching his, beseeching him to understand and accept her account.

"Are you saying a Nerean man killed the Nereans?" he

asked, not believing.

Effie nodded "yes" and unblinkingly watched his face, imploring him to believe her.

That made no sense, he thought, and felt a flash of anger that they'd think he'd believe something so stupid. Then how had Awk ended up with the knife?

"No. You lie," he shouted to them, pointing with his tied hands to Tabar's knife at his feet and then to Awk's side where it had resided. "Then how'd Awk get the knife?"

Effie put her hand up and made a noise that sounded like, "Ah yes." She said, "Man Nerea," and then pantomimed a man picking up equipment, dragging it all away, and then hiding it under rocks and dirt. "Man Nerea go. Krog find."

Although Moctu refused to believe the story, part of his mind began to question had Jabil done it? Could he have? No, that was just not believable. Even for Jabil. Ordu was his own uncle. Which was more likely, Jabil murdering three of his kinsmen for no reason, or these creatures attacking them. But even so, it was Effie...

"No. I don't believe it," Moctu blurted, still angry. "Why would a Nerean kill Nereans?" Another recollection suddenly flashed. "And how did a Krog spear end up in Samar's body?"

Effie seemed to understand the question, but instead of answering, turned to Awk and had another quick exchange with him.

She turned back to Moctu. "Nerean hunt Urda... um, bear. Lose bear. Angry. Make camp," she said haltingly. "After kill in night, in morning, man Nerea take Nerea spear... um..." At a loss for words, Effie enacted the events after the murders, as they'd been explained to her by Awk. She pantomimed Jabil taking a broken Krog spear from his pack, trying to push it into the dead body, then using his spear to puncture the body, and finally, sticking the broken point into the corpse.

As unbelievable as it was, Moctu admitted to himself that it would have been hard to make up such a convoluted story. Still, the bear story didn't make sense, and her explanation didn't convince him. Moctu shook his head, "No."

Awk made a sound and pointed toward the sun. It was almost time for the burials. They stood awkwardly for several moments, before Effie moved to Moctu and unbound him.

"Please Moctu. Krog... Effie true." She and Awk turned and left, walking toward the burial site. Moctu stayed behind, lost in a confusion of conflicting thoughts and emotions. After a long moment, he reached down and strapped on the knife. His father's knife. He moved to the entrance of the hearth, unsure what to do next. The cold cut through him as if he wore no tunic, forcing his thoughts to the present. He recovered a sleeping fur, and wrapping it around himself, he left the hearth and headed for the burial site.

Chapter Sixty

The burials were not nearly as elaborate as Nerean ones. No sacred red ocher or flowers, and almost no adornments were put with the bodies. The bodies were placed carefully and solemnly in the shallow graves, their knees flexed, except for the infant boy who was so small that didn't need to be done. Gut's mate was adorned with a few feathers, and the broken wooden part of Sag's spear was included with his body.

The crowd stood together in ankle-deep, loosely packed snow, their breath fogging in the cold, dry air. There was no real ceremony, but all in attendance were somber, and the hushed silence was broken only by moaning and low wailing by several of the women. That changed as Gut and another man began to cover Sag's body with dirt and stones. His burial seemed to elicit the greatest anguish, and after his grave was filled in, Gut placed the upper end of Sag's broken spear on the mound, apparently a sign of great respect.

Moctu's mind flashed on the broken spear he'd seen in Samar's body, but he shrugged it off as coincidence. His thoughts were in turmoil. He couldn't bring himself to believe that Jabil would cold-bloodily murder three of his fellow tribesmen, men who'd taught him how to hunt, track game, and knap flint into tools… taught him how to be a man. And Ordu was his uncle. No way.

But he couldn't believe Effie would lie to him either.

Was he being naïve? How well did he know Effie, anyway? She was from a completely different people, different culture. He paused, reflecting. But he did know her. He did, and she was... a good person. She'd never lied to him that he knew of.

The dark-haired Krog woman who'd lost her infant son came up to Moctu after the burial, her two older twin boys closely trailing her. She extended her hand toward him, holding three polished eagle talons strung together with thin sinew.

Moctu's brow furrowed, and he touched his chest. "For me? Why?"

The woman nodded and smiled then pointed to her twins. Wordlessly, she thrust the necklace closer to him and looked at him with a grateful smile, her eyes brimming with tears. Understanding, he gently accepted it and closed his eyes and nodded in thanks. When he opened his eyes, the woman had her eyes closed and was nodding in return. A tear stole down her cheek. He was deeply touched by the fine gift and the depth of appreciation the woman showed him for saving her two children. He found his heart softening toward her and the Krog in general.

Could these people kill my kinsmen and then lie straight-faced about it to me?

Rah had seen the exchange and came up beside him, smiling. She patted his back and smiled broadly to him, then touched her chest, bowed her head and closed her eyes.

She was thanking him too.

"You saved *my* life, Rah," he said touching his own chest, and pointing to her, quickly closing his eyes and nodding. She smiled and turned, headed for her hearth.

These people were such a mystery to Moctu. The Krog had just buried six of their clan, yet they seemed to focus on the good things that they had left. Did they kill his people? It had to be either them or Jabil. Could Jabil have done such a thing?

He missed his people. He still thought of Nuri often,

but he realized that by now she was sharing night furs with Jabil. She was mate to the leader of the Nereans and probably thought little, if at all, about him. He hoped Alta and Zaila were faring well. Alta no doubt had a new mate, her third in short order. How was she coping with that? And Palo and Seetu and all the others, what of them? He just wanted to find out how they were doing and tell them what he'd seen and learned.

It was bitterly cold and most of the people were filtering back to the warmth and comfort of their hearths. Despite his ribs hurting and being chilled himself, Moctu lingered, thinking of each of the departed Krog. Except for Sag, he knew little of them. Sag was perhaps his least favorite of the Krog. "Let's see," he murmured thinking back. "Sag threatened to cut off my manhood, he beat me, chased me, caught me and beat me again. He was always sour, grumpy and contrary. Why do I feel any loss for this man? Maybe because I could have saved him? I don't know."

New flakes of snow began to fall out of the dull gray sky. He heard someone approaching and turned to see Effie as she came up to him. Smiling, she took his hand in hers, and he realized how cold he was. Her hand was so warm. She gently pulled him away from the graves and they walked back to the hearth.

As they got to the opening to the hearth, Effie turned to him, and with her big blue eyes locked on his, solemnly said, "Effie true." Moctu wasn't sure why, but he believed her.

The fire was burning nicely, and a skin of stew simmered above it. After Effie pulled a skin over the hearth opening, the room became pleasantly warm and it smelled terrific. As cheery as the room was, Moctu could sense a melancholy in the two women. He felt it too. There was little conversation as the three of them reflected on the day's events. Days were much shorter now, and with the overcast skies, darkness fell on them quickly and heavily, and soon they sat on their separate sleeping furs staring almost hypnotized by the flickering, dancing fire. The shadows it cast on the hanging skins and cave walls were equally transfixing, moving and shifting like a thousand memories, present but transient, tenuous, and impossible to grasp.

The fire died to embers, and Moctu watched a somber-looking Effie restoke the fire and retire to her sleeping furs. Shortly thereafter, Moctu moved to his furs and Rah to hers.

Moctu awoke as Effie crawled in next to him, her back to his chest as he lay on his side. She was shivering and she took his upper arm and wrapped it around her, and she nestled into him. The fire had died down, and the room was cold. She felt good next to him. Not just her warmth, but... her. He breathed in the fresh flower and wood smoke scent of her soft blond hair and pulled her closer to him. His breath caught as she reached behind and began stroking his manhood.

Chapter Sixty-One

Da's hunting party had been gone for more than half a moon and Moctu had overheard Effie and Rah worrying that they'd met up with the fierce Shiv. There was widespread relief when one of the hunters returned brimming with excitement. It was a cold midmorning, and an eager crowd quickly grew around the man. With rapid signing and grunts they showered him with questions. Moctu could understand more Krog now, but the people were speaking so fast and talking over one another, he couldn't follow the conversation. Effie explained that a group of mammoths had been spotted near the *killing place*. This was a site with ideal topography for killing the huge beasts.

Moctu was intrigued and wondered how, exactly, topography could help with bringing down one of these massive beasts. As he questioned Effie about it, she grabbed Awk's arm and asked him a quick question to which he nodded affirmatively. She turned to Moctu and asked him, "Awk say yaw help with hunt?"

"Absolutely! I mean, yes, I'd like that," Moctu replied excitedly. "But I have no spear or..." He paused, and remained silent, deciding he wouldn't use or mention the atlatl that Awk was so curious about.

Awk was watching and smiled at Moctu's enthusiasm. Effie asked Awk something about spears, and the big man shook his head no. Effie persisted, and Awk's apparent obstinacy began to crumble. Finally, he nodded, and Effie turned to Moctu and became very serious. She took both his hands in hers.

"Member Krog see man Nerea hide weapons?" she asked tentatively.

"What? Oh… umm, yes, I remember what you told me about that," he said, his mood souring.

"Yaw want Krog spear or yaw father spear?" she asked, stunning him.

"What? You have my father's spear?" he asked incredulously, his thoughts racing.

Well, of course they did, he realized quickly, angry at himself for not recognizing that they'd have kept more than just his father's knife. Whether they stole it from the bodies or dug it up from where Jabil buried it, they'd have kept all the fine weapons and gear.

"Where is it?" he said fiercely. "Where's my father's spear? Where's the rest?"

Awk eyed Effie, then motioned Moctu to follow him. Together, Awk and Effie led him back to an empty hearth, directly behind a large public fire pit that the Krog seldom used. There, Awk knelt and moved some rocks and furs, exposing a cache of weapons and gear, most of which Moctu recognized. On seeing the pile of gear, Moctu's mind immediately flooded with the same questions he had been struggling with.

Did these people kill his father and friends or did Jabil? It had to be one or the other. Then he saw something that swung his mind momentarily away.

"There's Tabar's spear!" he exclaimed, taking hold of it excitedly. He looked at them and said, "My father's spear." They nodded in understanding.

"A fine piece," he went on, hefting it and smiling. "Tabar made good equipment. And there's Samar's spear, and Ordu's," he said, putting Tabar's down and, in turn, lifting each of the other two spears. "I recognize his work. Tabar made good equipment, but Samar's was exquisite. He made both of these. But this one was my father's," he said, happily retrieving the first spear. "This is the one I want."

A treasure trove of memories had resurfaced along with the fine equipment. It was all still in excellent shape, and it brought back recollections of earlier, simpler, and happier times when he was young and learning to hunt.

Awk made some loud grunts and Effie interpreted, "He say we go kill mammoth now."

Caught up in the thrill of a potential mammoth hunt, Moctu temporarily sidetracked his other turbulent thoughts and focused on his preparations for the event. Effie brought him extra skins to wear and astonished him when she explained that much of the hunt could take place in the frigid evening or nighttime. No Nereans had ever hunted at night by choice. It was just too dangerous.

Shortly before noon the hunters, six including Moctu, all heavily clad in skins, had gathered at the north end of Uhda and soon thereafter headed out at a fast pace to the northeast. Some of the men carried large bundles of sticks which baffled him as to their purpose. Awk stayed close to Moctu, and he wondered if Effie had encouraged him to do so. No matter the reason, Moctu was thankful for his close presence. He was embarking on a trip in freezing weather to kill a massive and thoroughly dangerous beast, perhaps at night, with men of a different people, that he didn't know well, and with whom he could barely converse.

"What could go wrong?" he muttered to himself, smiling. He thought he'd never been this excited.

Chapter Sixty-Two

For all their brawn, Moctu had no trouble keeping up with the Krog men. In fact, at a rest stop in mid-afternoon, after climbing a good-sized hill, some of it through knee-deep snow, most of the Krog men were considerably more winded than he was. Their breath vented explosively like clouds in the brisk air. Awk was looked to as the leader of their small group, and in a snow-cleared area in the dirt he explained to the men where the kroag-kroag were and some of the topography and plans.

Moctu wished he could understand more of it. He was only getting about half of it.

After going over the plans with the men, Awk came and sat next to Moctu. The other men had gone back to talking amongst themselves. Awk pointed to Moctu, then himself, then taking two fingers, wrapped his other hand around them.

He's telling me to stick close to him, Moctu thought, a sense of relief washing over him. He nodded to Awk.

The hunters again set off at a fast pace and by late afternoon, near the base of a large hill, they heard a hailing whistle from some of Da's group higher up the slope. Awk's group all waved, but Moctu couldn't see who they were greeting. They hiked to near the top of the hill and met up with two of Da's men in a small clearing. The place offered a broad panorama over a narrow valley with a large, frozen-over stream in the middle. Moctu could tell that even before this past warm summer, the ice sheets had retreated into the mountains, leaving a tundra of low scrub on both sides of the stream, all now covered by snow.

In low voices, the groups gave each other updates, which obviously included news of the sickness and deaths, because both of Da's men let out soft moans and noises of grief. Moctu was moved by the heart-rending scene as several of Awk's group embraced the two men, and there was a long moment of shared anguish.

Awk made a noise like clearing his throat, and the men returned to the task at hand. From a large diagram in the dirt, there was a long exchange of information which involved a great deal of pointing and discussion. During the discussion, one of Da's men motioned at Moctu, scowling and grunting in surprise—and perhaps disgust—that he was among the hunters. Awk gave a sharp response and the man's attitude changed abruptly.

From what Moctu could gather, the kroag-kroag, the mammoths, had been spotted to the north making their annual migration southward as winter set in, from the high steppes and valleys to the lower, warmer valleys in the south. There was at least one hand of the beasts, and Da's other men and women were positioned to try to direct them down the west side of the valley toward Awk's group. As Moctu wondered how mere people could *direct* the huge animals, he heard Awk use the Krog word for fire as he pointed to the bundles of sticks and all became clear.

The men seemed to understand the plan and their duties. Several picked up bundles of the dry sticks and left, moving downhill, evidently to assume their agreed-upon positions. Moctu moved closer to Awk, who was now by himself, and in labored sign language, Moctu took the opportunity to ask him what the series of bent lines on the diagram represented.

Awk moved a flat hand, palm down, horizontally in front of him several times and then turned it sharply vertical and plunged it downward.

"Ah, cliffs," Moctu murmured. "They're going to try to run the beasts off some cliffs. That's what the *killing place* is." As Awk stood and motioned for him to follow, Moctu modified his earlier comment. "Hmm, *they're* not going to run them off the cliffs. *We're* going to do it."

Twilight set in, and a light snow began to fall. The air grew so cold that it hurt Moctu's throat to breathe through his mouth. While they hiked, the freezing temperature seemed tolerable, even pleasant. Much colder now, it felt as if death were caressing his face, yearning to drag him to darkness. Although Awk had large icicles hanging from his red beard, he didn't seem as troubled by the frigid temperatures. As they got halfway down the hill, Moctu saw the gleams of two small blazes ignite almost in unison in the gray light some distance to the north.

They were driving them, and Moctu's heart beat faster. Perhaps they did this in the dim light so the beasts wouldn't see the cliffs. Far ahead, a mammoth trumpeted, and he could hear shouting and the gleams of firelights waving and moving in the dusk. As he and Awk reached a lower elevation, he saw the cliff. It wasn't really a cliff, but rather a steep embankment off an alluvial terrace that ran along the hill, with rock walls and forest on one side and the steep slope on the other. A short stone's throw south of them, the terrace narrowed and had been blocked completely by high piles of brush and limbs, obviously placed there earlier by the Krog hunters. Awk pointed to the barrier and then to himself and Moctu and indicated that he and Moctu were the ones to drive the beasts over the embankment.

Oh, Spirits. Spirits be with me! Moctu thought in near panic.

Awk saw his trepidation and clapped him heartily on the back, smiling, and, Moctu could swear, laughing.

Awk knelt and immediately set to making fire from his

spindle and flat board. As Moctu nervously waited, he examined the drop-off and could make out that, although it was steep and as high as six or seven tall men in most places, there were scrub oaks and small pines growing intermittently on it. The one gentler slope he saw in front of them had also been barricaded with high piles of brush, tree branches and thorn bushes.

Moctu shivered as he waited for the fire and the mammoths. He didn't think he'd ever been this cold before.

Was it cold or fear? Both, he decided—a lot of both. His feet felt like blocks of ice and he could barely move his fingers. Earlier he thought with his heavy furs and spear, he had everything he needed to escape to Etseh. Now, he realized that without fire, no one could survive a night of such cold.

Then Moctu felt it. The ground was moving, it was rumbling! It had to be the beasts. Shouts went up from men in some of the closer positions and new torches blazed. The thundering rumble increased, and in the murky twilight, he could sense Awk's tension. The end of Awk's spindle glowed and he blew on it into some shredded bark. A tiny fire blazed and Awk quickly built it into a small but stable fire. He stuck two small bundles of sticks into the blaze and when they ignited, he handed one to Moctu.

The ground vibrations got stronger and Moctu felt a mix of intense fear and exhilaration. A mammoth trumpeted loudly not far away and Awk positioned himself and Moctu near the forested hill, motioning that they would charge out at the beasts with their torches and try to maneuver them over the edge. Moctu's bundle of blazing sticks gave off tiny shooting embers as his hand shook uncontrollably.

Chapter Sixty-Three

Moctu could see the hulking shapes in the near dark, appearing not as animals, but as giant, moving parts of the mountain. He tried to swallow, but his mouth was too dry.

They're huge! Moctu thought, bile rising in his throat. He was awestruck at the size of the first beast that lumbered into view in the gray darkness. It was taller than two hunters at the shoulder and it had curving tusks that extended a similar distance forward. Moctu could also see a smaller but still huge figure behind the first.

Screaming loudly, Awk charged out at the big beast, spear in one hand and waving the torch in the other. Moctu realized this was his cue, but his feet seemed frozen in place. As Awk's torch lit the area near the huge mammoth, Moctu saw that it was a large female, and she appeared more angry than scared. She slowed to an amble and faced off with Awk, who immediately began to back up. Suddenly Moctu's legs began to work and he charged out as Awk had moments before, spear in one hand, torch waving in the other, and screaming as loud as he could. The mammoth had started to come at Awk, and backing up, he stumbled and went down. As Moctu got closer, he threw his spear, hitting the beast in the neck, but doing little damage. The beast was now enraged by this pain-dealing newcomer, and despite Moctu waving his torch frantically, she loped toward him. The mammoth took an angle that precluded Moctu running for the forest, and she picked up speed, wanting to bash him with her huge tusks or trample him underfoot.

Moctu threw his torch at the beast, hoping to slow her, while he turned and ran. His back to the enormous beast, he sprinted as fast as he could in the uneven snow, but by the feel of the ground vibrations and thunderous noise, he could tell that the animal had gained speed and was closing on him.

There was just no place to run. Completely out of options, he gritted his teeth and went over the edge, hoping desperately to grab some brush or a tree on the way down. Moctu hit hard on a thinly snow-covered, gravelly slope and desperately clutched for brush or rocks to slow his descent. He heard a trumpeting shriek as the beast apparently lost her footing at the lip of the embankment as it crumbled under her vast weight. There was a great commotion, then a tremendous whump from just behind and below him that sent a shock wave through the brush and rock to which he tenuously clung. Another immense whump followed from farther down the hill, just as a second bulky figure toppled over the edge, shrieking as it, too, crashed against the hill close behind him.

A chorus of cheers and whistles went up from the men positioned to the north. They couldn't have seen the events in the near blackness, but they'd undoubtedly heard and felt the thunderous crashes that the beasts made as they slammed down the steep slope.

"Moctu," Awk called out plaintively. "Moctu?"

"Yes! I'm all right," Moctu yelled back. "For the moment," he muttered to himself, wondering how securely rooted the small bush was to which he clung, and how far it was back up to the terrace.

"Brud Moctu!" Awk called out relieved, and Moctu wondered what *brud* meant.

He heard heavy footfalls approaching the area above him and knew there were more mammoths.

This isn't over yet, he worried. If any of them slip and come down on me, I'm dead.

But the remaining animals had heard the noises below and sensed the threat from the embankment. They milled around above him, trumpeting in dismay, apparently listening for any sound from the two fallen members of their herd. After a great deal of mournful-sounding and unanswered roaring and trumpeting, the mammoths slowly moved southward, broke through the barrier, and continued on their way.

Cheers broke out again, louder now, as hunters began to congregate above him, most still waving their torches. Two torches flared below him as well, and looking down, he could see the shadowy remains of the two mammoths, now enormous heaps of flesh, bones and tusks.

"Moctu? Brud Moctu," Awk yelled from above as he held a torch over the edge of the embankment, looking for him.

"Here! Awk, over here," he yelled hoarsely. Soon a wiry hunter he didn't know appeared, scrambling above him. In the flickering torchlight, he watched the man clamber down the slope, holding onto a thick spear shaft extended downward by several others above him. The man then stretched the butt end of a second spear shaft toward him, offering Moctu a lifeline back to level ground. After he grabbed it and began scrambling up the slope, the men above him pulled up their spear and both he and the wiry man had little trouble making it to the terrace. As soon as he was up, Awk embraced him in a bear hug.

"Brud Moctu," he roared, jarring Moctu with jubilant back slaps. The entire group was euphoric and celebratory. Moctu was as happy as he'd been in a long time, and he felt a strong bond of brotherhood with these men. He was joyful just to be alive. He felt a tremendous sense of accomplishment, and he could see that the other men did as well. Awk jabbered to Moctu and Da and the other hunters, but the words were said so fast that he understood little of it. Awk's tone, however, was unmistakably happy. One arm still around Moctu's shoulder, he pointed to him several times while he smiled, laughed and talked with the other hunters.

The men had removed the barricade and cleared a pathway on the one gentle slope Moctu had seen earlier, an apron of debris that formed from a broad drainage off the terrace. Torch lights descended the slope, and soon thereafter, a large fire blossomed near the bodies of the mammoths. Awk guided Moctu to the slope and finally gave up his hold on him, as they separately made their way down to the fire and the huge carcasses.

It was the first time Moctu had been warm since they climbed up the other side of the hill earlier that afternoon.

Was that just this afternoon? Moctu thought in amazement. It seemed like moons ago.

The hunters immediately started hacking into the carcass of the smaller mammoth, which turned out to be an adolescent female that had followed her mother off the edge. One hunter had also cut the prized tongue from the big mammoth, and with two bloody hands, he offered it to Moctu. Moctu was stunned by the honor, but he gratefully accepted it and raised it over his head to the cheers of the men.

It weighed as much as one of his legs, Moctu thought in astonishment. With some help, he skewered the tongue lengthwise on a long sharp stick and rested it over the fire on two Y-shaped sticks on the periphery.

The men feasted and celebrated all through the night, and in the morning two men were sent back to recruit help from Uhda for the huge effort of butchering and transporting the meat.

Chapter Sixty-Four

"Hello, sister-friend Nuri," Avi called as she approached Jabil's hearth.

"Hello, Avi!" Nuri said, happy to see her. "Come here and sit. I'm alone right now."

"Ah, you have a nice fire going. That's good. I'm so cold these days."

"Yes, I'll bet you're glad to have Jondu back safely from the southern trip. It's difficult for the hunters in this kind of weather."

"Uh huh, and I've missed his warmth in my sleeping furs," Avi said without thinking.

After a slight, but noticeable and uncomfortable pause in the conversation, Avi said, "Um… are things any better in that regard between you and Jabil?"

"No, he spends almost every night with Leuna. But I'm not really complaining. I can't say I enjoy the time he does spend with me."

"I'm so sorry," Avi said, moving to put her arm on Nuri's shoulder. "I'm sorry he doesn't… um… I'm sorry he mistreats you. And I'm sorry I brought the subject up."

"No, that's all right. It's kind of nice to be able to talk about it. I… I really don't want him to… take me. It's just so… humiliating not to be wanted. Does that make any sense?"

"No, I understand completely. I just wish there was

something I could do to help. I want you to be happy again."

"Thanks, Avi," Nuri said, trying to wipe a small tear away without Avi seeing. "You're a good friend. And it's nice to see you looking so happy and healthy."

"Uh… yes, about that. There's… uh… something I need to tell you, but… um…" Avi faltered.

"You're pregnant! That's it, isn't it?" And seeing the confirmation in Avi's eyes, Nuri continued, "Oh, I'm so happy for you. Really Avi, I am."

"Oh, thank you, Nuri. I've been worried about telling you. But I'm really happy about it, and so is Jondu."

"It's wonderful news, and this is the happiest I've been in days. Congratulations Avi."

"Thanks, Nuri. Well… speaking of Jondu, I'd better get back. Since the hunting was poor to the south, they're planning another trip soon to the north, and he wanted me… uh… to stay close for the next few days."

"I understand. Thanks for the great news and congratulations again Avi. You're going to be a wonderful mother."

After Avi left, Nuri found herself awash with conflicting emotions. Another tear escaped her, and she angrily wiped it away.

"I'm genuinely happy for Avi," she murmured, shaking her head in confusion. "Why do I feel so miserable?"

Chapter Sixty-Five

Krog men handled most of the butchering, skinning, and transport of the meat, fat and skins. Women took charge of drying and storing the meats, and scraping and preparing the hides. Even the mammoths' long hair was saved to weave into twine. It was an enormous undertaking. The meat and fat taken from the two carcasses weighed nearly as much as the combined weight of every person in the Krog tribe. One thing was certain—there would be no starving time this winter.

People feasted while they worked, and the celebration seemed to go on and on. To anyone who would listen, Awk had extolled Moctu's role in the kills, and he was given most of the credit for both. Effie and Rah were pleased and very proud of Moctu. It humbled Moctu to learn from Effie that *brud* meant *brother*. Awk had called him a brother. He searched out Awk to thank him.

"Ah, brud Moctu," Awk said, smiling as he saw Moctu approach.

"Brud Awk," Moctu called. "I come to thank you for the honor. I'm very pleased for you to call me brud Moctu."

Awk nodded, smiling, understanding most of what he said, and pleased by it.

"I have one favor to ask," Moctu went on.

When Awk nodded, he asked, "May I call you *Hawk* instead of *Awk*? Awk means nothing in my language, and Hawk is a fierce bird. It suits you better and sounds almost the same."

"Yaw say me Hawk?" the big red-haired man asked, touching his chest and then moving his hand questioningly through the air like a bird.

"Yes, a very fierce bird that kills other birds and animals," Moctu said, hoping he hadn't insulted the man somehow.

"Yaw brud Moctu, I Hawk," he said thoughtfully.

"Brud Hawk," Moctu added brightly.

"Brud Moctu, I brud *Hawk*," the big man said smiling broadly and pointing proudly to himself. He unexpectedly hugged Moctu.

Although Moctu enjoyed his temporary celebrity status, he chastened himself by remembering his abject, frozen terror when he first saw the mammoth.

I couldn't even move, he reminded himself. Still, he did have fun imagining arriving at Etseh with a huge travois of choice mammoth meat and fat and telling Jabil it was his manhood rite meat offering.

More than half a moon had passed and workers still toiled processing the carcasses. Wolves howled mournfully in the nearby hills every night, smelling the blood and flesh, frustrated by the fires and activity. Mammoth bone and tusk huts had been constructed near the kill site to house the workers. Although it continued to snow every few days, the path from the carcasses to Uhda was marked by a deep, travois-rutted furrow with high snow banks on each side. Not all the meat had been taken back to Uhda. The ice had been broken on a nearby lake and a substantial amount of meat, including both front legs of the larger beast, had been submerged in the frigid water and weighted down with rocks.

Back at Uhda, smoking fires burned all day and night. The rich smell of roasting and smoke-dried mammoth meat pervaded the air. Women worked to cut the meat into thin strips, less than the thickness of a little finger, after first removing all the fat. The strips were then placed on racks over a smoky fire until the dried meat was crisp enough to break in half.

They don't use salt, Moctu thought, surprised. In fact, they don't appear to have any salt.

The nights were extremely cold, but Moctu and Effie kept warm, enjoying sharing furs together. Beginning with that first night when she had crawled in next to him, they had made love every night since. Besides their ardent lovemaking, Effie's bulging stomach seemed to give off as much heat as a campfire, and their night furs never felt cold. On more than one occasion, especially if the hearth fire had gone out, a shivering Rah had joined them in a platonic effort to stay warm.

It was a pleasant time, and although Moctu continued to miss and think of Nuri, Alta, and all his friends and relatives at Etseh, it happened with less frequency. In his mind, Nuri had moved on as mate to Jabil, and Alta was a survivor. She'd make any situation work out well, including having a new mate. Even so, whenever he thought of Jabil, there was an uneasiness, a misgiving he couldn't quite grasp, that tugged at his mind. He knew it had something to do with the murders. After all, it had to be him or the Krog that perpetrated the atrocity, and he couldn't bring himself to believe it was the Krog. He felt as if he were missing something.

He was kept very busy with the butchering and transport of the meat. Then Da and two of the men from his hunting party became ill with fevers and blotchy skin. With Rah's and Effie's help, Moctu treated the men, and although one of them had become extremely sick with high fever and delirium, all survived.

He struggled to teach himself how to make fire with a spindle and board, but with no success. He was embarrassed to ask Hawk for help because he didn't want to admit to him that Nereans didn't know how to do it.

If he could make fire, he could leave for Etseh any time he wanted. But would he? Moctu pondered that again and again. It was a simple question with no easy answer. He didn't think he could leave Effie. At least he didn't want to. Maybe she'd come with him, but he wasn't sure.

It was during one of these fire-making efforts that Effie saw him struggling and she gave him the secret.

"Yaw stick, wood need dry-dry. More dry." She led him to a hearth where appropriate sized sticks and wood planks were kept, along with kindling, out of the weather. "These dry. Put near fire, get dry-dry. Then make fire easy."

Sure enough, using the very dry wood, he was excited to see a wisp of smoke curl up from his spindle, and soon thereafter, he created his first fire. He was as elated as he'd been after the mammoth kill.

"I can make fire," he marveled. "I can really make fire!"

Chapter Sixty-Six

Jondu smiled as he heard the report from one of his scouts about two hands of horses not far to the north. His group had traveled into the lowlands and north toward the foothills of the Alpeetans looking for game to help Etseh through the winter. Rats had ruined some of the Nerean meat stores, and his people would be hungry by spring without at least one more successful hunt. The earlier trip to the south had been a waste of time, so these horses could be a lifesaving source of meat for the tribe.

A light drizzle of icy rain began as Jondu addressed the assembled hunters. "We'll divide into three groups. I'll lead one that will approach the horses from the southwest, and we'll keep as hidden as possible. Palo, you have a team that'll do the same thing from the southeast. The third group is just Nabu and Seetu, and you have probably the hardest job." Looking at Nabu he said, "You two will circle to the north and attempt to drive the horses toward us. There's a slight breeze from the north, which ought to help. Even in this rain it'll carry your scent and scare the horses our way." It was a good plan and there were smiles among the excited men. Jondu was proving to be a good hunt leader. With a little luck they would finally be bringing fresh meat back to Etseh.

Nabu and Seetu did their work well, and Jondu's group managed to wound two horses, which the full hunting party pursued and killed some distance to the west. The exultant men quickly built a fire from the skull ember which Seetu carried, and the butchering and feasting began. In this weather it was unsafe to travel alone, so rather than send two men back to Etseh for help, Jondu told the hunters that they'd do the work themselves.

The men set to work processing the two horses and building travois to transport the meat. Late on the second day of this effort, the weather broke and the dull, gray clouds receded southward, replaced by a clear blue sky with thin, wispy clouds high above. It was still cold, but the afternoon sun shone brightly, adding to the happy mood of the hunters.

Nabu saw it first. Far to the north, at least two columns of light gray smoke trailed up from the white, snow-covered Alpeetans.

"Look! Smoke. Up there. It's the Pale Ones," he said in a loud voice while pointing. As his fellow hunters saw it, they began to point and chatter in a frenzy of hostility and vengefulness, tinged with some apprehension as well.

"We will finally avenge Ordu, Samar, and Tabar," one shouted, and a roar of agreement followed.

"How many of them do you figure are up there?" asked another.

"At least now we know where they are," Jondu exclaimed. "We can figure out which pass and which valleys to use. We'll hit them after the snows melt a little." He immediately dispatched Nabu and Palo to get closer and ascertain the best route to take once the snow wasn't so deep.

"This trip has been guided by the Spirits," he said to the happy and excited men. "We've been doubly blessed. Besides fresh meat and fat, we have important news to take back with us to Etseh."

Chapter Sixty-Seven

The winter moons passed slowly, with much more snow than usual. During the earliest part of winter, snow fell every few days and included several huge accumulations. Gathering firewood became nearly impossible, as many of the drifts were taller than a man. But the Krog, with Moctu's earlier, involuntary help, had stored an immense amount of wood at the north end of Uhda and, with their ample meat stores, they persevered in relative comfort.

For Moctu, any thought of leaving for Etseh had been dashed by the first huge snowfall. He was now convinced that Jabil had indeed killed Ordu, Samar, and Tabar.

It was difficult to accept that he would side with the Krog over a Nerean. But on one hand there was Jabil, and Moctu knew what he was like. On the other was… Effie. And Hawk.

He just knew Effie wouldn't lie, and he'd gotten to know Hawk, and he trusted them both now. If he was right, then Nuri, Alta, and the rest were being led by a murderous, lying madman and they were in danger.

Nuri's probably sharing furs with him, he thought. That lying scum! But if… but when… when I return, can I convince anyone about Jabil? All I have is the word of… the People Eaters. That's what they'll say in Etseh. I can tell them that the Krog use broken spears ceremonially, and that Jabil probably found one and used it to fool us. I didn't see the other end of the broken spear shaft when I was there. Maybe... hmm. He trailed off envisioning the confrontation. No. My story sounds... unlikely, even to me, and pathetically weak. How am I going to get people to believe me? He was again lost in thought.

Everyone knows the bad blood between Jabil and me, and they'll just think I'm trying to undermine him with this... ridiculous story. That I'm trying to become leader myself.

He shook his head. If I show them I can make fire from sticks... how could that help? Maybe some might think I have the power of the Spirits, and the Spirits rarely lie. He shrugged, giving up on that idea.

And what if I'm wrong? Could I be wrong? Could Effie, or at least Hawk, have done this and be lying to me? No, they didn't do it. Why am I so sure of that? There's something, something I'm missing.

Rah came into the hearth carrying some dried mammoth meat. She watched him for a moment as he remained lost in thought, muttering to himself.

"Yaw no happy?" she said, showing off her improving Nerean speaking skills.

Moctu's Krog had similarly improved, and he answered her in Krog, saying he was fine, just thinking.

"Yaw Krog good," she said smiling, and went about her stew-making activities.

"Where's Effie?" he asked.

"Make basket. Get ready for baby."

Moctu smiled, thinking of Effie's round belly and his coming baby. He'd convinced himself that the baby was his. He felt real affection for Effie, and with her only other partner, Sag, dead, he knew he'd care for her and the baby even if it turned out to be Sag's.

Although he hoped the baby would be a boy, he didn't care about the sex that much. He just wanted the baby to have Effie's strikingly blue eyes, which he found mesmerizing.

And he hoped it would be an easy birth.

He wondered if they did Odel-emits, and an involuntary shiver coursed through him at the memory of the penile stitching. He hoped it wouldn't come to that.

Moctu went out to look for Effie and get away from the smoky air in the hearth. Hawk, Da and some other Krog men were gaming and betting, seeing who could throw a round stone closest to the center of a circle drawn in the dirt. Moctu was still sore from yesterday, when they had wrestling matches. Hawk had encouraged him to join in, and Moctu initially declined, thinking the brutes would kill him, even if unintentionally. After some cajoling, however, he participated, and had enjoyed it and learned a lot of moves. He could tell that the Krog men held back and didn't use their full strength, but even so, they always won.

Chapter Sixty-Eight

It was another cold, gray evening, made miserable by a freezing rain that had kept people hearth-bound once again, this time for three days. The long winter brought cramped confinement with increased hostilities and more arguments. Even Nindai's flute playing did little to calm the cooped up, irascible tribe.

Just beyond Jabil's hearth entrance, water dripped steadily from an icicle at the top of the overhang, plunking every few moments into a small pool lined with orange lichen. Leuna was in labor in the Red Hearth, and Nuri worried about her as she added dried rhino meat to the dinner stew. She looked at Jabil as he tied a shaft point in place with mouse gut.

"When the baby comes, I can move to that corner," she said pointing, "so that Leuna is closer to the swaddling skins and dried moss for the baby."

"I don't need your advice," Jabil said, not even looking at her.

"I was just…" Nuri started.

"I don't care what you think," Jabil interrupted her. "I need you for two things, only one of which you do adequately. And that's the cooking."

Stunned and outraged, Nuri said, "Well, we can change that." And she spit into the stew.

Jabil lunged at her, slapping her hard against the cheek.

As she tried to claw at him, he grabbed her hair and forced her to the ground. Still holding her hair, he kicked her midsection, causing her to collapse to the ground, gasping for air. Aroused now by the power he felt, Jabil roughly stripped her clothes off, then his own. His hand to her throat, he took her brutally, savagely enjoying her sobs as she quit fighting him.

He climaxed quickly, withdrew, and looked at her for a long moment. "I'm tired of your insolence," he said scowling. "If you ever dishonor me again, I'll... I'll make you a Rejected Woman, I promise you that." His teeth clenched, he continued. "Then, after all the men in the tribe get finished using you, you'll die of starvation in the winter." He got up, quickly dressed, and left.

Nuri lay where she was, angry and completely humiliated, trying to quell her sobs and regain her composure. She didn't believe that Jabil could alienate her extended family from her, but his Rejected Woman threat still chilled her to the bone.

"Spirits, why do you torment me with this man?" A sob escaped her despite her effort at control. "Please give me guidance and wisdom. Please give me hope."

* * * *

The weather cleared overnight, and the bright morning sun and indigo sky seemed to lift the tribe's mood which was further swelled by the sight of three heavily laden travois of fresh horse meat. Jondu's group had followed the edge of the storm southward and arrived in the dark with their huge prize. Women were already busy unloading the meat, roasting some, and setting up drying racks for the rest.

Near midday, a weary Jelli came out of the Red Hearth clutching a bawling baby boy with one arm and supporting Leuna with the other. The healer helped the dazed-looking new mother gingerly walk to Jabil's hearth, and guided her to the sleeping furs. She could tell the baby needed to nurse, so she placed him close to Leuna and encouraged his efforts to clamp onto her nipple. Leuna's swollen breasts indicated that her milk had come in, and with Jelli's expert assistance, the boy was soon sucking happily.

Nuri had left earlier with other women to brave the shin-deep ice and snow to gather firewood. In the spring, men had ringed many of the nearest trees in the west woods by chopping completely through the bark all around the base of them. Now these trees were all dead, and although the women seldom attempted to fell any of the trees, they could pull the heavy lower limbs off.

Jabil entered the hearth soon after Leuna had suckled the baby. Jelli finished stoking the fire and left after nodding wearily to Jabil. Leuna smiled up drowsily at him, happy, but still exhausted from a lengthy labor.

"Well, what do you think?" she asked, her speech slow but sounding deeply contented.

"A good-looking, healthy son," Jabil said, as he studied the boy's features closely. The head was cone-shaped from the birthing process, but he knew that was temporary.

It was definitely not Samar's nose. The baby had Jabil's nose and chin.

"He's wonderful," Jabil said heartily, and Leuna smiled again, her eyes closing halfway. Nursing the baby had relaxed her, and all she wanted to do now was sleep.

"I think we'll call him *Itzal*, since he was conceived in the shadows," Jabil said to the sleeping Leuna.

"Jabil! Leuna!" Jondu called from some distance away. Jabil went to the hearth entrance and met him, speaking softly.

"They're both asleep. But everyone is healthy and happy."

"That's great news," Jondu said slapping Jabil's shoulder. "How do you feel about your first child being Samar's?"

he asked in a lower voice.

"It's an honor," Jabil replied convincingly, suppressing a smile. "You got back late last night. Sorry not to meet you but, I was... um... occupied with other matters. But I hear you had a successful trip, praise the Spirits. Two horses. That'll feed the tribe through the rest of the winter. You're a hero, Jondu. Plus, I hear that there's other news, something the men were secretive about. They said you wanted to tell me?"

"Yes, that's what I'm here for, besides congratulating you and Leuna on your son. I have great news, important news. I know where the Pale Ones are. We've located their camp."

Jabil was quiet for a long time and Jondu worried he was about to have another episode. But then Jabil began to fire questions.

"Where is it? How close are they? How many of them are there?"

"We don't know too much yet because the snows are really heavy in that area and we weren't able to get close," Jondu replied. "But there was smoke from several fires, big fires. When the snows melt in the spring, I'll take a war party and we'll scout them. If there aren't too many of them, we'll attack. That is, if you agree."

"Yes, I agree. I definitely agree," said Jabil.

Chapter Sixty-Nine

It had been sunny for four days in a row and the snow was melting fast. The creeks had risen and were flowing strongly. In most areas, there was no snow left on the trees. Even though the air was still crisp, many Krog could be found enjoying the sunshine, having discarded their clothing from the waist up.

Effie wasn't enjoying the few remaining days before her baby came. Her belly seemed huge and she suffered from its discomfort, as well as from leg cramps and early contractions. Moctu and Rah often took turns massaging Effie's legs, trying to ease some of the cramping.

Hawk and Moctu sometimes spent whole days together, teaching one another the secrets of rock knapping and fire building, among many other things. Moctu had developed a respect and fondness for the burly, powerful man and Hawk, likewise, clearly respected Moctu, typically referring to him as brud Moctu. Moctu had developed a reasonable fluency in Krog, and surprisingly, Hawk had made the effort to learn rudimentary Nerean.

One of Hawk's two mates, Lok, a short but sturdy blond, had recently given birth to her first child, a son. She spent a lot of time talking and commiserating with Effie.

"What yaw do, Ef baby look Sag?" Hawk had asked him recently.

"Effie baby, my baby," Moctu said in Krog, hitting his chest, but his answer left Hawk wondering if he meant he was sure it was his baby or that it would be his baby even if it looked like Sag.

"Yaw go Etseh, stay Uhda?"

"I need to go back to Etseh soon. Bad man leader. Dangerous for my people. Dangerous for Krog. Need kill." Moctu had only recently realized that if he could prove Jabil killed his father, or get him to admit it, then he would kill him. He'd kill him without reservation. It was only the ambiguity of who murdered his father that had forestalled that decision. But now he was convinced, he knew it had been Jabil. He just couldn't prove it.

"Nereans think Krog kill our people. Very angry. Want to kill all Krog. I used to feel that way too," Moctu admitted.

Hawk nodded his head in understanding. "Want Hawk help, kill bad man?"

"Thank you," Moctu said, closing his eyes briefly and lowering his head. "But no. I think they'd kill us both if you're with me."

"Yaw go, Ef go?"

Moctu had given the subject a lot of thought. "We'll see," he said. "Effie decide. Dangerous, but she's my mate and I want her with me."

"She go," Hawk predicted, nodding. "Yaw go, Ef go."

That night in the furs, Effie said she was feeling better than usual. Moctu rubbed her legs briefly before settling back to sleep. Moctu hadn't discussed the trip back to Etseh, because Effie had enough to worry about right now. They could discuss all that after the baby came.

Moctu had fitful dreams of Tabar and himself, surrounded by wolves. Tabar's spear had been broken during the mammoth kill, and Moctu had yet to fix it. In his dream, both he and Tabar were worried that the wolves were getting closer and Tabar's spear was broken.

Moctu sat up in the furs.

"That's it. That's it!" he said loudly, but Rah and Effie only stirred.

"The broken spear! Jabil said that the red-haired beast had broken Ordu's spear in half... but I've seen it. It's whole. And what else did he say? The spear point broke as it hit a boulder. But the point's whole. And no one makes points like that. That's Samar's work!"

It seemed too good to be true. "Am I dreaming this? No. And that's really what Jabil said, and he said it several times. He lied. That scum lied to us all! And if he lied about that, he lied about everything. He killed my father. And Ordu. And Samar. I'll kill that piece of hyena dung!" Moctu had a sudden terror that he'd forget all this by the morning.

"Effie, Effie! I need you to wake up. I'm sorry... I'm sorry, but please, I need you to wake up."

"Wha?" Effie said groggily.

"Effie, I have proof that Jabil killed the Nereans, and not the Pale Ones... the Krog. It wasn't the Krog. I can prove it!"

"Um... that good," Effie said, still only half awake. "What proof?"

"Ordu's spear! It's not broken. It's there! It's... there. It's... fine. We can prove that Jabil was lying. He said a Pale One... a Krog broke the spear," Moctu gushed in excitement.

"That good," Effie said. "Krog no kill Nereans. Now sleep."

"I'm worried this is a dream or that I'll forget this by morning," said Moctu agitatedly. "Will you make sure I remember this in the morning?"

"Oh, I 'member this all right," Effie said grumpily.

Chapter Seventy

At first light, Moctu was up and looking at the cache of weapons and gear that the Krog had uncovered after Jabil hid them. "There it is," Moctu said happily as he carefully extracted Ordu's spear from the pile. A sudden worry that the fine spear point would break swept over him. He couldn't let anything happen to this spear. He'd take it back to the hearth and wrap it in skins.

When he got back to the hearth with the spear, Effie was awake.

"So yaw 'member," she said, with only a slight tinge of grumpiness.

"Yes, sorry about that. I was just… just so excited. This is the spear. Jabil said it was broken in the fight, but apparently there wasn't any fight. This is my proof," he said hoisting the spear slightly higher in the air.

"That good," Effie said. And then she let out a soft moan as another contraction took her.

"Pains coming faster," Rah said in Krog. "Baby soon."

"The baby's coming now?" Moctu said in consternation.

Rah nodded and Effie gasped again.

"Yaw go now," Rah said, directing Moctu to the hearth entrance. "Ef have baby soon. Only us here—no man."

No Red Hearth, Moctu realized. They're going to have the baby right here.

"Effie… she'll be all ri—"

"Yaw go now," Rah interrupted with a sterner tone. "I get yaw if Ef need."

Moctu did as he was told, even as visions of bloodletting resurfaced. But Effie's labor progressed quickly, and by late afternoon, she was suckling her new baby daughter. A distinctly darker than usual daughter for a Krog mother.

"My daughter," Moctu whispered to himself, dumbstruck with happiness and pride. He yearned to tell his mother, Palo, and all the other Nereans about his daughter and to show her to them. "She's such a beauty," he thought with deep satisfaction.

His happiness was short-lived. As he was admiring his baby girl, an alert was raised. Da's mate Zat was missing after working the south woods gathering firewood. Tracks had been found in the vicinity—huge tracks, tracks of a cat, probably a hiss-gaw. Moctu volunteered to join a search party to help look for her and kill the beast if it came to that.

He wasn't sure how helpful a spear would be against a hiss-gaw, and he shuddered as memories of his desperate encounter with the hiss-gaw resurfaced. Not wanting to risk damage to Ordu's spear, he went to the cache and retrieved Samar's spear, which was, if anything, of even finer quality.

He met a grim-faced Da with Hawk and one other man at the path leading to the south woods. Calling Zat's name, they entered the woods and began looking for tracks, hers and the cat's. Hawk was the first to find her tracks, in the mud near a creek that she'd jumped across. The men trailed the vestige of her imprint on the land and soon found a troubling, new set of tracks, a huge hiss-gaw that had begun to follow her. Crossing another small creek, the men rounded a bend in the trail, and Da let out a cry of dismay. There, at the side of the trail, was Zat's wood-gathering skin. Her tracks showed a longer stride, indicating she'd begun running. Not far ahead, at a tree with a projecting lower limb, they found bloodstains on the ground and deep scratch marks in the bark on the trunk and lower limb.

She'd climbed the tree to try to escape. Unbidden, terrifying memories flooded back to Moctu. He gripped his spear tighter and scanned the woods carefully. Moctu knew the poor woman hadn't stood a chance against the hiss-gaw.

Da, although deeply distressed, maintained his discipline and, spear at the ready, he scoured the area for further signs of his mate. It wasn't long before he found bloody drag marks and a shredded scrap of her tunic. On seeing the scrap of leather, his self-control broke down and he let out a soul-piercing moan of grief. Moctu and Hawk went to him and tried to comfort him, but both were convinced that his two small children were now motherless. After some time, Da indicated that he wanted to continue, and the four men edged along the gruesome trail and to the boundary of a dense thicket of small conifers, scrub oak, and blackthorn. The Krog's long spears would be useless in the confines of the underbrush, so the men stopped to consider the situation.

Moctu's Nerean spear was shorter, and although it wouldn't be much more effective in the thicket, he volunteered to go in a short way. Swallowing hard, with his spear pointing ahead, Moctu bent low and entered the narrow parting in the brush. His senses screamed for him to stop and go back, but he slowly moved through the hole in the congested thicket. Although he was less than three spear lengths from the other men, he could no more see them than if they'd been back at Uhda. Moctu's heart beat faster as he followed a turn in the crude path, and then another.

It was there he saw her. Or what was left of her. Her face was chewed off, as was her whole left midsection. Vomit rose in his throat, but he managed to keep it down. The narrow parting in the thicket widened, and Zat's body was in the middle of the beaten down brush. Moctu apprehensively swung his spear from side to side for a moment, before becoming convinced the beast wasn't present.

"Oh Spirits! She's here Da, but she's… dead," Moctu called back.

Da had already been sure she was dead, so he was quiet at the news.

Moctu lay his spear lengthwise on the body and grabbing Zat under her arms, with great difficulty he dragged her out to where the men stood. When Moctu emerged with the body, the fierce-looking Da lost his composure, doubled over with grief and nausea and vomited violently.

A simple burial was conducted the next day at Uhda, the seventh in less than four moons.

Chapter Seventy-One

Nuri smiled as she finished the baby backpack she'd made for Avi. It was made of soft skins with holes for the baby's legs and straps to go over Avi's arms. It was easy to put on and take off, and Nuri was sure that Avi would find it useful.

"Hello, Nuri," Avi called from outside.

"Hello, Avi, come in! This is good timing. I have something for you."

Avi entered the hearth and Nuri was shocked at how big she was. "Little" Avi looked about twice her normal size, and Nuri wondered if she were carrying twins.

"You're so big!" Nuri said with a broad smile. "Has Jelli listened to see if there are a handful of heartbeats in there?" Although said in jest, this was a compliment, as multiple births weren't uncommon among the Nereans, and they were considered harbingers of good fortune.

"I feel like I'll provide Jondu with a litter of babies!" Avi said, sitting awkwardly on a boulder near the hearth.

"I may have to alter this for more leg holes," Nuri said chuckling and giving the carrying skin to Avi. "It's for carrying your son or daughter—just one of them—around. I'm pretty sure it'll fit you well."

"Oh, Nuri. It's wonderful. You're so thoughtful. Thanks so much. You're always so sweet to me." Avi paused and then said, "Are things any better for you? Your black eye is gone."

"Well, he hasn't hit me anymore lately, so that's good. And he hasn't made me a Rejected Woman yet as he threatened."

"That will never happen," Avi said. "There are too many people in this tribe that love you and would care for you."

"Thanks, Avi. I think you're right, but it's nice to hear that anyway. Who would have thought my life would come to this?"

"You deserve better—so much better. Even Jondu was upset by this last… fight, and what Jabil did. And Mother Alta. Alfer beat her again too. The son isn't much different than the father, huh? Is there anything I can do for you Nuri?"

"No, you've got enough on your mind right now. And you've helped just by stopping by and talking."

* * * *

Four hearths away, Jabil approached Jondu. "Hello, Jondu. How are your plans coming?"

"Well, Jelli says the signs are mixed and confusing, but she sees some misfortune," Jondu replied. "We wanted to leave tomorrow, but it may be good to wait."

"The longer you wait, the more you miss the opportunity for surprise," said Jabil.

"Yes, I know… and the men want to leave now. They don't want to wait."

"Then go," Jabil advised. "If the signs turn worse, I'll send a messenger to you."

"So, you still don't want to come, Jabil?" Jondu said, his voice neutral.

"I've been having too many attacks, too many episodes," Jabil responded, honestly wishing he could go, and feeling upset and diminished as a near-invalid. "I think I might be a burden. I really do wish I could go. I miss being out there hunting and exploring with you, Jondu."

"Yes, we've had some great times through the years," Jondu said, smiling and putting his hand on Jabil's shoulder. "Maybe when we get past all this, we can get back to hunting and exploring together again."

"That sounds good," Jabil replied. "And I can go on this trip if you really need me."

"You're needed more here at Etseh," Jondu said politely, but both men knew it was a lie.

Chapter Seventy-Two

"She's beautiful, Effie," Moctu said sitting beside his mate as she lay in the furs, nursing their baby girl.

Effie nodded and smiled contentedly. The baby was indeed attractive, with deep blue eyes, light hair, and healthy-looking, light olive skin.

"What we name her?" she asked, staring into the child's sweet face as if looking for the answer.

"I've been thinking about that a lot," said Moctu. "She's such a beautiful mix of both of us. How about Elka? It means *unite* in Nerean."

"What means *unite*?" Effie asked.

"It means mix together, or from two, make one," Moctu answered.

"Mmm. I like name," Effie said, smiling at her daughter. "How yaw like Elka?" she asked the baby. Looking at Moctu, she said, "I like name Elka. What her totem?"

"We'll have to decide that later," said Moctu. "I know that some will say she's of the saber-tooth totem because of the recent events, but I don't want that for my daughter. The saber-tooth is a man's totem, a powerful man, and, also, it would have too much sadness attached."

"No saber-tooth totem," Effie agreed. "Maybe Kroag… mammoth?"

"Maybe," said Moctu. "We can decide that later. Listen,

I… need to talk with you about… um… something else. Effie, I have to go to Etseh. It could be dangerous and I don't know if you'll want to come. Travel can be tough on a mother and new baby, but I want you to know that you're my mate and I want you along if you want to come."

"I go," Effie said simply. "Elka, I go. Be fine. Where yaw go, I go. Yaw people, my people."

"I'm looking forward to showing you two to Alta and… all my friends." He'd almost said, "and Nuri and all my friends," but he didn't know how Nuri would take to Effie and Elka. And Moctu planned to kill the man who was probably her mate now.

"Then as long as the weather holds," Moctu said with both excitement and trepidation, "we'll leave at dawn, the day after tomorrow. We'll take it nice and slow."

The next day, as they made their plans and preparations for departure, word got out and Hawk, Da and Rah all offered to come along for part or all the trip. Da wanted to show his appreciation for Moctu's help in locating his mate's body, and both he and Hawk thought traveling in a group would be safer with the hiss-gaw stalking the route. Both insisted on seeing them at least to the pass at the head of the lowlands. Thinking about the hiss-gaw and the safety of Effie and Elka, Moctu readily agreed. He knew Rah wanted to go for other reasons. She was going to miss her daughter and granddaughter.

"But Rah, you're needed so much in Uhda," Moctu said. "I know you'll miss Effie and Elka. They'll miss… we'll all miss you too. But I'll do my best to bring them back to visit you. Often."

"Is right Ef go with you," Rah said, her eyes welling with tears. She hugged Moctu. "Keep safe. Ef, Elka, you."

All night long, Moctu's mind raced with thoughts and plans. He would take both Ordu's and Samar's spears, as well as his atlatl and Tabar's shafts. He'd keep Ordu's spear carefully wrapped in skins so that it didn't get damaged. It had to be in perfect shape when he got to Etseh. He needed to take his fire-starting equipment and keep it dry as they crossed the streams, which would be difficult since they were running fast and high with snowmelt. They'd have to take it slow for Effie's sake. They would need food for four adults to the pass and for two thereafter. Hawk and Da would double back to Uhda after they got safely to the pass. When he, Effie and Elka got near Etseh… what then?

The darkness was just beginning to recede when he arose, stoked the fire, and left the hearth to check the weather. The sun had yet to crest the eastern mountains, but the still beauty of the dawn was like a tonic to Moctu's agitation.

It was midmorning before the group got off and only after a long, tearful embrace from Rah. Even though they rested frequently, they made good time, enjoying seeing all the things that the Earth Mother now unveiled, after having buried the land in white for several moons. The morning was cool, but not uncomfortably so, and much of the snow had melted, allowing them to find paths in most places, where they could bypass any deep snow. The sterile smell of winter air had been replaced by a sweet-smelling herbal scent as buds sprang out on trees and fern fronds broke through mossy banks. Everywhere it seemed that trees and shrubs were pushing out their buds, vying for the best sunlight. The whole group, including Elka, enjoyed the day, the fresh air, beautiful scenery, and companionship.

The men continually scrutinized the ground for tracks, hoping not to see fresh hiss-gaw prints. With any luck, the beast had moved on. Happily, they saw none of his tracks, and that evening, they camped on a treeless knoll where they built a small fire. Da would take the first watch, then Moctu, then Hawk. Although they heard wolf howls, none came close, and they passed a peaceful night.

At dawn they were off again, chewing on dried mammoth strips while they walked. The morning was much cooler than the day before, and all of them kept fully cloaked in furs, even on the uphill stretches. It was midday when Hawk saw it, a huge print in a muddy part of the path. It was a hiss-gaw print, and it was fresh. Moctu was immediately thankful to have Hawk and Da along. At the rate they were going, it was two more days to the pass, and he was grateful to have the two powerful men with spears beside him.

All three men were deeply unsettled by the tracks, and with their spears raised, they scanned the nearby brush carefully. Moctu made his atlatl and shafts more readily available. Throughout the day, as the group continued their trek, they saw several more sets of hiss-gaw tracks, all fresh, and all traveling the same direction as they were.

Chapter Seventy-Three

"There's the pass we take to get to where the smoke was coming from," Nabu said to Jondu as he pointed toward the valley between two large foothills that each led upward to snow-covered mountains. "I don't see any smoke now, but I'll bet they're still there."

"We can get to the pass by this evening if we push," Jondu said, turning to the other men in the group. Somewhat surprisingly, Alfer had come along, as well as Seetu, Sokum, and Palo. All had their faces and arms painted in red and black Spirit paint, and all were nervous yet excited and full of bloodlust to avenge Ordu, Samar, and Tabar.

"I know you all feel as I do," Jondu said, looking fierce with his eye sockets darkened and red zigzag lightning bolts on his cheeks and forearms. "We're here for revenge. Three of the best men in our tribe were brutally struck down by these savages… these People Eaters. Ordu. Samar. Tabar. All gone now, because of these… filthy hyenas. Each of us can think back to times when those men touched our lives. But it's not just about revenge. The Pale Ones intrude on our hunting grounds and raise the chances of starving times for us and our families. We live each day having to worry whether our mates and children are safe from them. Or will they be stolen away to be eaten? Now is our chance to strike back at them for Ordu, Samar, and Tabar, to repay our debt to those great men, yes. But it's also our chance to drive these vile creatures away forever and make our families safe again."

The men roared their approval and Jondu smiled. "Then let's go hit these beasts!" he shouted, and the men cheered again.

They walked at a fast pace, each of the men periodically checking and rechecking their spear points, atlatls, and shafts to ensure they were ready. In the early afternoon, the men stopped for a rest, and looking to the west, Jondu saw a red hawk being chased and badgered by five crows.

He rubbed his chin. It was probably an omen, but was it a good omen or a bad one? Nuri's totem was the red hawk. He considered that for a while, but his thoughts soon came back to the matters at hand.

By evening, they were inside the pass, on the eastern hillside where it met a flat valley with lakes scattered along the length of it, and thick, low brush and marshes in between.

"There'll be no fire tonight," Jondu instructed, "or any night while we're in this area, unless we can find sites where boulders or trees completely block the light and disguise the smoke. We can't risk being discovered by the People Eaters. Surprise is one of our best weapons."

Seetu, who carried the skull ember, located a good site a short way up the hill, where a semi-circle of tall boulders surrounded by trees allowed them a small fire without fear of detection. The men had agreed to keep their voices to whispers, but few spoke at all, as they chewed on dried horse meat, rechecked their gear, and envisioned their planned assault.

Jondu took first watch and was awakening Alfer to take the second when a piercing roar cut the night, causing several of the sleeping men to jump to their feet, spears at the ready.

"What was that?" Seetu asked in a high state of anxiety.

"That, Seetu, was a saber-tooth, and he sounds angry," Alfer said, enjoying the distress of the younger men, but furiously rubbing his auroch totem, a piece of horn that he wore around his neck.

"It… it came from the north," said Palo. "How close do you think it is?" He tried to sound casual, but he was nervous too.

"Not that close," Alfer said. "But probably within a day's trek in this country."

"Well, that's something else we'll need to be careful about," said Jondu. "But for now, let's try to get some sleep."

Chapter Seventy-Four

Moctu, Da, and Hawk were all up, each with their spears pointed to the south, the direction from which the roar had come. Effie too was alert, but the baby slept on, undisturbed by the threat.

"That was close," Moctu said more to himself than the others. Anxiety flooded through him as he recalled his battle with the monstrous cat. Seeing the other men with their spears ready, he went to the fire and added wood, building it to what he thought was a level that would discourage the hiss-gaw from approaching.

"Thank you for coming with us," Moctu said in a low voice to the two men. He knew Hawk would understand the words and Da would understand the tone of appreciation. They heard no more roars, but they decided that two would stand guard from now on. Even so, no one got much sleep for the rest of the night.

When the cold, windy morning arrived, they were all huddled close to the fire, with only Elka sleeping. Moving out cautiously to the south, they soon came upon tracks of the hiss-gaw. He'd come within several stone throws of their camp. His tracks indicated he'd circled the camp at least twice.

Awk and Da exchanged Krog words and signs that Moctu didn't catch.

"Da say, go fast, make lowlands dark time," Hawk interpreted.

"Sounds like a good plan to me," Moctu agreed. The thought of the hiss-gaw attacking Effie or Elka was almost too much for him to bear. The sooner this was over the better.

They moved out at a fast pace, focused on the ground, looking for tracks, and on the nearby brush, vigilant for a charging saber-tooth. The cold wind bit into them, and they pulled their furs tighter around their heads and shoulders. They traveled east of the lakes and marshes, following the same route by which Moctu had nearly escaped many moons before.

Moctu's mind drifted back to that time. He'd been so desperate to escape from the Krog and get back to Etseh, to his relatives, friends, and... to Nuri. It was amazing to him how the Spirits toyed with him, how they'd turned his life up-side down, and taken him from bleak despair to... deep happiness. He'd ended up with a truly wonderful mate and she'd given him the most beautiful daughter in the world. And he'd learned how to make fire! That thought still sometimes made him think he was dreaming.

He still missed Nuri, but she was Jabil's now, no doubt had been for a long time, and she'd probably hate him once he'd done what he had to do—kill her mate.

They were moving along a narrow path in the low brush near the boulder-strewn eastern hillside when Hawk stopped the group with a loudly whispered, "Wait!"

"Hear sound," he continued, and they all listened intently, alert for any sound of the cat.

Moctu fitted a shaft on his atlatl, put one in his teeth and made another ready in his spear hand. He edged forward, aware that Hawk eyed his atlatl activities with great curiosity. His focus was on a tall thicket of brush that ran along the west side of the path, between it and a large lake. Moctu was examining a large parting in the brush when, from the other direction, a shaft took him in the left shoulder. It spun him around, and he went to one knee, glimpsing two more shafts hit, one just in front of him, and another at the ground by Hawk's feet.

In an instant, Moctu had registered movement from the rocky hillside and thrown a shaft. Instinctively, he rapidly launched two more before the pain from the protruding shaft in his shoulder registered, and his mind screamed, Effie! Elka! Have to get them to safety!

He scrambled back as more shafts rained down, one taking Da in the leg. Effie was on her knees near the edge of the brush, protecting Elka with her body. As he got to her, she let out a grunt of pain as a shaft took her in the side. Moctu let out a primal scream of rage and distress, grabbing both Effie and Elka and pulling them back just as another shaft landed where they'd been. Stumbling backward, with Hawk and Da following, the group reached a low hedge that offered a modicum of cover.

A shaft protruded from Effie's left upper rib cage and she was breathing with difficulty.

"Noooooo!" Moctu screamed again in rage and frustration. Looking back, he could see dark shapes retreating southward on the hillside. In an eruption of fury, he ran down the trail in their direction screaming and launching the rest of his shafts up at them.

When he got back, a hobbled Da was holding Elka while Hawk attended to Effie. Moctu knelt by Effie and she looked at him and tried to smile. She coughed trying to say something to him, then coughed again, bringing up blood.

"Don't try to talk Effie, just breathe," Moctu said in a choked voice, a wave of desperation sweeping over him.

But Effie shook her head and in a croaky whisper said, "Take care... Elka."

"Yes, Effie, I'll take care of her. We both will. Effie, please don't leave me!" Moctu was sobbing now, racked with uncontrollable grief.

"Effie, please! Oh Spirits, please! Don't do this. Don't

take her!"

Effie struggled to get air, each breath a wheezing effort.

"Spirits... Spirits, I'll do anything," Moctu pleaded. "Please don't take her!"

Effie coughed violently, more blood seeping from the corner of her mouth. A sigh escaped her and she lay still. Moctu convulsed in an agony of anguish. Hawk's eyes were wet as he knelt by his sobbing friend and patted his back.

Chapter Seventy-Five

"I'm all right," Palo said to Seetu. "How is Jondu?"

Both had been hit by shafts from the Pale Ones, a shocking development. To this point, they'd believed that the creatures didn't have or use atlatls.

"He's bad. Hit in the upper leg," said Seetu. "Shaft's still sticking out. We need to get him back to Etseh, to Jelli."

"But you're all right?" Sokum asked Palo again.

"Yes, the shaft was sticking through my arm, but I broke it off and pulled it out. I have two holes in my arm though," Palo said, almost smiling when Sokum looked ill.

"I didn't think they had atlatls," said Seetu.

"Me neither," said Palo. "And they're pretty good with them! The shaft they hit me with looks like one of Tabar's. If it is, it proves this is the group that killed him, Ordu, and Samar."

"The one in Jondu looks like Tabar's," Seetu said.

"We hit 'em hard, didn't we? We got those hyenas!" Alfer interjected loudly, still coming down from the adrenaline rush. "Killed at least two of the beasts and wounded a bunch more. I'd say we took a big step toward avenging my brother… all our men today."

Despite the wounds to Jondu and Palo, the mood of the group was mostly upbeat. They'd finally retaliated.

"That scream was weird," said Palo.

"Yeah," said Seetu. "Sounded… like it came from the Spirit world. Sounded like… um…"

"Like Moctu?" Palo offered tentatively.

"Yeah!" said Seetu. "That's what I was going to say."

"I heard it too. Made my skin crawl," said Sokum, joining in.

There was a pause in the conversation while they reflected on the matter.

"Do you think they'll get reinforcements and more of the beasts will come after us?" Sokum asked anxiously after some time.

"I would if I were them. Wouldn't you?" Alfer asked. "But it depends how many more of them there are. Plus, they have to get back to their camp. That'll take time."

As he said that, Palo pointed to a column of dense, gray smoke that rose not far from where they'd attacked the People Eaters.

"They're signaling," he said. "We'd better move out for Etseh. Now! Well, as soon as we can build a travois for Jondu."

Jondu moaned in pain. He was conscious but in shock.

"Put some more skins around him. But watch out for the shaft. Don't jar it," Palo said, taking control, since no one else was.

When Jondu was loaded onto the travois, the small group set a fast pace toward Etseh.

Chapter Seventy-Six

A heavy, dark cloud of gloom had descended on Moctu, threatening to shut him down. His actions seemed mechanical, spiritless, and ploddingly slow.

While Hawk built a signal fire, Da and Moctu helped each other extract the shafts from their bodies. Da's wound was less serious. The shaft had gone through the outer, fleshy part of his leg, and they easily broke off the point and pulled it out. The shaft in Moctu's shoulder had hit the top of his collarbone, cracking or breaking it, and then lodged in his shoulder muscle. Working together, the two men were able to remove the shaft, but the process caused a lot of bleeding and immense pain. Grief-stricken, Moctu almost welcomed the pain, as it forced his mind, at least momentarily, away from the ruin of his world.

Hawk got the fire burning strongly and heaped it with green branches full of wet pine needles. When it was giving off massive clouds of thick, gray smoke, he said with a grim face, "Signal fire burn. We go Uhda now. Bad men see fire, maybe come."

Elka had begun crying during the shouts and commotion of the attack, and she hadn't stopped. She cried even louder now, furiously demanding attention. With the shafts extracted, Moctu gingerly picked Elka up and held her tightly to his right side. He murmured to her, trying to calm her, all the while lost in a desolation of thoughts.

The event had happened so fast that Moctu was only now realizing that it was undoubtedly Nereans—his people—who did this. Retrieving the bloody shaft he and Da had pulled from his shoulder, he realized with shock that it was Palo's!

Had they seen him? Or did they think he was Krog… a Pale One? He was furious at the Nereans for their attack and angry at himself, because he, too, had long ago favored an assault on the Pale Ones.

"Jabil," he muttered savagely. "He's the one who provoked this hate." But deep inside, he knew he shared some of the blame.

His emotions moved from anguish to rage and back again. He twice knelt by Effie's body, convinced that he'd wake up from this nightmare and she'd be fine, smiling, laughing and wanting to nurse Elka.

How would they feed Elka? he wondered with a sudden rush of worry. They had to get back to Uhda fast. He couldn't lose Elka too! His despair lifted somewhat as this new purpose supplanted it.

"We need to move fast," he said to Da and Hawk. "We have to get Elka back to Uhda. Some of the women there can wet-nurse her. She'll need feeding soon and…" his voice faltered as he looked down to his dead mate's body. "We'll have to walk all through the night…" his voice trailed off again, thinking of the hiss-gaw. Without a word, he left the two men who were fashioning a travois, and he went to collect some of the Nerean shafts. With his wounded shoulder, it was difficult while holding Elka. Hawk saw what he was doing and came to help.

"Yaw teach Hawk, throw small spear?" he asked.

"Maybe Hawk. Let me think about that," Moctu replied. "Right now, we need to figure how we're going to get to Uhda fast-fast."

"I pull travois," Hawk said. "Yaw, Da walk fast."

"You and Da get started," Moctu said. "I need to give Elka some water. I'll catch up with you."

Moctu took Elka to the edge of the lake and dipped his little finger in the icy water. He touched it to the baby's lips and her crying stopped while she moved her lips to the moisture. He found that if he balled his fist and extended his little finger, he could slowly dribble water into her mouth. This worked briefly before Elka decided she wanted milk and started to cry again.

He caught up with the two men easily. Hawk was slowed by the travois, Da by his leg wound. Moctu's wound pulsed with pain, and he could feel wetness dripping down his chest and side. Elka fell asleep as the men wordlessly made their way, but the silence didn't bring peace, it brought heartache.

At the rate they were going, it would be more than two days back to Uhda, even if they walked through the night. And that was if they didn't get slowed by the hiss-gaw.

He wondered how long babies could go without feeding. He had to move faster.

Elka woke and began crying at dusk. She was angry, and nothing Moctu did helped. Elka wanted her mother's milk. Completely frustrated, Moctu considered leaving the two Krog men behind so that he could move faster. But his shoulder throbbed awfully, night was falling, and there was a hiss-gaw out there somewhere. It was better to stay together, at least for tonight.

After trying to give Elka water at a rest stop, the men resumed their trudge while Elka cried in loud, angry wails. As they walked, Moctu thought forlornly of how the Spirits had once again perversely upended his world.

What was their reason? Why did they do this? Did they enjoy his misery that much? Why did they let him become happy only to overturn his life?

"Spirits, I don't understand your ways," he prayed, softly whispering the words to himself. "If you're testing me, I'm failing. No, I've failed… and this test has… has left the world darker… and uglier. You've taken a really wonderful…" he paused shaking his head. "You've taken her from me, from her family, from her people." He paused again. With his teeth clenched he continued, "I will never understand why you did this. Never. But please, please give us strength to get Elka to safety. She's… she's all that's left of—"

At that moment, a massive roar split the night, electrifying the men, causing Hawk to drop the travois as he fumbled for his spear.

Chapter Seventy-Seven

The three men huddled together in the darkness, their spears pointed outward. The roar had come from nearby to the south.

"Hiss-gaw smell blood," Hawk said. "Hear baby cry. Easy kill."

The men thought about that for a while.

"I don't think we should go any farther tonight in the dark," said Moctu. "Can you build us a fire, Hawk? A big one."

As Hawk worked on a fire, Moctu had a revelation. As bad as things were, they would have been much worse if these two men weren't with him. There was no way he could make a fire with his injured shoulder.

Once Hawk had a fire going, the men could see that they were near a break in the woods, and not much farther ahead was a meadow. They decided to move their fire to the center of the meadow to allow them better visibility and more time to react if the beast got close. They carried several burning branches to the meadow and, near a fallen tree, soon had a blazing fire there, while the first fire gradually died down to embers.

Elka's crying had been replaced by a much softer, but more worrisome, whimpering. She needed water, Moctu knew, but he couldn't risk going to the stream. Between watching for the saber-tooth, stoking the fire, and listening to Elka's distressed whimpering, the men spent a wretched night. At first light, after getting a dribble of water into Elka, the men were off at a fast pace. By midday, the pace of the two Krog men had slowed considerably, and Moctu worriedly examined Elka's declining health. Her skin was gray and she looked exhausted. She wouldn't drink much water.

"I'm going to have to move faster," he said to Hawk and Da. "I'm going to have to go on ahead and get Elka to Uhda sooner than we can get there together. Hawk, can you make a fire so I can take an ember with me? I can't build a fire with this shoulder."

Hawk complied, and Moctu had soon encased a large ember in crumbled chunks of rubbery, dry, rotten wood between two arcuate pieces of moist bark tied with a leather strip. Not nearly as good as a skull, but it would probably work. Taking another close look at Elka made him certain he was doing the right thing. It was her only chance. With Hawk's help, he fashioned a crude sling that would take most of Elka's small weight. It would allow him to move faster and partially free his hand to hold Samar's spear. Ordu's spear, still wrapped in skins, was strapped to his back.

Before leaving with Elka, he patted Da on the shoulder and said, "Good luck."

"Gaw lac," Da tried to say it back to him.

Moctu moved close to Hawk and extended his right arm saying, "Good luck brud Hawk!"

Hawk started to embrace him, then remembered Moctu's shoulder wound. He grabbed Moctu's extended arm, patting his good shoulder and said, "Brud Moctu."

After wishing the men luck, Moctu was off, moving fast despite the throbbing pain in his shoulder and the still-oozing blood. He estimated that he could be at Uhda by late the next day if he walked through the night and maintained his pace. In the late afternoon, he stopped to check his ember and blow it back to life.

After getting Elka to suck a trickle of water from his finger, he was off again, following a trail made muddy by the bright afternoon sun and the melting snow. The mud caked on his foot skins making his feet twice as heavy as usual. If he could just slog through it, with some luck he thought he would have Elka back to Uhda by this time tomorrow. She was pale and sluggish, but she could make it.

His heart sank when he saw the track. It was the hiss-gaw, and it was ahead of them. He was being stalked by a saber-tooth again, and this time he had a baby and a terrible wound. The beast had walked along the trail for some distance, heading north as Moctu was doing. As he cautiously followed the trail, Moctu noticed that the right front paw prints were shallower, and in some cases absent altogether. The cat was limping. It was his beast! He'd heard it grunt in pain as it descended from the tree that night.

"I may be hurt, but so are you," he whispered. "And I may have a baby to worry about, but I've got fire this time. And my weapons."

Chapter Seventy-Eight

The twilight faded to a murky grayness and coming to a broad open space he decided to stop for the night. There were several downed trees that offered a good source of firewood. Considering the risks to Elka, right now the threat of the saber-tooth outweighed that of her dehydration. Using the ember, he soon had a good fire, and he easily gathered a large pile of firewood. He'd have a big fire tonight, really big. He readied his weapons, even unwrapping Ordu's spear, which he'd use only as a last resort. Night fell, and the stars came out in full splendor, adding some light to that of the campfire.

It wasn't long before Moctu heard movement in the brush, and he knew it was the cat. He fitted a shaft onto his atlatl and focused on the sounds. He could tell the beast was circling the camp area moving from left to right. If he could hit it with a shaft, maybe, once again, it would decide he was more trouble than he was worth.

After two complete circles, the beast let out a frustrated roar. It didn't like the fire. The roar woke Elka from a light sleep and she began crying again. Her crying seemed to excite the cat, and Moctu saw it edge closer, still circling, but staying in the deep shadows. The thought of the beast's claws, teeth, and savageness as it tried to kill him on the tree filled Moctu with worry for Elka.

"I have to protect Elka! Spirits, please help me protect

this child. Please."

The creature circled the camp enough that the fire wasn't the deterrent it had been initially. At one point, it was close enough that Moctu could see it limp!

"You still carry the pain from our last meeting, old friend! Come closer and you'll get more," Moctu yelled to the cat. The beast let out a throaty growl and surged closer, feigning a charge. Moctu let loose a shaft but missed. It hit close enough that the creature retreated deeper into the shadows. Moctu listened intently but heard nothing.

Elka's raspy crying had dwindled to whimpering and then no sound came. Moctu worried that she wasn't just sleeping, but that she might be unconscious or dead. He held his ear close to her face and thought he could hear faint breathing. Moctu was emotionally exhausted and physically spent. The blood loss had been substantial, and his whole left side was stained and wet with it. His eyelids felt leaden as he waited to see if the huge cat would return. His eyes had begun to flicker shut when he heard movement again. Instantly alert, he held his atlatl ready and listened intently. Not wanting to diminish his night vision, he added wood to the fire without looking at it.

It was nearly dawn and the cat was circling again, and it was closer. He saw a flash of movement as the beast began a charge or a feint, and he threw a shaft at it. The cat screeched and veered away.

I hit it, he thought with a soaring sense of hope and joy. I hit it!

The saber-tooth growled loudly in frustration and pain as it went back to circling the camp. Moctu knew it was unlikely that he could kill the beast with an atlatl shaft. It would take a perfect strike. Maybe several.

Moctu was almost pleased when Elka began whimpering again. It meant she was still with him, still fighting for her life. Just as he was.

"Come close and I'll sting you again," Moctu screamed, his fury growing. "You're not getting this baby!"

The beast growled from deeper in the shadows. Moments later, it let out a guttural roar from much farther away. It was leaving. Moctu let out a triumphant yell, "Arrrruuuu!" Once again, he'd thwarted the huge cat. Once again, the cat had left injured. He'd saved Elka.

Kneeling to examine her as she softly whimpered, he saw that she was extremely weak. Even in the dim, shifting firelight he could see that her sparkling, deep blue eyes had retracted inward and changed to a dull, sickly gray. Her breathing was shallow, and everything about her looked drawn and dry.

He had to get her water, but more important, he had to get her to Uhda tomorrow or she'd die, he realized, overwrought with worry. She had to have milk. Soon. He readied his equipment to be able to move out at first light. Even though he was worried and exhausted, his deep desolation was gone. The challenge from the saber-tooth, last night's confrontation, and his renewed purpose to save Elka had swept away most of his depression.

At first light, Moctu stoked the fire with wet, green leaves and branches, which began to pour a column of dense gray smoke into the morning sky. He secured an ember, and he moved out fast after first dribbling more water into Elka's mouth. The trouble was, she just wouldn't accept much of it. She wanted and needed milk. He hadn't gone far when he heard noises ahead to the north. Noises of people.

It was a rescue party sent out from Uhda. It had to be, he thought, and a deep sense of relief flooded through him.

"Here!" he yelled. "We need help. Elka needs help."

He saw them—two older, limping Krog hunters that he knew from the days of butchering the mammoths—as well as Rah. And worried about Elka, she'd brought Awk's mate, Lok with her baby boy.

"She can nurse Elka!" Moctu realized, and his worries for Elka began to abate.

When Rah saw Moctu rush to Lok with Elka, she went to her knees in grief. If Effie wasn't with Elka, she knew her daughter was dead.

Moctu whispered, "Awk good," as he extended Elka to Lok, and she let out a quick gasp of relief briefly closing her eyes and tilting her face skyward. Taking Elka quickly, the short woman showed a gentle calmness and competence. Even with a child in each arm, she was soon nursing Elka. In moments Moctu made his way to Rah and knelt beside her. No words needed to be said as they embraced each other, Moctu fighting tears as Rah sobbed softly on his good shoulder, his other one grotesquely stained and caked with blood. Finally overcome with emotion, Moctu sobbed openly, despite Nerean culture scorning such action.

In short order, Moctu regained his composure, as did Rah.

"Awk and Da?" she asked him, and the others in her party listened in closely.

"Awk fine, Da has leg wound. They pull Effie... Effie's... body," Moctu said, his voice choking on the last word. But hiss-gaw. Hiss-gaw hunts them." Having just lost Zat to the hiss-gaw, the party was profoundly concerned for the men's safety.

"You go help Awk and Da. I take women back to Uhda," he suggested to the two hunters. They readily agreed and were soon off.

Chapter Seventy-Nine

"They had Tabar's shafts?" Jabil questioned Palo in alarm. "How'd they…" his voice trailed off, as he realized he couldn't ask how the Pale Ones got them.

"Yes, and they threw them well. They were good! We withdrew, but only after we hit them hard. Alfer thinks we killed several, and wounded most of the rest," Palo replied.

Jabil's brow furrowed—his mind was in turmoil. How had they gotten those shafts? They couldn't have found them, he'd hidden them too well. They must have been watching him! The thought made him shudder. The beasts had been watching him. They could have attacked him. And they probably saw it all, the whole horrible… He began to tremble and his breath caught. He felt nauseated.

He's having one of his episodes, Palo thought, rolling his eyes imperceptibly. He was grateful that Jabil hadn't been with them during the attack. He'd have been a liability.

"Ordu, Samar, and Tabar are avenged," Palo said, ignoring Jabil's illness. "But we need to be on guard against them. They may decide to retaliate."

"Yes, yes, good," Jabil said in a weak voice, waving him off.

* * * *

With Jelli's doctoring, Jondu was healing well. He could already walk on the leg, but Avi continued to encourage him to rest it. She'd have her baby any day now, and Nuri spent a lot of time with her. Nuri had also brought by some delicious stew to show support for Jondu and to help his healing.

Palo's wound healed and his arm was nearly as good as ever. He'd been embarrassed by the attention and adulation the war party had received on their return. Nereans were thrilled to hear that the men had located the People Eaters and inflicted some retribution. The spirits of Ordu, Samar, and Tabar could now rest.

Palo, Seetu, and Sokum continued to discuss the eerie sounds they'd heard during the fight, and they wondered what kind of omen they represented. All of them agreed the screams sounded ghostly, and uncannily like Moctu.

"Do you think the Pale Ones memorized Moctu's scream when they attacked him and killed him?" Seetu theorized. "Or was Moctu's spirit there to help us during our ambush?"

Itzal was healthy and growing well. Nuri helped Leuna by doing more of the chores and all the cooking. She also spent time with Alta and Zaila, who was now walking and speaking. She was a beautiful child, and Nuri wished Tabar and Moctu could see her now. Alta was doing better, and she'd found herself surprised when she worried about Alfer while he was on the war party expedition. She didn't know if she could handle another mate's death. And she knew if Alfer died, no other man would take her as a mate, as some already believed she was cursed. All the same, it had been relaxing not to be beaten for nearly half a moon.

Nuri watched as a scout breathlessly ran past, shouting that caribou—lots of them—had been spotted to the north-west.

Chapter Eighty

Elka was a healthy, happy baby again. A half-moon ago, Moctu had held her as she cooed and gurgled, oblivious as men buried her mother, a wonderful woman that Elka would never get to know. Since Moctu had brought Elka back to Uhda, Rah remained close by her side, worried that she, too, could disappear from the world. During the quiet evenings, Moctu and Rah wordlessly grieved together.

With help from the two hunters that went to meet them, Awk and Da had gotten back safely with Effie's body a day and a half after Moctu. Although they'd seen tracks, the men had not encountered the hiss-gaw. If they had, it would have slowed them even more. Rah was convinced that Elka wouldn't have made it that long, and for that she was grateful to Moctu. For his part, Moctu berated himself for taking Effie on a dangerous trip.

Moctu had decided to attempt the trip again, and soon.

He had to go. He would avenge Tabar. And Ordu and Samar. And now Effie. Jabil was a murdering scum, and who knew what he could do next? Alta could be in peril, or Palo or… Nuri. Nereans could attack Uhda or Krog hunting parties. It had to stop. But he wouldn't take Elka. He couldn't. If he was successful, he'd come back for her.

Shortly after the burial, Hawk had taken Moctu to a hearth where his sister Tas, Sag's former mate, worked on weaving a basket. The men had talked about toolmaking briefly, where-upon Hawk pulled Moctu outside the hearth and offered his sister to Moctu as a mate.

So that was why Hawk had brought him here. That had been his purpose all along.

"Tas good worker and look like Effie. Yaw like?" Hawk asked.

"Krog people don't have a Mourning Moon?" Moctu asked, surprised.

"Mourning Moon for women. Men don't need," Hawk said smiling. "Yaw like Tas?"

"Of course, I like her, and I'm honored. But no, I'm not ready. Thank you, brud Hawk."

"Yaw shoulder better. Yaw go Etseh. Yaw go soon?"

"Yes, very soon. Elka stays at Uhda. I'll return later," Moctu replied, thinking, if I survive.

"I go with," Hawk stated.

"No, no… I'm not going to risk anybody else with…"

Hawk waved his hand and interrupted, saying, "No." Then slowly, with his hands on Moctu's shoulders, pronouncing each word distinctly, he said, "I… go… with… brud… Moctu!"

Seeing that the big red-haired man would not be dissuaded, Moctu agreed and the men began to plan the trip. Moctu was adamant that Hawk not come near Etseh with him, it was just too dangerous. Nereans were killing Krog on sight.

Hawk told him that Da and Ronk, Da's best friend, wanted to come, and the three Krog men could hunt in the lowlands while Moctu entered Etseh. Moctu got Hawk's word that the men wouldn't come near Etseh, as every scenario he envisioned in that regard ended in disaster.

That settled, it seemed like a good plan, and they decided to leave the morning after next. Moctu appreciated the help getting through hiss-gaw territory. This time they'd be focused on the threat of ambush. They wouldn't be taken by surprise again.

Rah wasn't surprised that Moctu again planned to travel to Etseh, but she was visibly relieved when he asked if she'd keep Elka while he was gone.

"I keep. She healthy, bigger, yaw come back," Rah said with a smile.

It was a bright sunny morning when the men said their goodbyes and departed. They'd started a bit earlier, but were delayed when Moctu had a thought, and went back for a large skin full of dried mammoth meat.

It would be his manhood rite meat offering if they asked for it, he thought smiling to himself, relishing the idea of telling Jabil and the Nerean men that he'd satisfied his obligation by killing a mammoth.

But later, as the men began their trek, Moctu was downcast and somber as he recalled leaving the last time, in much better spirits, with Effie holding Elka.

"Oh Spirits. What will you bring me this time?" he whispered. "Please be with us. Guide us and give us wisdom and strength." He stopped the group to bury a choice piece of dried mammoth meat as an offering to the Earth Mother and other Spirits.

There was still snow and ice completely covering the higher elevations, and in the darker valleys, but almost all the trails the men took were clear and largely dry. They made excellent time and saw no evidence of the hiss-gaw, not even old tracks or distant roars. They were slowed only by the precautions they took, including extra scouting, to avoid potential ambushes.

By the fourth day, they were well into the lowlands.

Chapter Eighty-One

"Well, hello, Mother Avi. I guess there was only one in there after all," Nuri said, smiling, as she came to Jondu's hearth.

"Hello, Nuri! Come in," Avi replied, looking tired, but beaming, obviously pleased by the *Mother* appellation.

"Are you feeling better? We were worried at how hard you struggled to deliver that big boy."

"Oh Nuri, you and Jelli were wonderful to help me through it. You're probably about as tired as I am."

"I know that's not true. You worked hard!"

"Yes, this boy has his father's big head," Avi said grimacing. "It took a long time and was pretty painful," she continued, nodding seriously. "I wanted to scream so many times. Well, you know, you were there. I hope I didn't leave bruises, gripping your arm so tightly."

"I'm just sorry you had to go through all that, but today you have a beautiful son."

"Yep, having this little boy next to me makes it worth all the trouble and pain," Avi said leaning back. "I can say that now. But yesterday, I had a very different opinion."

Nuri laughed and looked closer at the boy who stared back at her with serious eyes. "He has your eyes, Avi! That's wonderful. You have such fantastic eyes."

"Thanks, Jondu's pleased by that as well. I hope they stay that way. He'll be disappointed if they change. We'll see.

They look kind of hazel to me," she said, twisting to peer into them. "Jondu's also glad it's a boy. He's already named him Indar because he's so strong. He cries so loud."

As if on cue, Indar started crying lustily, and continued until Avi fumbled open her tunic and began to suckle him.

"Having a strong son has helped Jondu get over not going on the hunt. His leg's getting better, though, so he'll be able to hunt soon," Avi said.

"The hunt went well," said Nuri. "Three caribou–and Jabil got one of them so he was happy when he got back last night. He's still sleeping."

The two women heard a loud commotion and Nuri went to the hearth entrance.

"It's Seetu," she said. "Coming from the north. What's he yelling about?"

Then she heard it.

"It's Moctu!" Seetu was yelling. "It's Moctu. He's back!"

At first, Nuri thought she'd heard him wrong. Then she thought this was some awful attempt at humor. Even so, she became light-headed and sat down on a rock in the hearth.

"Did he say what I think he did?" Avi said in amazement.

"Oh Avi, do you think it could be Moctu?" Nuri said, still having a hard time catching her breath.

"Don't get your hopes up, Nuri. It's Seetu. You know how he likes to play tricks. If this is one of those, I'll kill him myself. It's sick."

Just then, Alta went rushing by, holding Zaila.

Chapter Eighty-Two

"It's Moctu! And he's carrying a big pack," Seetu continued yelling, overflowing with excitement. "I was at the northern lookout. He called and waved to me. I know it's him."

People streamed out of their hearths to see if any of this could be true.

"It's true! It's him. Moctu's returned," several others joined in the shouting.

Jabil was stunned and not pleased. Before he, too, went out to greet Moctu, he donned his finest tunic and grabbed his spear.

He needed to look formidable. This could only bring problems, what with Nuri and all.

Alta was the first to Moctu, even weighed down by Zaila. As she got near him, he rushed toward her, weighed down by a pack that was well over half his own weight. Alta set Zaila down and swallowed him in a bear hug, overjoyed, and squealing in exultation.

"Where have you been? We thought you were dead. Oh, thank the Spirits! You're back!" Alta shrieked as tears flowed down her cheeks.

"Mother! It's so good to see you!" Moctu started. "Whoa. What's this?" he said, pushing her away slightly to examine her black eye and scuffed cheek. "Who did this?" he said, his voice taking on a steely tone.

"It's nothing," Alta replied, pushing Zaila in front of her. "Look at your sister. She's grown, hasn't she?"

"Zaila!" Moctu said in surprise.

He'd figure out who to deal with about the bruises later, he thought grimly.

"I wouldn't have recognized you," he said, hugging the little girl. "You've grown so big."

Others were surrounding him, peppering him with questions and comments.

"Where were you? We gave up on you."

"We thought you were dead! What have you been doing all this time?"

Then he saw Nuri. She was running toward him. He made room and moved toward her. She melted into his arms, tears streaming down her cheeks, unable to speak. They stayed that way for a long moment.

"That's my mate you're holding," Jabil called, and Nuri immediately, but regretfully, pushed herself away. "She's frigid, anyway," he chuckled as Nuri moved away, turning her back to them both.

Moctu looked over to Jabil and his blood ran cold. This was the scum who killed Tabar. And Ordu and Samar, he thought, his teeth clenching hard. The urge to charge at him and kill him right then was almost unbearable.

"Jabil," he said, his voice icy.

"Where have you been? We thought you were dead. What have you been doing all this time?" Jabil asked with a distinct edge to his voice.

"I'll answer that soon," Moctu said. "At a Council of Warriors. I call for a Council of Warriors this afternoon."

"You have to be a man to sit at the Council of Warriors, much less call for one," Jabil said, his voice verging on a sneer.

Moctu threw a large skin at his feet. "Here is my meat offering." Inside, was nearly half a man's weight in dried mammoth meat, a huge prize. Carrying such a heavy pack had caused his shoulder wound to reopen and ooze blood, but this moment was worth it.

"Mammoth meat?" asked Ono, one of the first to taste a piece.

Moctu nodded, and a flurry of questions ensued from the crowd.

"How did you get mammoth meat? Did you kill it?"

"How could you kill a mammoth? Did you come across a dead one?"

"Did you get that wound from the mammoth?"

"It died trying to kill me," Moctu said honestly. He paused to hug Palo who'd just arrived.

"Where have you been?" Palo asked him, still incredulous that his best friend was back.

"As an elder, I declare Moctu a man!" Ono shouted, and those nearby cheered except for Jabil.

Moctu looked at Ono, ignoring Jabil, and said, "I call for a Council of Warriors this afternoon."

Trying to reassert his authority, Jabil cut Ono off, and said, "We'll have a Council this afternoon, just after the sun starts down from its high."

Chapter Eighty-Three

Curiosity reigned as the men arrived at the Council, but the atmosphere also had a distinct element of tension. Moctu had yet to tell anyone of his whereabouts or actions during the many moons of his absence, despite all the questions.

"Where could he have been?"

"It was a bad winter… how did he survive all this time?"

Jabil had shown up early, his spear placed upright against the rock face of the wall against which he leaned. He sat on a small boulder with the cave bear skull positioned prominently in front of him. Much of the tension emanated from him. He did not look pleased.

When Moctu showed up he brought his long bundle, wrapped in skins and placed it beside him. His arrival brought new questions from the men. Women and older children on the periphery of the Council circle edged closer to try to hear.

"Now will you tell us where you've been? Why were you gone so long?" the men showered him with questions.

"What have you been doing? How'd you kill the mammoth?"

"Yes, please tell us these things," Jabil said. "I want to get back to my mates."

Moctu knew the last line was thrown in to provoke him, and it did.

"I'll tell you all, but first I ask a favor," he said to the gathered men. "I'll tell you things that'll shock you. Some will no doubt make you angry. Will you agree to hear my whole story before you make decisions?"

All the men respected Moctu, and they were curious beyond measure, so all concurred. Even Jabil was so curious that he gave no objection.

"Well," Moctu said, taking a deep breath. "Long ago, when making my manhood kill, I wounded a red deer. I tracked and chased it, but my whipping injuries..." he paused and looked at Jabil, who smiled inscrutably, "had given me fever and I passed out. Several times."

Moctu knew his next sentence would cause an uproar. "I was captured and healed by the Pale Ones, and then forced to be a slave."

The resulting furor was even greater than he'd expected. Again, the questions and comments came from every side.

"What?"

"Those savages!"

"You're lucky they didn't eat you."

"How'd you get away?"

"I'll tell you much more about that in a little while," Moctu continued. "I want to tell you an important story, but before I do, let me just say that the Pale Ones are more advanced in some ways than we are."

More pandemonium.

"No!"

"They're animals, they're not like us."

"People Eaters? I don't believe it."

"They taught me how to make fire," Moctu said, and the circle went completely silent for a moment. The men were stunned.

"You say you know how to make fire?" Jabil asked.

"And the Pale Ones taught you?" Jondu followed up, disbelieving.

"Yes," said Moctu. "The Pale Ones showed me how to go

into a cold, fireless hearth and make a blaze from dry wood."

Now Jabil knew Moctu was lying, and he relaxed. Man couldn't make fire, much less the People Eaters. Only the Spirits could, with fire bolts from the sky. Here was his chance to bring his rival, this lying little braggart, down. "You have to understand how hard it is for us to believe this," he said. "You must show us this."

"Oh, I'll show you. I'll show the whole tribe. But first, let me tell a story. One that all will find of great interest. Let's go back to that horrible day, the day when my father, and Ordu and Samar were killed." A hush fell over the men, and many looked to Jabil to see if he'd have one of his spells, but he was still preoccupied with Moctu's assertion of being able to make fire.

"Jabil has told us what happened when our men were overrun by the vicious People Eaters, and how he *bravely* came to their aid," Moctu said, stretching out the word *brave-ly*. "How Ordu threw his spear and the spear point broke against the boulder, how the red-haired creature picked up the spear and broke it over his knee."

Jabil didn't like where this was going and said, "This is reviving bad memories. I see no purpose. Let's see this fire-starting that you boast about."

"Soon, Jabil, soon. Now four of us came later and searched the area for tracks and clues. Did any of you see either piece of Ordu's spear? Or the broken wooden end of the Pale One's spear? We found just the spearhead, embedded in Samar."

He saw Nabu shaking his head, with a frown on his face.

"So, the Red-haired one took the pieces with him," Jabil offered. "What are you insinuating, anyway?"

"Only that we found no broken spears, just the one spear-head. And while I was with the Krog… um, the Pale Ones, I saw that they leave a broken spearhead like that as an honor on the graves of their great hunters."

Jabil sputtered in mock outrage. "You dare to imply that I'd lie about such a thing?" At the same time, he cast a worried glance toward Jondu, and saw that the remark had registered with him, and he'd cocked his head sideways in suspicion.

"I think we've heard enough from this blustering fool," Jabil exclaimed, but Moctu was unwrapping his bundle.

"Now the Pale Ones told me they didn't kill our men. They told me a Nerean man had killed our men," Moctu said.

"We've heard enough! We can't believe this man. He's lived with the Pale Ones. He's one of them," Jabil screamed trying to get Moctu to stop.

"I didn't believe them," Moctu continued in a louder voice, talking through Jabil's hollering. "Until I saw this." And with that, he held up Ordu's spear. It took a moment, but the implication soon dawned on the men. The spear was in beautiful condition, with an unbroken spear point and shaft. It was clearly Samar's work, the spear he had made and given to Ordu.

"They saw Jabil hide our men's equipment and they retrieved it later," Moctu said. "Unbroken."

One by one, the men turned to look at Jabil. Even the women, who'd crowded closely behind the men, strained to see what Jabil would do.

"It's not Ordu's," Jabil shouted, standing. "He's had almost a year to replicate the original spear. Don't you see? Moctu wants to be leader, so he's trying to smear me. He made that spear. It's not Ordu's."

"I wish I could make a spear of this quality," Moctu said, shaking his head wistfully. "But only one man could. All of you can see it's Samar's work—the one he made for Ordu." He turned, pointing the spear at Jabil's neck.

Chapter Eighty-Four

The men were convinced, and they turned angrily on Jabil.

"You lied!"

"Kill him."

"How could you kill our men?"

"Kill the lying murderer!"

"Do it, Moctu. Do it."

"A quick death's too good for this scum," Moctu said. Moving the spear point away from Jabil's neck he shoved Jabil and said, "I want to know why. Why did you have to kill my father? And Ordu? And Samar? Why Jabil? I think we all want to know."

Jabil's mind screamed for him to escape. He had to get out of there.

Palms up, he lifted his hands about shoulder high and protested, "But I didn't do it. There's been a horrible mis-understanding." When he said the last word, he lashed out hard at Moctu's bloodstained shoulder, causing him to stagger backward in pain.

Jabil leapt toward the right, his closest pathway to free-dom, and into a crowd of women that had gathered on the periphery of the Council circle. Ono snagged one of his feet as he went by and Jabil crashed into the women, knocking two of them to the ground, including Nuri.

Ono and Petral corralled Jabil and dragged him back to

the Council circle. On the way, Jabil surreptitiously grabbed a handful of sand. Moctu was seated, holding his aching shoulder. But Jondu was up now, holding a spear to Jabil's chest.

"Where is the broken spearhead we found together, Jabil?" Jondu said menacingly. "Did you use it on Samar? You killed our kinsmen, didn't you?"

"No Jondu, you know me," Jabil replied. "I wouldn't do that. Come on, we've been friends forever."

His mind was racing, desperately searching for the best means to escape. If he could just get away, he would head south to meet up with Ordu's son's group.

He edged closer to Jondu and said in a low voice, "Jondu, I'm telling the truth. Hey, best friend, it's me. Come on Jondu, we're like brothers. Who're you going to believe?"

With that, he threw the sand into Jondu's eyes and kneed him in his wounded leg. Jondu groaned in agony, a hand clutching his leg, and sank part-way to the ground. Jabil wrenched the spear from Jondu's other hand and swung it around on the crowd, threatening anyone to move. Waving the spear, he bounded out of the circle of men and into the crowd of onlookers, knocking Poza and Nindai over. It was utter chaos. The men rose to follow, but Jabil grabbed the closest woman to him.

"I'll kill her," he screamed, "Or any man that comes close."

It was Avi. She shrieked in fear, and her baby, Indar, in the sling Nuri had made for him, awoke and began crying loudly.

"Avi!" Jondu rose in alarm and began staggering toward Jabil without a weapon, his hands together, extended forward. "Jabil. Don't do this. Oh, Spirits. You were my best friend. You know how much she means to me. And my son. Come on, please Jabil. Don't hurt Avi or Indar." His voice cracked near the end.

"All I want is to get out of here," Jabil said, edging backward, again bumping into Poza and Nindai who'd gotten up with the help of his cane. "I'm taking her for insurance. No one better follow me, or I'll kill the baby first."

"Noooo!" Avi shrieked, and Jabil shook her savagely.

"No Jabil," Jondu exclaimed. "No one's going to follow. Just don't hurt my son or Avi."

Jabil smiled. This was going to work. He'd get out of here and head south. He'd keep Avi for insurance, so they didn't follow. He might even have some fun with her along the way.

"Then get back, Jondu," Jabil said. "And Nabu, I see you circling around with your spear. If you want me to kill the baby right now, just take one more step."

Nabu stopped where he was.

Jabil had just started to wonder when he should kill the baby. He thought he'd do it early on, so it didn't slow them down. Maybe the first time he saw one of the men following, to serve as a warning that he was serious.

"Huuaww!" he groaned, expelling air. Something painful had hit him in the side. Now he saw Nindai, pulling Avi and her baby away from him, and he felt frozen, unable to stop the broken man from taking her. Jabil felt at his side and found a shaft protruding. "But what...?" The shaft had a curved end. As he went to his knees, he realized it was Nindai's cane, but most of it was buried in his side. He fell face down in the dirt and gasped for air.

Avi was in Jondu's arms. "Spirits, I was so worried," he said. Avi was still sobbing, but now it was largely in relief, after she'd checked and rechecked Indar to make sure he was unharmed.

Moctu moved toward Nuri but saw that she was already being comforted by Palo and Nabu. He briefly watched her sob in Palo's arms as Nabu patted her shoulder whispering, "It's over. It's over." Was she crying for Jabil or something else? Was she that upset about her mate being speared, or was she crying in relief that Avi was safe?

Nuri saw Moctu as he turned away, and she quickly re-gained her self-control. She wanted to go to him but couldn't gracefully extricate herself from Palo and Nabu. She was disappointed to see him move toward another group of people.

Looking down near Avi's feet, Moctu could see the discarded thick leather wrap that Nindai kept around the base of his cane. It had covered a spear point, he thought in astonishment. The spear point of a warrior.

Chapter Eighty-Five

Jabil was still alive in the late afternoon, groaning in agony for someone to end his life. Jondu guarded him at spear point and fiercely forbade anyone to give in to Jabil's pleas. In a small but savage act of retribution, he roughly cut off Jabil's signature hair braid and tossed it in the fire. During the afternoon, Jondu got the whole sordid story out of Jabil as he pleaded for relief.

Hearing Jabil's piteous groans was too much for many.

"We all wanted him to suffer, Jondu," Palo said. "But he's had enough now. Let me end him."

"Un-uh, Palo. He betrayed us and then nearly killed my mate and baby today. I'd ram hyena dung down his throat if I could find some. He's going to suffer." Palo couldn't dissuade him. Later, Jabil's father, Alfer, tearfully pleaded with Jondu to end his son's pain and allow him to pass on to the Spirits, and Jondu finally complied, ramming his spear brutally into Jabil's neck. Jabil died instantly. Afterward, Jondu roughly dragged the body to the refuse pile and left it for the vultures and other scavengers. Alfer recovered his son's corpse and buried him not far away in a shallow grave.

Moctu didn't really know how Nuri felt about losing her mate. When she was sobbing in Palo's arms, what was that for? Was she crying for Jabil? Or something else?

He had a lot to tell her and everyone else, some of which

people might find hard to accept. The rest of that afternoon, he spent his time with Alta, Zaila, and Nuri, in Alfer's hearth, telling them, and the other people eavesdropping from nearby hearths, about his time with the Krog.

"You have a granddaughter, Mother," he told Alta, watching Nuri's face for her reaction. "She's wonderful. Her name is Elka."

"Who's the mother?" Alta asked. "A... Pale One?" Alta was unsuccessful in keeping the shock and contempt from her voice.

It was going to take a while for her and the rest to not hate the Pale Ones, he knew. It had taken him some time.

"Yep," he answered. "And she was a truly wonderful woman, but she's... she's dead now." He hung his head. It still hurt to think about Effie.

Nuri had seemed startled to hear of his daughter. "Tell us about your daughter, about Elka," she said, her voice neutral.

"She's beautiful. She has big blue eyes and lighter skin and hair, but not as pale as the Krog. Rah, her grandmother, is taking care of her with help from Lok, another Krog woman. Krog is what the Pale Ones call themselves, by the way. It means *mammoth people*." He looked at Zaila.

"Did you know you were an aunt?" he asked her, touching her shoulder.

"Aunt!" she said with enthusiasm, and everyone laughed.

"Do they really know how to make fire?" Alta asked. "And you can too, now? Is that really true?"

"Yes," said Moctu. "They're behind us in a lot of things, but they really can make fire. They have some great medicines, too. In fact, Elka's grandmother is a great healer. And they know how to kill mammoths at least as well as we do."

"Welcome back, Moctu," said Nindai as he hobbled up to the hearth.

"Nindai!" they shouted in unison.

"I didn't get the chance to thank you, Nindai," said Moctu, standing and moving to hug the man. "You were the true hero today. You have a warrior's heart. Thank you."

As the group murmured in agreement, Nindai beamed at the praise, especially the part about having a warrior's heart.

"I understand that the Pale Ones have some excellent tonics and medicines. I'd be grateful to learn more from you," he said.

"I'd love for you to come with me when I go back to Uhda... um, I mean the place where the Pale Ones live," Moctu said.

"You're going back?" Alta said, sounding alarmed.

"Of course I'm going back, Mother," Moctu replied. "I have a daughter there. But I'm not planning to stay there."

"I'd love to go," Nindai exclaimed. "If you think I can make it."

"It's rugged, especially the last part, I don't want to mislead you. I don't think Jelli would make it. But I really want you to come. We'll figure out something," said Moctu, enthused. "You and Rah will get along great. She's their healer. You two will learn so much from each other."

"Hello," called Palo, walking up. Moctu got up and embraced him warmly.

"We have a lot to talk about, my friend," Moctu said. "It's crowded, but we can fit you in. Come join us."

The group talked long into the night. Moctu became somber when he told them of the ambush that killed Effie and wounded him and Da.

"I don't like talking about it or even thinking about it," Moctu said, his voice choked with emotion. "It was a horrible time. But I don't blame any of you. If I hadn't been captured, I would have been there throwing shafts at the Krog too. We all thought they were murdering savages. Jabil's at fault. But even before him, before... what he did, we were considering an attack."

The group was quiet for a long time contemplating his

words.

Palo broke the silence. "So that was you. Making the sounds and throwing the shafts at us?"

"Yes, that was me," Moctu acknowledged, bleakly remembering the day.

"Well, you hit me and Jondu. You'll be pleased to know you're still a good shot."

"Yes, and the shaft I took in my shoulder was yours," Moctu replied with no trace of anger. "You're a pretty good shot too."

"Hard to believe we almost killed each other," said Palo, the realization setting in.

Chapter Eighty-Six

The next morning, Moctu was in the middle of the Council circle again, this time with his fire-making equipment. Virtually all the men of the tribe were there, many still unwilling to believe that Moctu could build a fire.

Just as he'd been taught, Moctu readied his shredded bark, flat wood, and spindle. The men paid rapt attention, but many had their arms crossed, still convinced this was some sort of hoax. Moctu began turning the spindle, expectantly awaiting the men's reaction when the smoke started rising.

He almost chuckled with anticipation. He knew they were going to be as stunned as he'd been when he first saw it.

They were. As a thin wisp of smoke rose, several of the men pointed and shouted.

"There. Look!"

"Whoa, that's... smoke!"

Moctu redoubled his efforts and soon had an ember in the bark, which he blew into a flame. He looked up to see the men astonished, eyes wide, several holding their hands to the top of their heads or over their mouths. He smiled in deep satisfaction, remembering the amazement he'd felt. He knew these men recognized how important this knowledge was to the tribe.

He spent the rest of the morning working with all the men who wanted to learn the procedure. One by one, he shared their exhilaration as the men began to master the technique. He could still vividly recall his first time. How awestruck he had been to realize *he could make fire*.

At noon, Petral rose and said, "Ono, Jondu, Nabu, to you as elders, I ask to make this a Council meeting to choose a new leader. I nominate Moctu, and I encourage all the men here to make it unanimous."

Moctu's head swung around and his eyes found Petral beaming broadly. There were immediate shouts of acclamation. Even Jondu appeared disinclined to argue for himself as an alternative.

After looking at his son, and seeing his reticence, Ono said, "How many men here support Moctu as leader, please stand." Every man stood, including Jondu.

"Then it's my pleasure to announce Moctu as our new leader," Ono said.

Spirits, what just happened? Moctu thought, staggered by the speed of this development. Palo, then Nabu, then Petral, then each man in turn embraced Moctu and congratulated him and wished him well.

Moctu had a sudden thought. "I know the first thing I'd like to see us do," he said to the men. "I'm pretty sure you'll all support this. I think Nindai has earned the right to sit at the Council of Warriors. What do you say?"

"He's one of us," Jondu exclaimed, and there were widespread shouts of agreement.

"Then at the next Council meeting, after Nindai does the Song of the Tribe, we'll ask him to stay and sit with us," Moctu said, smiling as he envisioned the surprised look on Nindai's face.

Alfer was conspicuously absent from the group, as Moctu had confronted him on his return from burying Jabil the evening before.

When he arrived at the crowded hearth, Alfer had begun to berate Alta for so many people being there and for not having his meal ready. Moctu excused himself from the group and took him aside.

"Alfer, I'm sorry that you lost your son today," he started. "But I think even you will admit that he did evil things."

Alfer nodded sullenly, his eyes downcast.

"I've noticed the bruises on my mother's face and I know how she got them, Alfer," Moctu said, his teeth clenched and the last few words a snarl. He pushed Alfer hard in the chest. "If you ever... *ever* hurt my mother again, I'll hurt you so much..." he struggled to find something grisly enough to express his anger. "I don't know... I'm having a hard time keeping from bashing your skull in right now. Are you understanding me?"

Alfer looked to the ground again and nodded.

Chapter Eighty-Seven

Moctu awoke in Alfer's hearth and walked out to see the sun had already crested the eastern hills. Amber beams sliced through a soft blue sky and the birds were singing happily. As a gentle breeze rustled his hair, it seemed to Moctu that the Spirits were sighing with the pleasure of their creation.

Without exactly knowing why, Moctu made his way to Jabil's hearth, which was, for now, Leuna's and Nuri's. Leuna had already left the hearth, but Nuri was there, kneeling as she cooked over the small fire.

"You've always been a great cook," Moctu said as he approached. "Hello, Nuri."

Nuri rose, pulling her hair back from her face with both hands. "Hello, Moctu. This is a nice surprise. Congratulations on being leader."

"Thanks. That was… sudden. It still hasn't sunk in, I guess." He paused. "I wanted to talk with you about something else. I know I was… I was gone a long time, and I know a lot has happened. To both of us. I wanted you to know that the first part of my time with the Krog was miserable… really miserable, and the thought of you was… the only thing that kept me going."

"Oh, Moctu," said Nuri quietly. "I—"

"I realized after some time," Moctu continued, "that by then, you were surely mated to Jabil, and I… tried to get past those feelings and move on."

"I missed you, Moctu," Nuri said, her eyes welling with tears as she remembered the early days of wondering if he was alive or dead.

"I know you've just lost your mate, and there's the Mourning Moon—" he started up again.

"Mourning Moons are for people in mourning," Nuri said. "I'm not."

"I'll be going back to Uhda soon to visit and get Elka and—"

"I want to go with you," Nuri interjected.

"Well, I didn't want to… bother you during…"

She hugged Moctu and kissed him warmly and deeply, a kiss rich with promise. "Bother me Moctu. I want you to bother me. Now."

Notes and Annotated References

I would like to thank the following sources for providing information critical to the prehistorical accuracy of *Moctu and the Mammoth People*.

1. Benazzi, S. et al. (2011) 'Early dispersal of modern humans in Europe and implications for Neanderthal behavior' *Nature* 479, 525-528. Modern human remains at the Grotta del Cavallo in Italy date to **~45,000–43,000 years before present and are therefore the oldest known European anatomically modern humans.**

2. Higham, T. et al. (2014) 'The timing and spatiotemporal patterning of Neanderthal disappearance' *Nature*, 512, 306-309 Shows the **Mousterian** *(associated primarily with Neanderthals)* **ended by 41,030–39,260 years BP** across Europe, as did succeeding 'transitional' Châtelperronian (sites with some Neanderthal association). Data indicate Neanderthals disappeared at different times in different regions, starting in southeastern Europe, arcing through central Europe and ending in southern Spain (figure 1). The temporal overlap of EMHs and Neanderthals in Europe was only **2,600–5,400 years**, but there was plenty of time for exchange of cultural and symbolic behavior, as well as interbreeding between the two groups.

3. Churchill, S. et al. (2009) 'Shanidar 3 Neanderthal rib puncture wound and Paleolithic weaponry' *Journal of Human Evolution* 57, 2009 163-178. "**The wound that ultimately killed a Neandertal man between 50,000 and 75,000 years was most likely caused by a thrown spear, the kind modern humans used but Neandertals did not, according to Duke University-led research. Archaeological evidence also suggests that by 50,000 years ago humans, but not their Neandertal cousins, had developed projectile hunting weap-**

ons, Churchill said. They used spear throwers, detachable handles that connected with darts and spears to effectively lengthen a hurler's arm and give the missiles a power boost. **As human weapons technology advanced, Neandertals continued using long thrusting spears in hunting**" (Quote with permission from "Human Spear Likely Cause of Death of Neandertal" Science News, July, 2009).

4. The 1000 Genomes Project Consortium (2015) 'A global reference for human genetic variation' *Nature* 526, 68-74.

5. Wall, J. D. et al. (2013) 'Higher levels of Neanderthal ancestry in East Asians than Europeans' *Genetics* 194: 199-209. Documents that the similarity of both Europeans and East Asians to Neanderthals is the result of a recent admixture and not ancient population subdivision. Determined that the Denisovan admixture rate into East Asians is 40% higher than into Europeans. **Found that Neanderthal haplotypes were more frequent in East Asians than in Europeans (9.6% vs. 6.4%) and concluded that interbreeding between Neanderthals and modern humans occurred in multiple places and times.**

6. Walker, M.J. et al. (2008) 'Late Neandertals in Southeastern Iberia: Sima de las Palomas del Cabezo Gordo, Murcia, Spain' *American Journal of Physical Anthropology* 142, 261-72. **Skeletal remains of an individual living in northern Italy ~40,000 years ago are believed to be that of a human/Neanderthal hybrid.**

7. Fu, Q. et al. (2015) 'An early modern human from Romania with a recent Neanderthal ancestor' *Nature* 524: 216–219. **Analyzed DNA from a 37,000-41,000-year-old modern human from Romania and found 6-9% of the genome came from Neanderthals. That is more than any other modern human analyzed to date and indicates that the individual had a Neanderthal ancestor as recently as 4-6 generations prior. Documents that some of the first modern humans that came to Europe interbred with the Neanderthals.**

8. Brahic, C. (2014) 'Neanderthal demise traced in unprecedented detail' *New Scientist* 223(2983):10. Cites Thomas Higham and his colleagues (see reference #2) who dated materials from 40 definite and possible Neanderthal sites in Europe spanning the time when modern humans arrived and Neanderthals vanished. All were found to be at least 40,000 years old.

9. Currat, M. and Excoffier, L. (2004) 'Modern Humans Did Not Admix with Neanderthals during Their Range Expansion into Europe' *PLoS* Biol 2(12): e421 - **Estimates the maximum number of interbreeding events between modern humans and Neanderthals ranges be-**

tween 34 and 120 over the whole of Europe.

10. Wiik, K. (2008) 'Where did European Men come from?' *Journal of Genetic Genealogy* 4:35-85. **Uses R1b and other "old" haplogroups to show Basque population as perhaps the oldest in Europe, a form of whose language was likely spoken in the Paleolithic** throughout Western Europe and that was overrun by the progress of the Indo-European languages.

11. Zielinski, S. (2012) 'Neanderthals...they're just like us?' *National Geographic News*, Cites Pääbo et al. who analyzed Neanderthal DNA in modern Europeans to determine when Neanderthal genes may have mixed with those of modern humans. The date they came up with for the **gene flow was 37,000 to 86,000 years ago, and most likely 47,000 to 65,000 years ago.** The interbreeding may have aided modern humans in adapting as they moved into Eurasia. Other researchers have determined that **modern humans gained genes from Neanderthals that help our immune system fight off viruses.**

12. Gittelman, R. et al. (2016) 'Archaic Hominin Admixture Facilitated Adaptation to Out-of-Africa Environments' *Current Biology* 26:24 3375-3382. Identified 126 high-frequency haplotypes for use in investigating favorable genetic adaptations from interbreeding between EMHs, Neanderthals and Denisovans. OCA2 and OAS1/2/3 genes from Neanderthals affects skin color and the immune system respectively. **Demonstrated that hybridization helped EMHs adapt to their new environments.**

13. Kuhlwilm, M. et al. (2016) 'Ancient Gene Flow from Early Modern Humans into Eastern Neanderthals' *Nature* 530, 429-433. Documents that Neanderthals contributed genes to modern humans outside Africa 47,000-65,000 years ago. A population that diverged early from other **modern humans in Africa contributed genes to the ancestors of Neanderthals from the Altai Mountains roughly 100,000 years ago.** They conclude that in addition to later interbreeding events, the ancestors of Neanderthals from the Altai Mountains and early modern humans met and interbred, possibly in the Near East, many thousands of years earlier than previously thought. **There is evidence of EMH genes (including the FOXP2 gene that affects language development) entering the Neanderthal genome rather than the reverse.**

14. Liu, W. et al. (2015) 'The earliest unequivocally modern humans in Southern China' *Nature* 526 696-699. The newly excavated Fuyan Cave in Daoxian (Southern China) has provided **47 human teeth dating to more than 80 kyr** and with a likely maximum age of

120 kyr.

15. Simonti, C. et al. (2016) 'The phenotypic legacy of admixture between modern humans and Neanderthals' *Science* 351 737-741 **Genes we got from Neanderthals give us proclivities for depression and skin lesions resulting from sun exposure (actinic keratosis).** It is possible that some Neanderthal alleles *(like nicotine addiction – NTB)* provided a benefit in early EMH populations as they moved out of Africa, but have become detrimental in modern Western environments.

16. Sankararaman, S. et al. (2014) 'The genomic landscape of Neanderthal ancestry in present-day humans' *Nature* 507 354-357. Neanderthals have more genes affecting keratin filaments, suggesting that interbreeding may have helped modern humans to adapt to non-African environments. Their results suggest that **Neanderthal genes may have caused decreased fertility in hybrid males.**

17. Vernot, B. and Akey, J. (2014) 'Resurrecting Surviving Neandertal Lineages from Modern Human Genomes' *Science* Vol. 343:6174 1017-1021. **Estimate that the total amount of Neandertal sequence is less than 3% of the modern human genome. But the specific genes vary among individuals, so modern humans, taken together, span approximately 20% of the Neandertal genome.**

18. Green, R. et al. (2010) 'A draft sequence of the Neanderthal genome' *Science* 328:5979 710-722. Draft sequence presented composed of four billion nucleotides from three individuals.

19. d'Errico, F et al. (2013) 'Neanderthal acculturation in Western Europe? A critical review of the evidence and its interpretation' *Nature* 497:7449. **Bone tools, personal ornaments, and apparently modern stone tools in European late Middle Paleolithic or pre-Aurignacian Paleolithic contexts is sometimes attributed to technology transfer from modern humans to the final Neanderthal populations. Analysis of the data from Grotte du Renne, France suggests independent development instead.**

20. Lazaridis, et al. (2014) 'Ancient human genomes suggest three ancestral populations for present-day Europeans' *Nature* 513 409-413.

21. Callaway, E. (2014) 'Ancient European genomes reveal jumbled ancestry' *Nature*.14456. Studies indicate that **some early modern humans had dark hair and an olive complexion.**

22. Anthroscape Human Biodiversity Forum, (2009). Dolni Vestonice

ivory carving dating to ~26,000 years ago indicates EMHs had straight to wavy hair. The Venus of Brassempuoy (Figure 7) suggests that EMHs had wavy hair or possibly braided.

23.   Zubrow, E. (1989) 'The demographic modelling of Neanderthal extinction' *The Human Revolution* (ed. P Mellars and C. Stringer) 212-231. A consistent one percent difference in mortality (between H. sapiens and H. neanderthalensis), can produce extinction in as little as 30 generations (~1000 years).

24.   Vendramini, D. (2009) *Them + Us*, Kardoorair Press. Postulates Neanderthal Predation (NP) was key to EMH development in Levant area between 60,000-45,000 yrs bp. Has 800 references on human evolution. Describes a seminal transition about 46,000-47,000 years ago (Bar Yousef, 1996). A group of Upper Paleolithic behaviors suddenly appeared in Middle Paleolithic people living in present day Israel. Within just a few thousand years, these new behaviors had spread to Europe, Africa and Asia. Quotes Ofer Bar-Yosef and Bernard Vandermeersch as saying that **between 40,000-45,000 years ago the material culture of western Eurasia changed more than it had during the previous million years.**

25.   Diamond, J. (1997) *Guns, Germs, and Steel*, Macat International, Ltd. Discusses "Great leap forward" that happened 50,000 to 100,000 years ago, in which humans experienced huge advances in technology, art and culture.

26.   Goebel, T. et al. (2001) 'Masterov Kliuch and the Early Upper Paleolithic of the Transbaikal, Siberia' *Asian Perspectives* 39, 47-70.

27.   Boule, M. (1911) 'L'homme fossile de La Chapelle-aux-Saints' *Annales de Paleontologie* 6:111-172. Wrongly concluded Neanderthals were stoop-shouldered, bowlegged, and ape-like with opposable big toes, in part based on fossils of a severely arthritic Neanderthal.

28.   Krupka, F. (1909) 'An Ancestor: The Man of Twenty Thousand Years Ago' *L'Illustration; and Illustrated London Times*. Based on M. Boule's work, pictured Neanderthal as stooped, brutish, ape-like and primitive (Figure 2).

29.   Wells, S. (2003) 'The Great Leap' *The Guardian.* Around **60,000 years ago humans were on the brink of extinction. There were as few as 2,000 humans in existence at that time**. About that time dramatic advances occurred in human technology and culture. Tools became more finely crafted with a greater variety of materials. Art became much more common - evidence that our ancestors were using abstract and symbolic

thought. Mentions **Jared Diamonds, "great leap forward" in mental abilities and culture. Some attribute this to a favorable mutation in a language gene - such as the FOXP2 gene.** Wells claims these new abilities allowed us to leave Africa by two routes - one along the southern coast of Asia, which reached Australia around 50,000 years ago. The other route was through the Middle East leading to the settlement of Europe by around 40,000 years ago. Perhaps the most amazing thing to come from this research is the understanding that the billions of humans alive today expanded from a small population living in Africa some 60,000 years ago. **We're all cousins separated by, at most, a couple of thousand generations.**

30. From Eupedia.com / Genetics, "Neanderthals could have been cleverer than us. But that's not the whole story. Neanderthal's skull had a lower vaulted prefrontal cortex than most modern humans, and it has been speculated that they would have been less good at decision making and moderating social behaviour. On the other hand, **Neanderthals possessed a bigger occipital lobe, meaning that their visual abilities** (including the distinction of details and colours) were certainly better than that of modern humans. All Eurasian people apparently inherited various Neanderthal genes relating to the immune system (e.g. HLA types), including genes that increased **the risk for some autoimmune diseases such as type-2 diabetes and Crohn's disease. Physical features inherited from Neanderthal by Europeans and Middle Easterners include prominent eyebrows, big eyes, strong jaws and wide shoulders**. 70% of East Asians also inherited mutations in the POU2F3 gene, which is involved in keratin production and may be responsible for **straightening hair**. There are several genes influencing **skin colour**. Among them, the BNC2 gene, which influences saturation of skin colour and is **responsible for freckling**, was confirmed by Sankararaman et al. (2014) to have been come from Neanderthal. As for the genes for **light eyes**, there is a relatively high likelihood that they were inherited from Neanderthals too…" Here is a list of traits that distinguished Neanderthals from Homo sapiens, but that you could also have inherited if you are of European or Western Eurasian descent.

o **Occipital bun:** a protuberance of the occipital bone (back of the head) that looks like a hair knot. You have it if you can feel a rounded bone just above the back of your neck (same height as the ears).

o **Low, flat, elongated skull:** What matters here is especially the 'elongated skull', as opposed to the back of the skull falling almost vertically, like all East Asians, and most Anatolian, Caucasians and Eastern Europeans. Elongated skulls are particularly common in Scandinavia, in the British Isles and in Iberia.

o   **Retromolar space posterior to the third molar:** i.e., an empty space behind the "wisdom teeth."

o   **Supraorbital torus:** protruding eyebrow bone (including big deep eye cavity between the eye and eyebrow).

o   **Bigger, rounder eyes than average.**

o   **Broad, projecting nose:** angle of the nose bone going more upward than average (not falling straight like a "Greek nose").

o   **Bony projections on the sides of the nasal opening:** i.e., nose bone making a "triangle" between the nose and cheeks/orbits.

o   **Little or no protruding chin**

o   **Larger mental foramen in mandible for facial blood supply:** this means that the side jaw and cheek are bigger or better supplied in blood than average. This increased blood supply could result in the cheeks being red (like blushing) when doing physical exercise or when the weather is cold.

o   **Short, bowed shoulder blades:** i.e., shoulder bones curving toward the front more than average.

o   **Large round finger tips:** typically "flat" and wide finger tips, especially the thumb (e.g., if your thumb is more than 1.5 cm wide).

o   **Rufosity:** i.e., having red hair, or brown hair with red pigments, or natural freckles.

"**Fair skin, hair, and eyes**: **Neanderthals are believed to have had blue or green eyes, as well as fair skin and light hair**. Having spent 300,000 years in northern latitudes, five times longer than Homo sapiens, it is only natural that Neanderthals should have developed these adaptive traits first.

According to the Canadian anthropologist Peter Frost, the current level of hair colour diversity in Europe would have taken 850,000 years to develop, while Homo sapiens has been in Europe no longer than 45,000 years. This is evidence enough that **genes for fair hair were inherited from interbreeding with Neanderthals**.

DNA tests demonstrated that Neanderthals possessed fair skin, and **at least some subspecies had reddish hair** too." (Eupedia.com)

31.   Mick, J. (2014) 'Neanderthal breeding was hard but yielded benefits' *DailyTech, Science.* Although interbreeding with Neanderthals may have given modern humans better immunity and disease resistance, Neanderthals seem to have passed along some harmful genes, as well. **Studies suggest that genes associated with increased risk of lupus, biliary cirrhosis, Crohn's disease, and smoking addiction were all**

inherited from the Neanderthals.

32. Johanson, D. and Edgar, B. (2006) *From Lucy to language*, Simon & Schuster. At least 850 ~130,000-year-old **Neanderthal fossils from perhaps 80 individuals in Krapina Cave in Croatia showed 1) Most died between the ages of 16 and 24 years, 2) Some of these Neanderthals were butchered, cooked, and eaten. 40,000-50,000-year-old Neanderthal fossils from Amud Cave in Israel have features that are a blend of Neanderthal and early modern human.** 50,000-year-old fossils from La Chapelle-Aux-Saints, France of an individual with a deformed hip, crushed toe, severe arthritis in the neck vertebrae, a broken rib, and a damaged knee cap.

33. Cavalli-Sforza, L. and Cavalli-Sforza, F. (1995) *The Great Human Diasporas*, Reading Mass: Addison-Wesley. **Mounds of broken bones have been found that suggest Neanderthals ate brains and bone marrow of fellow Neanderthals. It's unclear whether they killed their neighbors in order to eat them, or they may have eaten their dead**, a form of cannibalism still widespread in Africa and some other parts of the world.

34. Ehrlich, P. (2000) *Human Natures,* Island Press. Skeletal remains show that **Neanderthals were much more injury-prone and subject to arthritis** than their modern human successors.

35. Wynn, T. and Coolidge, F. (2012) *How to Think Like a Neandertal*, Oxford University Press. **Neandertals cared for their injured and exhibited love. Almost all adults exhibited skeletal trauma and arthritis. They would have been wary of strangers. They had a concept of death and thought about it.**

36. Trinkaus, E. (1983) *The Shanidar Neanderthals,* Academic Press, New York. **Nearly every adult Neanderthal skeleton ever examined shows trauma.**

37. Bryson, B. (1990) *The Mother Tongue,* Avon Books, Inc. Mentions studies by Philip Lieberman (Brown University) suggesting that **Neanderthals were physiologically precluded from uttering certain sounds such as the ee sound of bee or the oo sounds of boot**. If they could speak at all, their voices would have been nasal-sounding and somewhat imprecise.

38. D'Anastasio, R. et al. (2013) 'Micro-Biomechanics of the Kebara 2 hyoid and its implications for speech in Neanderthals' *PLoS ONE* 8(12): e82261. Gross anatomy of the Kebara 2 hyoid from Israel is

very similar to that of modern humans. However, whether Neanderthals could use speech or complex language remains controversial. Their **findings are consistent with a capacity for speech in the Neanderthals**.

39. National Geographic Society Genographic Project, (2012) 'Basque roots revealed through DNA analysis' Press Room. Released a comprehensive analysis of Basque genetic patterns which indicates their uniqueness that predates the arrival of farming by 7000 years. The results of the study **support a genetic continuity of current day Basques with the earlier Paleolithic or Mesolithic settlers of their area**.

40. Khan, R. (2010) 'The Basques may not be who we think they are' *Discover* Gene Expression. Discounted R1b and Rh- stories and asserts Basques are not much different from other European populations, probably Neolithic farmers. His conclusions have since been disputed by Genographic Project results.

41. Behar, D. et al. (2012) 'The Basque paradigm: genetic evidence of a maternal continuity in the Franco-Cantabrian region since pre-Neolithic times' *American Journal of Human Genetics* 90(3):486-93. **Identified six haplogroups that distinguish Basques as different and older than their neighbors**. Their results clearly support a partial genetic continuity of today's Basques with earlier Paleolithic or Mesolithic hunter-gathers of their homeland.

42. Semino, O. et al. (2000) 'The genetic legacy of Paleolithic Homo sapiens in extant Europeans: a Y chromosome perspective' *Science* 290 (5494): 1155–59.

43. Morelli, L. et al. (2010) 'A comparison of Y-chromosome variation in Sardinia and Anatolia is more consistent with cultural rather than demic diffusion of agriculture' PLoS ONE 5 (4). Defends antiquity of R1b markers.

44. Karafet, T. et al. (2008) 'New binary polymorphisms reshape and increase resolution of the human Y chromosomal haplogroup tree' Genome Research 18(5) 830-838. **The haplogroup R1b originated during the last ice age at least 18,500 years ago and is most frequent in the Basque Country (91%).**

45. Viegas, J. (2015) 'Dogs and humans bonded earlier than thought' *Seeker* Website. **DNA dates dog domestication back 33,000 years.**

46. Pennsylvania Archaeology (2014) *twipa blogspot*. **In Europe, Asia**

and Africa based on cave paintings and the reduced size of spear points, the bow and arrow replaces the atlatl between 12,000 and 15,000 years ago.

47. Andrea, A. editor, (2011) *World History Encyclopedia*. The **bow and arrow were probably invented in the Late Upper Paleolithic, perhaps as early as 18,000-20,000 years ago.** The best evidence for this comes not from the bows but from projectile points that were too small to place on spears or darts.

48. Blitz, J. (1988) 'Adoption of the bow in prehistoric North America' *North American Archaeologist*, Vol 912, 127. There is **clear evidence for bow in North America only from 3000 BC**.

49. Waters, M. et al. (2011) 'The Buttermilk Creek complex and the origins of Clovis at the Debra L. Friedkin site, Texas' *Science* 331:6024 1599-1603. Documented tools and weapons that date to about **15,500 years ago, making them the oldest artifacts found in North America**.

50. Phelps, N. (2008) *The Longest Struggle,* Green Press Initiative. **Use of Atlatls is at least 30,000 years old but could be much older**.

51. Churchill, S. and Rhodes, J. (2009) 'The Evolution of the Human Capacity for Killing at a Distance' *The Evolution of Hominin Diets* (J. Hublin and M. Richards, eds.). Analyses of Middle Paleolithic points suggest that **long-range projectile weaponry (most likely in the form of spear thrower-delivered darts) was developed in Africa sometime between 90–70 ky BP**, and was part of the tool kit of modern humans who later expanded out of Africa.

52. Aronesty, J. (2015) *Deciphering the English Code*, Two Candle Press. **The earliest archaeologic evidence of an atlatl is 25,000 old, and the atlatl has been in use for some 40,000 years**.

53. Vutiropulos, N. (1991) 'Long-range weapons in Southeast Europe - The Neolithic to Early Bronze Age' *Internationale Archäologie* (C. Dobiat, ed.) Research indicates that **the throwing technique of the sling and the mechanics of bow and arrow were not developed before the Neolithic**.

54. Mellaart, J. (1967) *Çatal Hüyük: A Neolithic Town in Anatolia,* McGraw-Hill. **Probably the world's oldest depiction of a slinger with numerous radiocarbon dates between 6500-5700 B.C**.

55. Thoms, A. and Mandel, R., editors (2007) 'Archaeological and Paleoecological Investigations at the Richard Beene Site' *South-Central 2*.

Reports of Investigations 8 Center for Ecological Archaeology, Texas A&M University. Found **possible bola stones dating between 8500 to 7500 years ago.**

56.	Parents.com (2016) **Nine Birthing Rituals of the Past; Zuni Indian mothers were encouraged to remain silent**.

57.	Schele, L. and Miller, M. (1986) 'The Blood of Kings' *Archaeology* 39:3. **Bloodletting was commonly performed at** Mayan burials, marriages, and **births. It was done by piercing a soft body part, generally the tongue or penis**. The bloodletting was typically done on the body part correlated with the hoped-for result, i.e., **drawing blood from the penis would be done to increase human fertility**.

58.	Joyce, R. et al. (1984) 'Olmec Bloodletting: An Iconographic Study' *Sixth Palenque Roundtable* (V. Fields ed.) Univ. of Oklahoma Press. **Ceremonial bloodletting** was an important Mayan ritual, performed by drawing a cord through a hole in the tongue or by passing a stingray spine, **pointed bone, or thorn through the penis**.

59.	Varner, G. (2008) *The History and Use of Amulets, Charms and Talismans*, Lulu Press, Inc. Discusses the use of **amulets, talismans, totems, etc. as well known in Native American culture to provide luck, protection and good hunting**. Thought to give a direct link with gods or spirits.

60.	The Well-Rounded Mama blog, Images of squatting birthing mothers from ancient cultures (Persia, Aztec, Egypt, Native American Indian, India).

61.	Shroomery website: The Liberty Cap (Psilocybe semilanceata), is the most widespread wild **psilocybin mushroom** of the world. It grows in north temperate areas but it has been found even in Peru, India and also **at altitudes of 4000 meters in Italy**. Its effects are claimed to be very visual in high dosages and calming to the body.

62.	FactsandDetails.com (2016). **Otzi, the 5,300-year-old Iceman carried embers wrapped in maple leaves placed in a birch bark container. This shows that Neolithic people at least sometimes carried fire from place to place rather than starting new fires from scratch.**

63.	www.iceman.it website: Otzi's dagger is a 13 cm-long dagger made up of a small triangular flint blade in an ash wood handle. **The flint used for the blade came from quarries in the Lessini Mountains north of Verona. It was an important trade item during the Neo-**

lithic period in central Europe due to its high quality.

64. Henry, D., ed. (2003) *Neanderthals in the Levant*, Continuum Books. **Neanderthals** were the first humans to survive in northern latitudes during the glacial stages of the Pleistocene. They had domesticated fire, but their **hearths were simple, small and shallow and cooled off quickly, giving little warmth throughout the night**.

65. Rossano, M. (2013) *Mortal Rituals*, Columbia University Press. Neanderthal hearths at Abric Romani, Spain are small, about one foot across, and shallow.

66. Aiello, L. and Wheeler, P. (2003) 'Neanderthal Thermoregulation and the Glacial Climate' in van Andel and Davies, eds. *Neanderthals and Modern Humans in the European Landscape During the Last Glaciation*, McDonald Institute for Archaeological Research, Cambridge. Analyzed Neanderthal body type to determine cold adaptation. Results suggest Neanderthals could tolerate 2.5 degrees C (4-5 degrees F) lower temperatures than modern man. The small difference indicates **Neanderthals needed clothes and fire to survive Ice Age Europe**.

67. Wrangham, R. (2009) *Catching Fire,* Profile Books. Claims that **hominids became people—acquiring traits like big brains and dainty jaws—by mastering fire about 1.8 million years ago. Evidence for frequent use of fire by European Neanderthals between 400,000 and 300,000 years ago**.

68. Welsh, J. (2011) 'Cost of expensive human brain still up for debate' *Livescience.* **Our brain requires about 22 times as much energy to run as the equivalent in muscle tissue**.

69. The Genographic Project, 'Why am I Denisovan?' *National Geographic*. At least two of our hominid cousins—Neanderthals and Denisovans—had migrated out of Africa before we did it about 60,000 years ago. Genetic overlap is found between the Denisovan genome and that of present-day Southeast Asians. **Melanesian genomes in Papua New Guinea are 3 to 5 percent Denisovan. Some additionally inherited 4 percent to 6 percent of their DNA from Neanderthals.**

70. Ganan, R. (2012) **'What does an elephant taste like?'** *Adventures in Food, The Awl.com.* Quotes ancient rules whereby the head and right hind-leg of the kill belong to the one who inflicted the first wound. Describes an account of an elephant kill where the natives collected a ribeye the size of a plasma tv. The tribesmen would grab handfuls

of gushing offal and rib bones the size of canoe paddles. They would scream as they cut at the carcass with spears. They became more and more excited and some would jump inside the carcass in their eagerness to seize the precious fat, while others ran off, screaming, with huge pieces of bloody meat, threw them on the grass, and ran back for more.

71. Agenbroad, L. and Nelson, L. (2002) *Mammoths – Ice Age Giants,* Lerner Publications. **Adult mammoths typically had heights of 13 ft (4m) at the shoulder and weights up to 8 tons, while exceptionally large males could exceed 12 tons.**

72. Baraniuk, C. (2015) 'The Story of Rhinos and How They Conquered the World' *BBC.com Earth,* Woolly rhinos were around in Europe until 10,000 years ago.

73. Liesowska, A. (2015) 'Meet Sasha – the World's Only Baby Woolly Rhino' *The Siberian Times.* Baby Woolly rhino found preserved in permafrost. **Rhinos ranged from Scotland to Spain to Korea and became extinct about 10,000 years ago.**

74. Owen-Smith, N. (1984) in Macdonald, D., ed. *The Encyclopedia of Mammals* Facts on File. **Woolly rhinos had a thick, protective skin, 1.5–5 cm thick.**

75. Haines, T. (2001) *Walking With Prehistoric Beasts,* DK Publishing. Northern rhinos are larger than their African cousins. **Their thick winter coats and extraordinarily long horns are sometimes up to 2 meters (6.5 feet) long (see Figures 4 and 5).** All rhinos are short-sighted and easily startled.

76. Visual-arts-cork.com website: Prehistoric Art, El Castillo Cave Paintings (about 39,000 years ago). Some of the world's oldest cave art is found in the rock shelter of El Castillo, Spain. The red-ocher disk or **large dot below the hand stencils is dated 39,000 years ago. The hand stencils are dated to about 37,300 years ago.**

77. Unesco.org World Heritage List, Cueva de las Manos, Río Pinturas (Spanish for Cave of the Hands) in the Santa Cruz province of Argentina. The art in the cave dates from 13,000 to 9,500 years ago (Figure 3).

78. Aubert, M. et al. (2014) 'Pleistocene cave art from Sulawesi, Indonesia' *Nature* 514, 223–227. The earliest dated image from Maros is at least **39,900 years old. It is now the oldest known hand stencil in the world.** Additionally, a painting of a 'pig-deer' was dated to

35,400 years and may be the oldest figurative depictions in the world. Shows that humans were producing rock art by 40,000 years ago at opposite ends of the Eurasian world.

79. Bailey, M. (2013) 'Ice age Lion Man is world's earliest figurative sculpture' *The Art Newspaper.* The Lion Man of Hohlenstein Stadel is an **ivory carving of a lion-headed figure** and is known as the oldest anthropomorphic animal carving in the world. Discovered in Stadel cave in Hohlenstein Mountain in southwest Germany, it has been **dated to approximately 40,000 years ago**. Other important carvings discovered there include the Venus of Hohle Fels (33,000-38,000 years old), the earliest ivory carving of a mammoth, and **several bone flutes**.

80. Conard, N. et al. (2009) 'New flutes document the earliest musical tradition in southwestern Germany' *Nature* 460, 737-740. Report on the discovery of **bone and ivory flutes** from more than 35,000 years ago in southwestern Germany. The flutes document a well-established musical tradition at the time when modern humans colonized Europe.

81. Wilford, J. (2012) 'Flute's revised age dates sound of music earlier' *New York Times, Science Section.* Thomas Higham has **dated the flutes to at least 42,000 years old**. Higham and other researchers from Tubingen and Oxford have identified what they say are the **oldest-known musical instruments in the world. The flutes, made from bird bone and mammoth ivory**, come from Geissenkloesterle Cave in southern Germany which contains evidence for the occupation of Europe by early modern humans.

82. Crosby, A. (2014) *The Columbian Exchange,* The Gilder Lehrman Institute of American History. Epidemic among American Indians in New England, Native American populations in New England had no immunity to European diseases and were nearly wiped out by an epidemic—likely smallpox. Between 1616 and 1619, the populations of the **Massachusetts and other Algonquin tribes were reduced by as much as 90 percent by disease.**

83. Saltworks at www.seasalt.com website: History of Salt. Reports from Onondaga, New York in 1654 indicated the **Onondaga Indians made salt by boiling brine**. Settlers near Kanawha, West Virginia around 1755 reported that Native Americans made salt by boiling brine from salt springs.

84. Barber, J. (1829) *Interesting Events in the history of the United States,* "...a very mortal sickness raged with great violence among the Indians inhabiting the eastern parts of New England. Whole towns were

depopulated. The living were not able to bury the dead; and their bones were found lying aboveground, many years after. **The Massachusetts Indians are said to have been reduced from 30,000 to 300 fighting men**." As referenced in Loewen, J. (2004) *Rethinking Our Past,* Recorded Books.

85. Wolfe, M. et al. (2007) 'Origin of major infectious human diseases' *Nature* 447 279-283. Discusses **why most diseases come from the old world**. Greater proportion of diseases are transmitted by insects in tropics. Animal reservoirs are more common in the tropics. NTB: **May help explain why EMHs replaced Neanderthals. EMHs came out of Africa much later than Neanderthals and likely brought diseases to which they had more immunity**.

86. Wikispaces, *Colonial Disease Digital Textbook, Smallpox in Mexico.* In 1519, Hernan Cortes and his crew members reached Tenochtitlan, the Aztec capital and conquered their empire by 1521. An African slave aboard Cortes's ship had become ill with smallpox during the voyage to the New World, and the disease nearly wiped out the entire Aztec population. It's estimated **that the Aztec population in 1518 was 30 million, and by 1568 there were only three million left**.

87. Trinkaus, E. et al. (2014) *People of Sunghir: Burials, Bodies and Behavior in the Early Upper Paleolithic*, New York: Oxford University Press (Figure 10).

88. Radovčić, D. et al. (2015) 'Evidence for Neandertal jewelry: modified white-tailed eagle claws at Krapina' *PLoS One* 10 (3). Documents discovery of **eight white-tailed eagle talons from the Krapina Neandertal site in present-day Croatia, dating to approximately 130 kyrs ago. The talons were part of a necklace or bracelet**. Contradicts the argument from some researchers that Neandertals lacked symbolic ability or copied this behavior from modern humans. The find clearly demonstrates that the Krapina Neandertals made jewelry long before the arrival of modern humans in Europe *(as much as 80,000 years later - NTB)*. **This is the earliest evidence for jewelry in the European fossil record and shows a higher level of Neanderthal cultural sophistication than previously accepted**.

89. Zilhao, J. et al. (2010) 'Symbolic use of marine shells and mineral pigments by Iberian Neandertals' *Proceeding of the National Academy of Sciences* of the United States of America 107 (3) 1023–1028. Documented **use of pierced shells and pigments by Neanderthals** at the sites of Cueva de los Aviones and Cueva Antón, in southern Spain about 50,000 years ago.

90. Fabre, V. et al. (2009) 'Genetic evidence of geographical groups among Neanderthals' *PLoS One* 4(4). Neanderthals can be divided into at least three groups - Western Europe, a southern area, and Western Asia.

91. Adler, D. et al. (2006) 'Ahead of the game; Middle and Upper Paleolithic hunting behaviors in the Southern Caucasus' *Current Anthropology* 47(1). Traditional concepts of backward Neanderthal behavior are no longer valid. **Although Neanderthals and modern humans did differ in significant ways, the vast behavioral and cognitive gulf that was once believed to separate them has narrowed considerably.**

92. Frost, P. (2012) 'Were Neanderthals Furry?' *Evo and Proud website.* Cites references for **3 lines of evidence that Neanderthals were furry**: 1) Lack of tailored clothing - needles or awls largely absent. 2) mtDNA analysis of body lice (which favor clothing wearing organisms) originated no more than ~72,000 +- 42,000 years ago, roughly coincident with EMH encroachment. 3) Finger bone ridges in Neanderthals; Chimpanzees have ridges on their finger bones that stem from the way that they clutch their mother's fur as infants. Modern humans don't have these ridges, Neanderthals do.

93. ListVerse (June, 2009) 'Top ten misconceptions about Neanderthals' *Listverse.com's Ultimate Book of Bizarre Lists.* There is **no reason to believe that Neanderthals were hairier than modern man**. Computer models indicate that excess hair on Neanderthals would have induced too much sweating which would have thereafter frozen on the Neanderthals potentially leading to death.

94. Guatelli-Steinberg, D. et al. (2016) *What Teeth Reveal About Human Evolution* Cambridge University Press. Found 39% of Neandertals had hypoplasia (grooves in tooth enamel which indicate periods of famine or poor nutrition).

95. Reumer, J. et al. (2003) 'Late Pleistocene survival of the saber-toothed cat Homotherium in northwestern Europe' *Journal of Vertebrate Paleontology* 23: 260. Homotherium is an extinct genus of saber-toothed cats (sometimes called scimitar-toothed cats), that ranged through the Americas, Eurasia, and Africa from 5 mya – 11,700 years ago. **Homotherium** survived in Eurasia until about 28,000 years ago.

96. Sorkin, B. (2008) 'A biomechanical constraint on body mass in terrestrial mammalian predators' *Lethaia* 41, 333–347. Homotherium reached 1.1 m (3.6 ft) at the shoulder and **weighed approximately 190 kg or 420 lbs (Figure 9).**

97.   Ambrose, S. (2003) 'Did the super-eruption of Toba cause a human population bottleneck?' *Journal of Human Evolution* 45, 231-237.

98.   Rampino, M. and Ambrose, S. (2000) 'Volcanic winter in the Garden of Eden: The Toba super-eruption and the Late Pleistocene human population crash' in McCoy and Hieken (eds.) *Volcanic Hazards and Disasters in Human Antiquity*, Special Paper 345, Geological Society of America, 71-82.

99.   Gibbons, A. (2016) 'Modern human females and male Neandertals had trouble making babies. Here's why' *Sciencemag.org.* Y chromosome of male Neanderthal from El Sidron, Spain from 49,000 years ago weren't passed on to EMH's and suggests that female EMHs and male Neanderthals were not fully compatible.

100. Mendez, F. et al. (2016) 'The divergence of Neandertal and modern human Y chromosomes' *American Journal of Human Genetics* 98:4. Analysis of Y chromosome from Neandertal male from El Sidron, Spain from 49,000 years ago suggests the most recent common ancestor between EMHs and Neandertals was 588 kya. Identified several protein-coding differences which could cause male Neandertal-female EMH incompatibility and possible reproductive isolation.

101. Stringer, C. (2012) *Lone Survivors* Times Books. **The Campanian Ignimbrite eruption 39,000 years ago in Italy was perhaps the second most powerful eruption (after Toba) in the last million years. The eruption was closely followed by a Heinrich event in which large numbers of ice bergs broke off the northern ice caps and flowed south severely chilling Europe.**

102. Black, B. et al. (2015) 'Campanian Ignimbrite volcanism, climate, and the final decline of the Neanderthals' *Geology*, 2015, DOI: 10.1130/G36514.1. Suggests that 72 cubic miles of ejecta and nearly 1 B pounds of SO2 emissions from this violent eruption 39,000 years ago furthered the decline of the Neanderthals.

103. Fitzsimmons, K. et al. (2013) 'The Campanian Ignimbrite eruption: new data on volcanic ash dispersal and its potential impact on human evolution' *PLoS ONE* 8(6): e65839. Campanian Ignimbrite eruption was the most explosive in Europe in the last 200,000 years.

104. Rougier, H. et al. (2016) 'Neandertal cannibalism and Neandertal bones used as tools in Northern Europe' *Scientific Reports* 6. Goyet cave in Belgium has yielded evidence that Neanderthals butchered and cannibalized other Neanderthals between 40,500 and 45,500 years ago. There is also evidence they used some of the bones as

tools.

105. Zilhao, J. et al. (2017) 'Precise dating of the Middle-to-Upper Paleolithic transition in Murcia (Spain) supports late Neandertal persistence in Iberia' *Heliyon*, 3 (11). Neanderthals may have persisted in southern Spain to 37,000 years ago.

106. Otterbein, K. (2004) *How War Began*, Texas A&M University Press. Development of the atlatl and later, other long-range weapons, was probably the most important set of events in the last forty thousand years, allowing for Homo sapien migration out of Africa, the increase in their numbers, and the demise of Homo neanderthalensis and Homo erectus (p67).

107. Farmer, M. (1994) 'The origins of weapons systems' *Current Anthropology* 35, no. 5: 679-681. **Projectile weapons used by EMHs in the Levant circa 40,000 years ago were from darts thrown by spear throwers.**

108. Bronowski, J. (1973) *The Ascent of Man*, Little, Brown and Company. Even in historical times, a tribe has been found (pygmies on islands south of Myanmar) who carefully tend fires because they cannot create fire.

109. Longo, L. et al. (2012) 'Did Neanderthals and anatomically modern humans coexist in northern Italy during the late MIS 3?' *Quaternary International* 259: 102-112.

110. Condemi, S. et al. (2013) 'Possible interbreeding in Late Italian Neanderthals? New data from the Mezzena jaw (Monti Lessini, Verona, Italy)' *PLOS ONE* 9(1). Change in shape of the chin among the fossils of Mezzena and other late Neanderthals could be the result of a small degree of interbreeding with EMHs that happened less than 40,000 years ago.

111. Oppenheimer, S. (2003) *The Real Eve*, Carroll & Graf Publishers. Map on p. 70-71 shows early southern "beachcomber" route out of Africa. **Huge deserts in northern Africa and the Levant about 70,000 years ago precluded migration into Europe**. Map on p. 58 shows a later pathway from Africa through the Levant and into Europe as early as 45,000 years ago. Alternatively, based on genetic data, the map on p. 86 suggests that the earlier "beachcombers" escapees may have backtracked northwestward from coastal Asian areas across a greening Levant and into Europe. Cites data that early migrations (before 70,000-80,000 years ago) of EMHs from Africa died out and that EMH migrants into Europe may have come from

south Asia after earlier escaping Africa along a southern route.

112. Richards, M. et al. (2000) 'Tracing European founder Lineages in the Near Eastern mtDNA Pool' *American Journal of Human Genetics* 67(5) 1251-1276. The regional Early Upper Paleolithic components are highest in southern and eastern Europe, as well as in Scandinavia and the Basque Country. The majority of existing mtDNA lineages entered Europe in several waves during the Upper Paleolithic (50k-10k years ago), and there was a founder effect (bottleneck) that happened at the Last Glacial Maximum 20,000 years ago.

113. McBrearty, S. and Brooks, A. (2000) 'The revolution that wasn't: a new interpretation of the origin of modern human behavior' *Journal of Human Evolution* 39(5) 453-563. Many of EMH's cultural and technological innovations (such as bone tools, art and decoration) happened long before the "Great Leap Forward" proposed by Diamond and many other researchers.

114. Habgood, P. and Franklin, N. (2008) 'The revolution that didn't arrive: A review of Pleistocene Sahul' *Journal of Human Evolution* 55(2) 187-222. Disputes McBrearty and Brooks (2000) assertion that EMHs had a full package of cultural and technological innovations long before their dispersal from Africa.

115. NTB: Although some reports suggest remnant Neanderthal populations survived in southern Spain until ~28,000 years ago, these dates have been strongly discounted by more recent studies (see Higham and related references above) and are likely much older.

116. NTB: Recent studies indicate the Neanderthal gene (MC1R) producing red hair seems to be distinct from genes causing similar attributes in modern humans.

117. NTB: According to 23andMe, I am >3% Neanderthal, placing me in the upper 25% of their two million customers. After writing this book, I discovered that my paternal haplogroup is I-M438 which is found almost exclusively in Europe where it occurs in about 20% of the population. Like the character Moctu, men bearing this haplogroup were among the first EMHs to inhabit Europe some 30,000-45,000 years ago.

118. NTB: Recent publications have documented that much of the culture and technology that (may have) blossomed about 45,000 years ago had been developed much earlier (see McBrearty and related references above). Some technologies and culture may have been lost during the precipitous EMH population decline about 60,000 years

ago and been subsequently reinvented. Population growth and geographic dispersal about 45,000 years ago undoubtedly promoted innovation.

119.   NTB: EMHs may have used a southern "beachcomber" route to get to Southeast Asia as early as 70,000 years ago (see Oppenheimer or Richards references above).

120.   Powell, A. et al. (2009) 'Late Pleistocene demography and the appearance of modern human behavior' *Science* 324(5932) 1298-1301. Increased symbolic and technological complexity showed up 45,000 years ago as well as ~45,000 years earlier, and was the result of demography and population size.

121.   Soares, P. et al. (2011) 'The Expansion of mtDNA Haplogroup L3 within and out of Africa' *Molecular Biology and Evolution* 29(3) 915-927. **Fossils indicate that EMHs dispersed from Africa between 100 to 130 ka, but genetic evidence suggests that non-Africans come from a single successful later migration.** Haplogroup L3 provides an upper bound for the dispersal out of Africa with a **maximum at ~70 ka**, virtually ruling out a successful exit before 74 ka, the date of the Toba volcanic supereruption. This timing was likely related to climate changes.

122.   Villa, P. and Roebroeks, W. (2014) 'Neandertal Demise: An Archaeological Analysis of the Modern Human Superiority Complex' *PLoS ONE* 9(4): e96424. The cognitive/cultural/technologic gap between Neanderthals and EMHs was much smaller than previously hypothesized and not large enough to explain their demise. Neanderthals made use of ocher, personal ornaments, bone tools and complex hafting techniques before the arrival of EMHs in western Eurasia.

123.   Gibbons, A. (2014) 'Oldest Homo sapiens **Genome Pinpoints Neandertal Input**' *Science* 343(6178) 1417. 45,000-year-old EMH leg bone indicates an interbreeding event with Neanderthals that happened ~50,000 years ago.

124.   Brown, K. et al. (2012) 'An early and enduring advanced technology originating 71,000 years ago in South Africa' *Nature* 491 590-593. Advanced technologies were early and enduring. Any apparent "flickering" can be explained by a small sample size.

125.   Mellars, P. et al. (2013) 'Genetic and archaeological perspectives on the initial modern human colonization of southern Asia' *Proc Natl Acad Science* 110(26) 10699-10704. Data support a coastally oriented dispersal from Africa 60-50 kya.

126. Fu, Q. et al. (2013) 'A Revised Timescale for Human Evolution Based on Ancient Mitochondrial Genomes' *Current Biology* 23(7) 553-559. Analyzed mtDNA of ten securely dated ancient EMHs and recalibrated the substitution rate which now dates haplogroup L3 (the lineage from which all non-African mtDNA haplogroups descend) at 62-95 kya. Earlier EMH migrations from Africa did not thrive.

127. Reich, D. (2018) *Who We Are and How We Got Here*, Pantheon Books. Describes process for speeding the processing of DNA and the ramp-up in numbers of genomes analyzed. Examples show how ancient DNA is dramatically transforming our understanding of human prehistory.

128. Zilhao, J. et al. (2015) 'Analysis of Site Formation and Assemblage Integrity Does Not Support Attribution of the Uluzzian to Modern Humans at Grotta del Cavallo' *PLoS ONE*, 10 (7). Disputes 45,000-year-old EMH fossils at Cavallo, Italy and claims 41,400-year-old Romanian EMH fossils are the oldest yet found in Europe.

129. Trinkaus, E. and Zilhão, J. (2013) 'Paleoanthropological Implications of the Peştera cu Oase and Its Contents' in Trinkaus E., Constantin S., Zilhão J., editors. *Life and Death at the Peştera cu Oase: A Setting for Modern Human Emergence in Europe,* Oxford University Press; pp. 389-400.

130. Klein, R. and Edgar, B. (2002) *The Dawn of Human Culture* (Wiley, New York). Proposed **'fortunate mutation' hypothesis that a major genetic mutation (possibly to the FOXP2 gene involving language) occurred in EMHs 50,000-40,000 yrs bp that created the 'fully modern' human brain**.

About the Author

Neil Bockoven is an award-winning PhD geologist and journalist with 35 years of industry experience.

He has been featured in: Geological Society of America Bulletin, Association of Petroleum Geologists Bulletin, Virginia Journal of Science, and many other scientific journals. He is a repeat guest on some of the largest radio talk shows in the country. Neil is a member of the Archaeological Institute of America, the Archaeological Conservancy, and is an Impact Member of the Center for Study of the First Americans.

Neil worked as a geologist for Exxon/ExxonMobil in Denver, Midland, Houston, New Orleans and Albuquerque. He coordinated dozens of joint ventures with oil and gas companies, including rights to the entire King Ranch in Texas.

Neil attended The College of William and Mary, where he was a member of the state champion swim team, and received a Bachelor of Arts. From there, he went on to The University of Texas at Austin, earning a masters and doctorate. He has published articles on topics as diverse as the geology of huge volcanic calderas of the Sierra Madre Occidental Mountains of Mexico to sexual dimorphism in Astarte clams. His current interests center on the interaction between Early Modern Humans and Neanderthals during the Paleolithic Age, and the amazing related discoveries being made through archaeology and genetics.

For more about Neil Bockoven—and his books **Moctu and the Mammoth People** and **When We Met Neanderthals**—visit his web site at www.neilbockoven.com.

CPSIA information can be obtained
at www.ICGtesting.com
Printed in the USA
LVHW081715270819
629114LV00007B/83/P